INTO ALL THE WORLD

Books by F. W. Dillistone

CHARLES RAVEN

C. H. DODD

INTO ALL THE WORLD

A biography of Max Warren

by

F. W. DILLISTONE

HODDER AND STOUGHTON
LONDON   SYDNEY   AUCKLAND   TORONTO

The author and publisher are grateful to: Macmillan & Co. Ltd., of London and Basingstoke for permission to reproduce "The Coming" from *H'm* by R. S. Thomas; and to Gerald Duckworth & Co. Ltd., London, and Alfred Knopf, Inc., New York, for permission to quote an excerpt from a poem by Hilaire Belloc.

British Library Cataloguing in Publication Data

Dillistone, Frederick William
    Into all the world.
    1. Warren, Max Alexander Cunningham
    2. Church Missionary Society – Biography
    I. Title
    266'.3'0924   BX5199.W373

    ISBN 0 340 25479 3

Preface

MY ACQUAINTANCE WITH Max Warren spanned a period of exactly fifty years. After a brief encounter with him in Cambridge in May 1927 I do not remember meeting him again until late in 1943. Then a firm friendship developed and this was sustained through evenings periodically spent together. The last of these was in May 1977 less than three months before he died.

I never expected to be granted the privilege of writing his biography as I hoped that his literary executor, Douglas Webster would be able to undertake it. When it became clear, however, that other commitments would not allow him to do this for some time to come, he generously suggested my name to Mr. Edward England of the publishing firm Hodder and Stoughton and he in turn commissioned me to proceed.

I am deeply grateful to Douglas and to all the many others of Max's colleagues in the fellowship of the Church Missionary Society whom I have consulted. They still delight in every remembrance of him and have readily shared their memories with me. In addition friends who were undergraduates with him or assistants at Holy Trinity, Cambridge or fellow-adventurers in his enterprises outside C.M.S. or members of the Chapter of Westminster Abbey have all contributed to my attempts to record and interpret the successive stages of his career. So much more might have been written but my space was limited. I can only request the forbearance of those who may feel that important aspects of his life-story have been insufficiently treated or overlooked.

No one could have received more sympathetic co-operation than I have enjoyed from Max's daughters, Rosemary and Pat, and his niece Sheelagh. In particular, Pat and her husband Roger allowed me free access to the remarkable collection of letters which Max wrote to them in India during their period of missionary service in that country.

Most of all I owe an incalculable debt to Mary Warren for her complete open-heartedness from the beginning to the end of what I can honestly say has been a joint labour of love. She has opened to me her treasure-store of personal memories, letters, diaries and records. Besides this she has, through many conversations, guided me towards a deeper understanding of Max's personal life and relationships. Increasingly I have come to realise how large a part she played in his total ministry. A sudden remark of hers, remembered over the years by a friend who heard it, seems to me to summarise her achievement: "I must be one hundred per cent efficient for Max's sake." He was ever conscious of her whole-hearted sympathy and support; in moments of crisis she was always at his side.

When Max received news of the death of the American missionary leader John R. Mott he wrote in his diary: "It is not unfair to link him with St. Paul, Xavier and Carey as one of the few men who have caught the imagination of the Christian world from the point of view of the missionary enterprise." I dare to think that Max has the right to be accorded the fifth place in that succession. I regard him as the greatest all-round Christian leader of my own generation. To write about him has been what a recent biographer of Gladstone described as "an act of homage". I have often heard warnings about the perils of hagiography. I can only say that this man came nearer to my own conception of what constitutes a saint than any other I have known.

Finally, remembering my own dependence on the practical skills of others, I gladly record my indebtedness to Mrs. May Davis of Liverpool who has assisted our family in many ways over the past twenty-five years and has typed the manuscript of this book with her usual promptness and efficiency.

Contents

7

PART I

"To Thy great service dedicate"

1

Vision and Venture

MAX WARREN WAS born in Dun Laoghaire, Eire, on August 13, 1904. Though he was the son of an Irish clergyman (a graduate of Trinity College, Dublin) and of a mother whose family background was Irish, Max was never destined to spend any extended period in the land of his birth. Yet certain characteristics which are commonly associated with the peoples of Ireland – quickness of wit coupled often with darkness of depression, rugged independence combined with delight in other cultures, attachment to home and the family clan and at the same time a pioneering urge to explore other lands, above all a soaring imagination, sometimes, at least, allied with an intense concern for earthy details – all these were embodied, to a remarkable degree, in Max's own personality.

Within three months of his birth he was on his way to India, to which country his missionary parents were returning from furlough. They left behind in Ireland two sons aged nine and eight and this meant that for the first eight years of his life Max occupied the position virtually of an only child. He played with Indian boys and girls in the places where his father was stationed but did not meet them in school: the task of educating him in his early years was undertaken by his mother alone. He became familiar with the glare and the dust and the distinctive smells of Indian streets and markets and with the sounds of the rapid interchanges of the Hindustani language. But his mother's stories and then his books brought to his imagination the vision of the British Isles and their peoples. So he began himself to weave stories and to embark on that great adventure of discovering history which was to constitute one of the outstanding passions of his life.

"I remember," he writes, "I told myself stories which, as reading increased, drew on the world of other men's imaginings. Here I am sure was born that insatiable taste for reading, and with it the ability to read very quickly, which has been so great an asset ever since. What is more, reading has always been for me a form of listening. Books have always been 'persons' to me, not just the person of the author so much as the book itself talking, while I listened . . . always there is the magic of words, sometimes almost intoxicating in the vision they evoke and the explorations to which they beckon."

For figures he had no aptitude. Neither did he evince that curiosity about the natural world which characterises the scientist, nor that ability to handle material and construct models which makes the engineer. His was essentially a world of words – spoken, written, printed, patterned imaginatively on the mind. He was never happier than when reading or when sharing with others the fruits of his reading or of his own imagination. The boy who was often alone in the security of his home in Meerut or Allahabad, or alternatively was under the care of an Indian servant in the public places of the city, gradually built up an interior room of his own, into which he could withdraw with his own thoughts and imaginings at any time. No one in later years could have treated his friends more generously in opening his heart to them in conversation or correspondence. Yet there was always the sanctum, carefully guarded, into which no other human being was allowed to enter. The imaginative boy saw visions and dreamed dreams all through his life.

II

His parents belonged to that remarkable group of nineteenth-century men and women who regarded it as the highest privilege which earth could offer to spend their lives, without reserve or repining, in the foreign missionary enterprise. I have no figures to support my surmise but I suspect that Ireland's record in this area is as good as or superior to that of any other part of the British Isles. Since the days of St. Columba, the urge to spread the gospel seems to have been in the blood of Celtic Christians and none could have given themselves more wholeheartedly to the task than the Rev. and Mrs. J. A. F. Warren.

He went out to India in 1892 and she followed a year later. They served in North India with complete devotion and without any attempt to escape the cost involved. I find it hard to think of any mother having to bear more than Max's mother bore in her life as a missionary wife. Two fine boys had to be left behind in Ireland and

England for schooling when only nine and eight: one of them was to die on the battle field, the other from T.B. contracted while in the army and developing fatally after three years of missionary service. A little daughter died of bubonic plague in Benares and her husband, returning to India after the First World War, died there at the age of fifty three in 1920. Finally she was to face the ordeal of Max leaving for Nigeria, returning within a year a broken man. Yet I find no hint anywhere of complaint, no questioning of the conditions of missionary service. Father and mother were united in their response to the missionary call: their sons Jack and Max took up the torch and carried it on after them.

Max was devoted to his father. His was a gay and guileless character and, as Max recalls, he had a special ability to establish easy relationships with young people. In a letter some years after his father died he wrote: "He made joy wherever he went!" For six years from 1914 onwards he was constantly on the move around schools and youth organisations promoting the missionary cause. During this time Max was in boarding-school and their contacts must therefore have been confined to the school holidays. This however seems to have been enough to give the father a hero's stance in the boy's imagination. Sometimes absence from home at boarding-school makes a son's search for his own independence easier, avoiding the strain which often comes when father and son are in constant contact in the home. In Max's case there is no record of any kind of adolescent rebellion. Instead, his father was to him the best of men and one whose missionary career was the noblest of vocations. In the most natural way, it seems, Max wanted only to follow in his father's footsteps. This he did, not only through his own missionary dedication but also by his care for his mother who gave him up willingly to the mission field. Ultimately she came to live in her son's home until her death in her ninety-first year.

School holidays were also a time for getting to know his two elder brothers, both of whom were boarders at Dean Close School, Cheltenham in 1912. But the outbreak of war took them both into the army and only Jack survived. He came to play an increasing part in his young brother's life, especially when their father died. In many ways the opposite of Max – open, full of fun and good spirits, skilled in practical matters, a good instructor – he was able to draw out and impart confidence to a naturally reserved and somewhat shy boy. With the war ended and himself back at Cambridge he encouraged Max to share in the Christian activities in which he was engaged and the bond between the two brothers became even stronger.

Jack went out in 1924 as a member of a small band of reinforcements to the pioneer mission begun in Rwanda in 1920. "He came like a tonic to the tired little company, with a zeal and energy that far outdid his actual physical strength and there was no repressing him. Children flocked to him wherever he went, and he came with the love and gifts and prayers of many little English children behind him. Even his journey was fraught with excitement. He did conjuring tricks on the boat to crowds of excited little Belgian boys and girls, and preached to them in his 'extra special best French'.

". . . He arrived . . . to find a little grass shanty church and a handful of poorly trained teachers. With clear-sighted vision he drew up a policy for a future he would never see. There must be a boys' school to train evangelists and teachers from childhood. And there must be a solid beautiful church where little scattered congregations could gather for united fellowship and teaching. He then plunged into the work with such joyful intensity that he had a lung haemorrhage within the first few months and was ordered to rest. But prayer was made for him and he recovered and the best medical advice in the country bade him carry on."*

He shared the boys' activities and captured their hearts. "In him I first saw what the love of God was like," one of them said, and nearly half a century later in Kigezi faces would still light up at the mention of his name. Language study, tireless trekking around the villages, supervising the building of the church which to his delight was consecrated in June 1927, and finally the establishment of his own home – all this was too much for a weakened body. There were setbacks and disappointments, too, amongst the converts and by the spring of 1928 it was clear that he must return to England. On January 20, 1929, only two months after his young brother to whom he was devoted had also been invalided home, Jack died leaving behind his wife Kathleen and a baby daughter Sheelagh, little more than a year old.

III

Max has given us in his autobiography a graphic account of his schooldays, first at Heddon Court Preparatory School, Cockfosters, which he entered in September 1913 (up to this time his mother had

*Patricia St. John *Breath of Life* pp. 38 ff.

been his teacher), and then at Marlborough College, to which he went in 1918. It is hard to think of his receiving frequent beatings for "carelessness at work": there were certainly no signs of such "carelessness" in his subsequent life for as early as his undergraduate days the evils which he abhorred were "slackness, sloppiness and sloth". The truth probably is that he was too excited by all the treasures of the school Library to pay undue attention to Latin verbs. And he was constantly at work creating new stories in his imagination rather than concentrating all his energies on getting sums right.

Whatever the defects of the prep School may have been, Max makes light of them and, as always, pays tribute to the good which he derived from it. At least it prepared him for entrance to Marlborough and there can be no doubt about the immense influence which residence there exercised upon his whole future development. The town of Marlborough, with its main street so wide as almost to form a market square, must surely be one of the most attractive in England and on its east side the school buildings and fields form a kind of suburban village. Set in the midst of lovely country, with the Savernake Forest not far away, the whole environment seems ideal for study and recreation as one sees it today. Fifty years ago, however, not much attention was paid to physical surroundings or social amenities. To promote a godly discipline, which led to excellence in academic work and proficiency at games, was the dominant purpose of the school authorities. And at that time boys experienced a very spartan régime.

G. K. White, who entered Marlborough in Max's final year, gives this sketch of conditions at that time:

"The food was coarse, unappetising and inadequate. The central heating system was so poor that it left everything at best tepid except the class-rooms immediately above the furnace. About two hundred of us lived in a huge barn-like building called Upper School, heated solely by two enormous fires on the same side of the room. We used to do our preparation there in the evenings wearing big coats and gloves. Yet," he continues, "there was no unhappiness for 'we were all in it together'."* The fact that many of the boys were sons of parsons and had no knowledge of luxurious living may have helped some at least to accept their lot uncomplainingly.

Certainly Max was one who never complained and in retrospect wrote about it all with humour and tolerance. Clearly his was a

---

* G. K. White *The Last Word* p. 30. There is an even more horrendous account in Louis Macneice's unfinished autobiography.

successful school career according to the standards of the time –
playing for his house in rugby football, hockey and cricket:
becoming a school prefect in his final year: gaining an entrance
scholarship to Jesus College, Cambridge. But what he realised
mattered most were his friendships with boys of other traditions and
special interests, and still more his exposure to the interests and
teaching methods of some of the masters. Few men in public life
to-day have written more appreciatively about those who lit or
fanned for them the spark of knowledge, teaching them how to dig
for sources and to ask relevant questions.

In particular he pays a glowing and unqualified tribute to the
fellow Irishman who discovered his latent interest in the study of
history and so encouraged him in it that it became a ruling passion
of his life.

"He set to work to educate my imagination, guiding my reading,
lending me books, making his house a place to which I could come
at any time to browse, giving me an adult's friendship when I
needed it most, my father having recently died.

"Pat O'Regan was that rare kind of teacher who could by his
eagerness, his sheer enthusiasm for the subject, and his intellectual grasp, make the past come alive. You were 'there'. You
weren't hearing about it. You weren't reading about it. You were
there, part of the past itself. You were remembering where, in and
through your ancestors, you had been. This was great magic. It was
heady, intoxicating stuff. But it was also down-to-earth. For Pat
O'Regan the past was a clue to the present, with signals pointing to
the future. A medievalist himself, he insisted on us understanding
the forces making the world into which we ourselves were to go to
play our part. All his teaching endorsed the challenge of the
Marlburian poet, Charles Hamilton Sorley,

> We do not see the vital point
> That 'tis the eighth, most deadly, sin
> To wail 'The world is out of joint' –
> And not attempt to put it in.

To Pat O'Regan, with the exception of my father, I owe more than
to any other I have ever known." His father the Christian missionary, O'Regan the historian in action: to hold together, in vital
and continuous interaction, his Christian faith on the one hand and
his apprehension of history-in-the-making on the other hand,
became, I think, the dominant motif of Max's whole career.

He never tried to exploit his Old Marlburian status, but it

undoubtedly gave him useful links in the varying circumstances of his life. One of his closest collaborators in his days as General Secretary of C.M.S. was the President of the Society, Sir Kenneth Grubb, an old boy of the school. And in his travels around the world he was destined to meet again and again men who had been trained at Marlborough and now occupied positions of responsibility overseas. Preaching at the Old Marlburian Annual Service in the year of the Queen's Coronation he said:

"In the privacy of this company I hope I may be acquitted of presumption if I say that it has been part of the contribution of Marlborough to our nation's life that from its foundation it has sought to offer, and has in some measure been successful in offering to the public service, some in each generation of whom it can today be said that they have qualified as part of the royal blessing

'Wise counsellors and upright magistrates;
Leaders of integrity in learning and labour;
A devout, learned and useful clergy.'"

It was the final seal on Max's relationship with the School that the Old Marlburian Service on Passion Sunday 1978 should have been devoted to the commemoration of his life and ministry and that an extract from his last book should have been read by the Master. Moreover Mrs. O'Regan, who had been like a second mother to him in his Marlborough days and to whom he was utterly devoted, was still alive to welcome members of his family who came for the Service.

IV

One thing Marlborough failed to do for Max was to lead him to a personal relationship with Christ and a consequent commitment to his service. He has confessed that confirmation was scarcely more than a formality and that regular school worship left little impression upon him, at least consciously. This side of his developing personality was to depend upon his home life and upon the Christian activities in which members of his family were engaged.

His admiration for his father and his devotion to his mother – both of them completely dedicated missionaries – must have kept the call of Christ constantly before his imagination. His brother Jack had undergone a transforming spiritual experience in 1919 and the young brother could hardly have failed to be moved and attracted by his new enthusiasm. Jack himself felt a fresh responsibility for Max, especially after the loss of their father and, by allowing him to be drawn into and to share his own Christian concern, succeeded in enabling him gradually to find his own feet and to gain a new confidence. "Religion came alive for me for the first time." It was not a dramatic and sudden conversion. Rather what had been forming within him through the example and teaching of his father and mother, fostered too by the activities of the church in Gipsy Hill which the family attended, came to glad and conscious self-expression. He found that he could speak about his faith as his own personal commitment and that he could thereby know himself to be one within the fellowship of those who had joyfully accepted the responsibility of bearing witness, by lip and life, to their Lord and Master.

The family home was in Upper Norwood and the church in Gipsy Hill was Christ Church. At that time it was one of the most thriving churches in South London. Under the leadership of a noted evangelical, Canon R. C. Joynt, it often had more than a thousand present at morning and evening services and in addition had large Sunday schools. It gave more to the C.M.S. annually than any other parish in England. Joynt was essentially a pastor, meticulous in his regular visiting. At the same time he preached well constructed sermons centred in the gospel which was the heart of the church's life. There was no time for waving flags of protest against modernism or tractarianism. During holidays from school Max became accustomed to a form of positive evangelicalism which always remained his ideal.

V

As was common in London suburbs, there was in Upper Norwood a Crusader class for adolescent boys in secondary schools. Through his attendance at this when possible, and then in the summer holidays through his association with the Children's Special Service Mission led by his brother at Eastbourne, Max came under the strong influence of one of the most vigorous evangelistic movements of that period. Both the Crusaders and the C.S.S.M. were largely the products of lay leadership and this fact may well have helped to develop in him that profound respect for the Christian layman which he never lost. Men in the professions and in business gave their spare time to leading the classes, while the summer missions were usually organised by young men at the universities or London hospitals.

The C.S.S.M. at Eastbourne captured Max's interest and he became its loyal and enthusiastic servant from 1920 until his departure for Nigeria in 1927. It was in this context that he came to know his brother more intimately. Jack was then the leader and his joyous outgoingness communicated itself to the whole band of helpers. Max was present at first in a quite junior position but Jack entrusted him with tasks which, as he confesses, drew him out of the reserved shell in which he was in a measure encased. For many young men at that time the beach pulpit was the place where for the first time they bore witness to their faith in Christ. The testimony might be halting and almost incoherent but the children were uncritical and the parents usually indulgent. So as he proclaimed the gospel openly, without recourse to notes or pulpit aids, often with the background noise of wind and waves, a man sealed his commitment to Christ and took the first step forward along the pathway of missionary service.

In due course Max himself assumed the leadership at Eastbourne and this resulted in the least expected but the most providential meeting of his whole life. One of the most valuable aspects of a seaside mission was the opportunity it gave of easy relationships between the sexes at a time when, at least in evangelical circles, these were not frequent. It was normally the responsibility of the mission-leader to discover a senior woman to be house-mother and then to invite some one nearer his own age to become his assistant as leader of the girls' side of the work. This was the problem that confronted Max in the winter of 1925–6: whom should he invite to be joint leader for the summer of 1926?

Already, as Max recounts so charmingly in his autobiography, he had on his very first Sunday in Cambridge gone to the Freshman's Sermon at Holy Trinity Church and in the course of the service found his eyes riveted on a girl sitting under the gallery on the other side of the church. He did not know who she was and nothing further transpired at the time. But when he sought advice from a friend about a possible leader of the girls' work for 1926, he was told of two possibilities of whom one, it was recommended, should be asked first. When Max and Mary Collett met she proved to be the girl under the gallery, and the romance proceeded in real earnest.

It is no wonder that, for this and many other reasons, Max looked back towards the end of his life with profound gratitude upon all that his activities in the summer missions at the seaside had done for him. Like other organisations, the C.S.S.M. had its critics. Charges were made of social exclusiveness, of youthful indiscretions and (a criticism which Max himself was to communicate to the Mission headquarters) of too rigid requirements in matters of doctrine and conduct. Yet the large and wholesome benefits to many who gave willing service under the familiar red and white banner are admirably described in Max's own summing-up:

"To that joyful comradeship of young men and women, over-flowing with enthusiasm for Jesus Christ, I owe my life-long conviction that true religion is essentially joyful, precisely because it has for its basis the unwavering assurance of the utter trust-worthiness of Jesus. That indeed was the heart of the message, communicated day after day from the beach pulpit at Eastbourne as at many another seaside resort. The message was given with great simplicity. No doubt the simplicity was often very naïve, yet it was completely sincere and behind its delivery lay a great deal of private and corporate prayer. On the basis of such a very simple evangelical religion my Bible reading acquired what it had so far lacked, 'the warmth of desire', a warmth and enthusiasm which have grown down the years." And out of some of the grim realities of life on the mission station in Nigeria he wrote in a personal letter to Mary: "It's easy to think of the mission field as a C.S.S.M. It's absolutely nothing like it though the experience of C.S.S.M. is probably the best preparation in the world for the actual task ahead."

2

"Totally committed"

MAX WENT UP to Jesus College, Cambridge in the autumn of 1923. He had gained his history scholarship late in 1922 but, unlike many who either enjoyed a leisurely two more terms at school or left in order to gain some other kind of experience before entering the university, he used the period of grace to read voraciously in his chosen subject. This meant that in his freshman's year he was already in a privileged position. He was well ahead in his studies for Part One of the History Tripos; he came from one of the leading public schools; he was a keen and competent all-rounder at games; and he had many contacts in the religious life of Cambridge through his brother and other friends of the C.S.S.M. Few men have started their university career with greater promise.

To one with so deep an interest in history, the College which had elected him into a scholarship must have seemed almost a paradise. Though its foundation is officially dated as in 1496, some of its buildings were originally the Benedictine nunnery of St. Radegund, established in the twelfth century. In a beautiful setting, away from noisy traffic, possessing a lovely cruciform chapel in which the nuns had once sung their office, it is no wonder that the College laid its spell on Max. He became one of its loyal and devoted members and might well have one day found a place amongst its Fellows had he been so inclined. But he was too strongly committed in another direction. One of the highest distinctions which ultimately came to him was to be elected an Honorary Fellow in 1967.

The remarkable thing about his academic career is that he so resolutely kept his balance and refused to allow his missionary interests and evangelistic activities to interfere with time spent on his studies. This may have been partly due to his intense interest in the events of history and in patterns of historical development. Partly he owed it to tutors who, though kindly, maintained a firm discipline. Somehow he was already achieving that "mastery of time" which became the theme of one of his most significant books. Whatever might be the demands of his commitment to evangelism, they must not deflect him from his duty to inform his mind and to improve its expression in writing.

The achievement of a first class in both History and Theology and the winning of the Lightfoot Scholarship in Ecclesiastical History marked him out academically as one of the most successful under-graduates of that period in Cambridge. His athletic activities, however, were cut short in an altogether unfortunate way. He soon found a place in the College Hockey Eleven and by his third year was one of its most valued forwards. The team was well on its way to winning the inter-collegiate cup and in all likelihood Max would have joined the select ranks of the Cambridge Wanderers – those who just failed to get a Blue. But when playing centre-forward in the semi-final of the competition he was dashing for goal when the St. John's full-back, attempting to clear, drove the ball with immense force straight on his knee-cap. It was a sad ending to serious hockey for him but it incidentally had the effect of revealing the great respect and even affection that the "hearties" of the College had for him. Indeed it was being said at one time that he was the most popular man in Cambridge, though nothing could have been farther from his thoughts.

II

A first-class scholar and a fine athlete – these were the obvious terms in which to sum up Max's Cambridge career. But in fact these represented only those parts of his interests and activities that could be measured relatively easily. In addition he had freedom now to begin to work out the implications of his total commitment to Christ and his service. Some forty years later he was to say in a letter to Dr. Michael Ramsey, then Archbishop of Canterbury: "Ever since I was a school boy at the age of sixteen I have been totally committed to the missionary enterprise . . . From the evangelistic task of the Church in loyalty to the Church's Lord there can be no retreat." But commitment to the missionary enterprise did not imply marking time until the day arrived for going overseas. The evangelistic task had to be carried forward as faithfully as possible in Cambridge itself and all through his three years at Jesus and the following year at Ridley Hall he was concerned to find out how best to fulfil his responsibility in this respect.

There were two major Christian societies in the University at the time – the C.I.C.C.U. (Cambridge Inter-Collegiate Christian Union) and the S.C.M. (Student Christian Movement) with its subsidiary, the S.V.M.U. (Student Volunteer Missionary Union). The C.I.C.C.U. was the spearhead of evangelical Christianity and within its membership were many to whom Max was already known. Moreover his brother Jack had been a distinguished leader of it in his day. It would have been easy for him to throw in his lot completely with the C.I.C.C.U. and to confine himself to participation in its many activities. Yet surprisingly he already showed that independence of judgment and attitude that would not be confined within any single channel but claimed the freedom to witness and pray alongside all who acknowledged allegiance to Christ in sincerity. It was natural that his primary allegiance was to the C.I.C.C.U., but he was also a member of the S.C.M. and particularly active in its missionary involvement.

To some this seemed to be the way of compromise: agreement on certain doctrinal formulations, they held, could alone make it possible to pray and witness together in harmony. This absolute condition, however, Max never accepted. To worship God through Christ and to bear witness to his salvation were the only necessary preliminaries to fellowship. Once, having been "ticked off" by a stalwart member of the C.I.C.C.U. for his "liberal" attitude of working in with others, he wrote in his diary:

"I am learning very faintly and dimly something of what is my Cross. Once again I feel that the essential basis of co-operation is devotion to Christ. The men one works with may do much one regrets yet they cannot lightly speak evil of the Lord they follow, however mistaken I may think they be, and come what may Christ is preached." (More than once Max was confirmed in his own attitude by turning to Paul's words in Philippians 1:18). "I've unlimited faith in the power of that name however wrongly and inadequately expressed. Meanwhile I preach my own gospel and can do it in places other people can never reach."

Again, just before he went back to Cambridge for his year at Ridley Hall he wrote:

"My policy re C.U.M.C. (Cambridge University Missionary Council) and the mission field is just this. There is one simple basis for co-operation and that is – Devotion to Jesus Christ. Granted *that* in the first place – then be definite in one's own vision but unite for work with those who have that love but disagree in practice and detail: 'Come what may Christ is preached'. Coming out and being separate simply means one's testimony is never given and loveless-ness almost always follows. Loving Christ and living Christ is the real basis for unity. Let us rest on that and fight for that."

This, as his diary reveals, was Max's major struggle during his time in Cambridge. There were constant pressures from men senior in age to himself, and perhaps to a lesser extent from fellow under-graduates, either to concentrate attention on complete orthodoxy of belief or to direct all activities to the task of "winning souls". It was all the harder for him when these pressures came from men whom in so many ways he admired and whose friendship he valued. He wrestled with these questions, even agonised over them. "Why," he writes, "must they treat me as a pariah, an untouchable?" But somehow he could not give either of these concerns an absolute priority. He had already experienced the wonder of love in his family and amongst his comrades on mission teams and these human loves were transcended by his sense of an overmastering love for him "who first loved us". Nothing then or ever after could usurp the place of love, coming to its criterion and fulfilment in the love of Christ.

III

In his relation to dogma and orthodoxy it was, one would assume, the very width of his reading, especially in history, which made him question the validity of any narrow or unalterable verbal definitions. No undergraduate of his time could have loved his Bible more or studied it more regularly. Daily in his diary he first gave roughly half a page to what he had learned from his morning's devotional reading. Through most of 1926 he studied Isaiah, Jeremiah and other Old Testament books and there was never a day which did not yield some verse or theme of inspiration and illumination. On November 2 he reached Ecclesiastes 11.4 and was delighted with Moffatt's translation: "He whose eye is on the wind will never sow; he who studies clouds will never reap." "This is a priceless gem of teaching," is his comment. "It is the beatification of the element of chance which we must all recognise in every objective happening of life. If we are ever to get anywhere we must take our chance. Faith itself, even in the first analysis, is a leaping forth into the unknown darkness to find there not darkness but light. So in all we do let us not be over-cautious but with a simple trust in our heavenly Father let us launch forth on every task as v.6 has it 'Sow your seed in the morning of life, and stay not your hand till evening'."

Both in their spiritual insight and their felicitous wording many of his written meditations are astonishing as coming from a young man of twenty-two. Yet in spite of his sustained confidence that through the Bible he could listen to the voice of God, he did not enclose himself within a shell of verbal or historical inerrancy but wrestled with critical questions which were confronting Biblical scholars at that time. It is true that he adopted a conservative outlook generally and was sceptical about many of the historical judgments of commentators and teachers. For instance, he found Skinner on Jeremiah "brilliantly written but grotesquely arbitrary in his reasonings. The calm *a priori* assumptions of these Modernists amuse me." Yet a few days later he was finding it very difficult to justify the inclusion of such a "horribly sordid story" as Genesis 38 in Holy Writ. Even a chapter in the New Testament he found "muddled and involved" in its argument. He was frank about the difficulties which he encountered but made no attempt at this stage to set out any comprehensive statement about the relation between the Bible and his historical studies. His altogether dominant concern was to hear God speaking to him through the Bible and to respond in faith and obedience.

With the Creeds he was prepared to be more radical. "Was Nicaea a great mistake? A want of faith that come what may Truth would out? It seems as if that may be true." Again "the weakness of the Chalcedonian definition is obvious. Can we restate the creed in such a way as to safeguard the facts of God and Christ and yet make them less meaningless to us than is all the Greek philosophical terminology to the modern mind? I wonder how the problem affects the Muslim situation?" Instinctively he felt at home in the Bible with its method of story-telling to bear witness to the activities of the living God and his revelation in Christ. He was in a strange world when it came to the terminology of Greek philosophy and although he recognised the problem of communicating the gospel to those belonging to a different culture, whether that of Greek philosophy or that of Muslim theology, he clung to the story-method as conforming most closely to the biblical pattern and as most likely to convey meaning to the contemporary mind. Max was not a radical but his mind was never *closed*. How could it be when his reading was so persistent, so exploratory and so catholic?

IV

The other painful difference of opinion with many of his friends was concerned with the method of "soul-winning". Some seemed to have the ability to speak in season and out of season, to tackle the most unlikely people, to bring a person quickly to a point of decision and so to "win souls" for the kingdom of Christ. No one could have taken his responsibility as an evangelist more to heart than did Max. From the age of sixteen when the mission at Eastbourne had affected him so deeply, he had seen his future as that of a missionary and his present as that of training for that end. To obey the call to discipleship and witness was his deepest concern.

But in what way was this to be done? There emerged then a principle which stayed with him throughout his ministry: it was that of utter respect for the other *person*. He carefully guarded his own inner sanctum: he completely respected the right of the other man to guard his. So there could be no pressure, no hectoring, no attempt to dominate in however good a cause. The call of Christ must be presented but it must be done within the context of relationships which were truly *personal*.

Yet in Cambridge days he was often anxious about his own seeming lack of success. "I only wish I had half his zeal for souls." "I often worry about the lack of power in my life for winning other souls but I take comfort in the thought that God has given me certain talents which I am trying to use wholly for Him and those talents are making possible soul-winning by others better equipped than I for that work." "God does not ask us on eternity's morning the number of souls we've won but what have you done with your talents. We've all got different ones. God has given me in some small measure organising ability, something of writing and making friends and of speaking. I trust to use them to His glory."

Perhaps the key phrase in these confessions is "making friends". To say of Max that he had "a genius for friendship" is not just to use a trite phrase. He never spared himself in his effort to establish not just a pleasant acquaintance but rather a deep personal friendship. To achieve this nothing was more important than the unhurried person-to-person talk, if possible over or preceded by a meal. Days at Cambridge seem to have been a succession of encounters of this kind. "Brekker with a C.M.S. candidate. Lunch with a very keen C.I.C.C.U. Fresher. Tea with a lot of Anglo-Catholics and then a C.I.C.C.U. sermon followed by chocolate with Gray and McKay."

Visitors, especially missionaries, came to Cambridge and he was entertaining them at one meal or another. Men were constantly calling in to consult him on this or that matter. The wonder was that he was able to fulfil his ambition of six hours academic work a day and if possible two hours for his devotions.

This might have seemed enough for any man but still further there were letters to be written. This was another example of his intense concern for personal relationships. Here is a day in May 1927. "Played 84 games of tennis against Fitzwilliam. We won although James and I played putridly I'm afraid. After Hall wrote 31 letters and nearly passed out!" Or again in the previous year: "Six hours work, 22 letters and a good deal of other stuff done. My word life is full and no mistake. Well it is God given. I haven't sought it and I must carry on." He was meticulous in writing to his mother, his brother and close friends: he was involved in much correspondence about the C.S.S.M., which he was to be leading, and about missionary matters: and after May 1927 his pen became busier than ever for a new relationship, of unparalleled significance for him, had come into being.

He had seen the Girton girl on his first Sunday in Cambridge: he had met her in the winter of 1925–6 and secured her consent to lead the girls' work at Eastbourne: by the summer term of 1926, when she visited Cambridge (she had finished her History course in 1925), the diary records; "My word she is an ideal person and no mistake"; but it was to be more than a year before the oscillation of his feelings between hope of acceptance and dread of refusal was resolved. His whole desire was towards Mary but when could he dare to ask her to be his wife? By mid-May in 1927 "the strain of these days has been fearful". Then on May 13 the letter was sent and the next day a telegram brought him the word that transformed his whole outlook for the future. If there had been strain beforehand, far greater strains were due to be experienced before many months had passed. Under God, Mary's love and indomitable steadfastness supported him in the time of his major crisis and then continued to sustain and uphold him in all circumstances to the end of his life.

For Max, to write was freedom, joy, unburdening, conversation. Now to Mary he could pour himself out as never before. They were utterly at one in their love of history, in their sense of responsibility for Christian witness, in their unqualified ambition to devote themselves to missionary work overseas. For the time being Mary was teaching in Tunbridge Wells and they agreed that Max would go out to Nigeria for one term of service while she would undertake training in preparation for the time when, having been married on his first furlough, they could go out to work together in Nigeria.

Meanwhile his innumerable friends rejoiced with him and his fellow-students at Ridley made the most of the occasion. Some tried unsuccessfully to substitute "O perfect love" for the appointed hymn in Chapel but they did manage to get the Wedding March played as the voluntary. He had become the trusted alarm-clock for men on his staircase, rousing them regularly and often laying on tea. About one of them he wrote: "One awfully jolly fellow here whom I have to wake every morning and who is unbearably annoyed about each morning as he sleeps like a log – gazed at me the other morning in more than usual disgust, tempered with some thoughtfulness, and said: 'I do hope you won't get her up to pray at iniquitous hours in the morning' – in a tone of sympathy right from the bottom of his heart."

Yet anyone reading his Cambridge diaries in, say, the summer of 1927, could well have wondered whether he had not subjected himself to an almost intolerable strain and whether he was really fit to go off on missionary service. He was indeed physically strong, athletic, buoyant, but again and again the diary records a sense not only of tiredness but of exhaustion. He would be up at five thirty in the morning and drive himself through a day of prayer, study, writing, exercise, committees, personal conversations, without any let-up. Slackness of any kind he detested. "No one", he remarks, "has yet become a saint in their sleep." Yet, particularly from the early part of 1927, there occur such comments as "feeling so awfully tired", "the old mind simply isn't working at all. It hurts even to read for ½ hour." "I do hope and pray I'm not in for a bad mess up." An access of new life came with the engagement but by late July he was "feeling so very tired" perhaps "by overdoing myself physically and mentally": and in August "I cracked badly and my old nerves seemed to go right to pieces". Yet he was due to sail for Nigeria in November. He seemed to pick up again in his last weeks at home but it remains a question whether he was really fit to face the strain of parting from Mary and his home and taking up residence, under very difficult conditions, in a new land.

V

The words "totally committed to the missionary enterprise" were not lightly written. They expressed a priority which brooked no rival. History and proficiency in examinations, friends and their several potentialities, supremely the girl of his choice and his responsibility towards her – all were given as much time and attention as was humanly possible within his crowded life. But God had called him to share in the great missionary enterprise and if he were to be faithful to his calling he must, even in his days at university and theological college, do all that he could to promote its progress.

The commitment of which he speaks was made in the year of his father's death and shortly before his brother Jack had offered himself for missionary service. As Max felt a deep responsibility to take his father's place in the care of his mother, so he may well have felt a similar responsibility to carry on the task which his father had been unable to complete. Whatever the conscious or unconscious influences may have been, few men in this century can have had so strong a conviction of missionary vocation at so early an age and have continued to hold it undeviatingly to the very last days of his life. The only serious question for him was in what precise way his calling was to be fulfilled.

There was little doubt that it would be within the fellowship of the Church Missionary Society, for all his family's associations had been with that organisation and the church which he attended in vacations was its ardent supporter. But C.M.S. was working throughout Africa and the East. In what part were his particular talents and interests to find fullest scope? In one of his early letters to Mary he wrote: "Did I ever tell you that my first ambition was language work in Japan as the result of an appeal by Murray Walton? I was so depressed with life that I came to the conclusion the only job I'd ever be any good at would be inserting Christian advertisements in Japanese newspapers. It sounded an easy job though is probably a jolly hard one. Since then of course has come the Muslim call and with it the lesson that it isn't one's own capacities that count but His capacity and that is unlimited: So I'm going forward, to quote your message to the Reunion of a year ago 'to attempt things antecedently impossible in calm expectation of incredible success'. It sounds blatantly conceited but once you allow for the elimination – no not that but the filling of the human with His power, it is surely just normal Christianity or ought to be – with most of us and certainly still with me,`I fear, very much 'ought to be'."

The "Muslim call" came to him with suddenness and clarity at a surprisingly early stage in his university career. Just before going up to Cambridge, he and two others covenanted together to offer themselves for missionary service when the proper time came.

Then, in his first term, he was invited with a few others to a tea-party where G. T. Manley, the C.M.S. Secretary for Africa, told of specific openings there. In the course of his talk he appealed for a team of men to offer for service in Northern Nigeria. Thereupon Max wrote off to his two friends to ask whether this might not be the very mission to which they were being called. And, as he records, "the next term, to my great surprise, two men, both far senior to me called to say they had heard about our plan, and could they join. Soon there were six of us and, very much to Mr. Manley's surprise, and I suspect, some embarrassment, he found he was presented with six men prepared to go to Northern Nigeria directly they had qualified in their several professions." So there came into existence the Hausa Band, a group of men who soon began to be talked about in missionary circles and whose leader was unquestionably the youthful Max Warren.

1924, when the Band was formed, was a time of considerable significance in Anglican missionary history. So far as the Church Missionary Society was concerned it was a time of stress. The tension between conservatives and liberals within the evangelical section of the Church of England had already been felt before the War, but when the time of reconstruction came and evangelicals began looking towards the future, tensions increased and men organised themselves for biblical study and theological discussion on one side or other of the divide. This was serious enough in the country at large but it was critical in the extreme for C.M.S. This was the honoured evangelical society which for more than a century had been sending out missionaries of evangelical persuasion, without strict tests concerning doctrinal orthodoxy. Now, however, some were demanding assent to the verbal inspiration of the Bible and to a particular interpretation of the atoning work of Christ. Could the Society maintain its comprehensiveness in the face of these pressures towards a limiting orthodoxy?

The outcome was a painful split which led to the founding of the Bible Churchmen's Missionary Society in 1922. Max's whole philosophy of co-operation with others who were united in devotion to Christ kept him firmly within the society to which his father and mother had given such long and devoted service. But for a time at least the C.M.S. was prevented from taking full advantage of opportunities presenting themselves overseas by conflicts of opinion on doctrine and policy on the home front. Fortunately a man was found, Wilson Cash, who became General Secretary in 1926 and over a period of extreme difficulty in the Society's affairs, kept it (to use his own words) "in the main stream of the Church's life." A big man, in physical stature and in courageous leadership, he "took his stand on the intention of the founders to form, not an 'Evangelical Party' missionary society, but rather a church society whose special emphasis and message should be evangelical". (G. H. G. Hewitt. *The Problems of Success,* p. 443.) This "stand" was one to which Max gave his whole-hearted support from beginning to end of his association with the C.M.S.

This was the situation on one side. On the other side the Church of England as a whole was being made more aware of its missionary responsibility than perhaps at any time previously in its history. When one recalls the hesitations and questionings at the time of the Edinburgh Conference as recently as 1910, it is remarkable that only fifteen years later a World Call convention was held at Westminster, drawing together three thousand delegates of varying ages from all over the country, and creating a sense of enthusiasm and responsibility which was relayed back in many ways to dioceses and parishes. Moreover the Missionary Council of the National Assembly of the Church of England had been established in 1922 with Dr. St Clair Donaldson, Bishop of Salisbury (a man of striking presence and wide vision gained from overseas experience) as its first chairman. The mid-twenties saw large numbers of undergraduates from Oxford and Cambridge going on student missionary campaigns to Carlisle, to Portsmouth and other cities. The war with all its devastation had opened up new vistas of the world's needs and of the responsibility of young men and women to respond to those needs as they had done in offering themselves for military service.

Max, then, with his call to missionary service and his full commitment to C.M.S. was in many ways a marked man already. The Society maintained specially close contacts with Cambridge and secretaries or missionaries were often there on visits. Manley, who had first sounded the call for recruits for Northern Nigeria, was very able but a somewhat austere man and Max could not be on easy terms with him. H. D. Hooper, however, who succeeded Manley in the African Secretariat in 1926, was very different in temperament and won his complete confidence and affection. For him, as Max said, "Northern Nigeria was not just an office file but a living reality," a pregnant statement which summed up so many of his own attitudes when he came to sit in the General Secretary's chair. Then, late in 1926, Temple Gairdner, the apostle to the Muslim World in Cairo, came to Cambridge and was invited to tea. "He seems most sympathetic to my ideals about literary evangelism in West Africa. O to be allowed a share in putting right the great misunderstanding of 13 centuries." S. A. Morrison, who was making a notable contribution as a lay missionary in Cairo, also came and talked over policies for Muslim work. Through these many personal contacts Max was building up his own theology of missions as well as constructing guide-lines for the work in Nigeria. In addition "I must read and read", books of travel, books about Islam, anything to give him a clearer vision of the best policy to pursue.

He had assumed responsibility for organising the Hausa Band and this involved constant correspondence with C.M.S. Headquarters about their deployment. He also saw to regular dissemination of information to the members of the team. He inaugurated a *Crusade Report* and arranged for frequent prayer meetings. One of the senior men who had, to his surprise, asked to join the Band was Guy Bullen, already at Ridley Hall. Without question the gift of his friendship at Cambridge, followed by his sympathetic understanding in early days in Nigeria, proved to be one of the outstanding benedictions of Max's life. Though he described the Hausa Band at one time as "a collection of weird birds" there was nothing weird about Guy. He was strong and vivacious, able to sustain Max when he was depressed, sharing his hopes and ideals, supporting him as an older brother while deferring to him as the leader in policy and planning. His death by accident at an early age after becoming Bishop in the Sudan robbed the Church of one of the most promising missionary leaders of this century.

Max felt the loss deeply. In a beautiful essay in the book of recollections by Guy's friends, he speaks of his administrative "ability", his complete integrity, his humility and "good companionship". Then, more personally: "It is one of the gladdest memories of my life, which has been enriched out of all measure by undeserved friendship, to look back on a day, now eighteen years ago, when, as a mere schoolboy, I was asked by Guy Bullen to go for a walk with him over the Downs behind Eastbourne. What those years of friendship have meant can easily be guessed by those who for longer or shorter time have called Guy Bullen friend." And in Cambridge days he had written to Mary: if "unselfishness is the distinguishing mark of any man it is his". Guy and his brother Jack were his boyhood heroes. Neither possessed his intellectual gifts nor the sweep of his imagination but each revealed to him a pattern of natural and whole-hearted dedication to the service of Christ. They trusted Max unreservedly: his life matured and blossomed within the warmth of their friendship.

Because those in positions of authority recognised the unusual gifts and promise of this young man, they invited him to speak on missionary themes and to participate in conferences where policies were being debated. He was asked to be a speaker at the Salisbury Diocesan Conference. He was chosen as a delegate to an important missionary conference in Belgium where for the first time he became acquainted with Dr. J. H. Oldham who had so successfully organised the Edinburgh Missionary Conference of 1910. He found time to study phonetics, to learn typewriting, to read the Qur'ān, to take a course in dispensary work – all in preparation for the great day when he would sail for Nigeria. November 22 was his last day at home when his prayer for Mary and his mother was that they might have "the joy of a more intimate companionship than ever before with the Friend on the Road". The next day they journeyed with him to Liverpool, little dreaming of the kind of homecoming that was in store for him in Plymouth eleven months later.

3

The knock-out

THE STORY OF Max's brief period of missionary service in Northern Nigeria contains many of the elements of tragic drama. Its pattern has constantly reminded me of the scene on the hockey-field at Cambridge when the dashing young centre-forward (at the time the key man of the team) was racing for goal and then was stopped short by the devastating blow on the knee which put an end to his athletic career. So this young missionary, allowing nothing to deflect him from his ambition to preach the gospel of Christ amongst the Hausa tribes of Nigeria, boarded the *Apapa* at Liverpool and then less than a year later landed at Plymouth, apparently defeated, with bodily health destroyed.

It was a drama in which a large number of actors were involved. First of all, though this may seem strange, there was the British Government. Nigeria was a British colony and the Government was highly concerned about the problems of its administration. Traditional tribal structures were tightly-knit and had to be handled with great care. More important still were the often fanatical religious sensitivities, the result of Muslim infiltration. Colonial officials, bearing the responsibility of keeping the peace and of promoting prosperity within their territories, looked with a good deal of either suspicion or apprehension upon missionaries who seemed intent on disturbing the hallowed allegiances and customs.

Possibly as an outcome of his careful study of history, Max had already come to feel a healthy respect for the administrator in his task and had no wish to clash with him unless matters of large principle were at stake. In a letter to Mary not long after their engagement he wrote:

> Dearest, never get an anti-government complex. Almost every Nigerian missionary has got it and it is doing more harm to the

cause of Christ than anything else over there. 50% or more of the mistakes are on the missionaries' side, due to the most flagrant tactlessness and bad taste. It is going to mean so much if we can help to bridge the gulf.

Again, when the Governor of Nigeria invited Max to meet him as representing the Hausa Band, he wrote:

You've come into something which will have plenty of excitement. I think Northern Nigeria is the test case in the Mission field to-day on the question of Government and Societies. It may well make all the difference to missionary effort all over the world if a real stable sensible settlement is made here. This is one of the reasons why we've got to be very very sensible about Government and not get carried off our feet.

This may sound over-confident as he had not yet set foot in any colonial territory but it indicates already that in his missionary leadership his policy would be to work along with the government of the day just as far as that was possible.

Then there was the C.M.S. in London. His relations with its officials and particularly with Handley Hooper, the Africa Secretary, had been altogether cordial. He knew how dependent missionaries overseas were on the home staff for their welfare in every domestic way – finance, education of children, furloughs – but still more for guidance about their responsibilities within the overall strategy of world-evangelisation. It was always easy for those on the spot to think that they knew best and this was particularly true when dioceses were being formed and individuals were given new authority as bishops. At the beginning of his own missionary work, Max kept in close personal contact with headquarters, a process he was destined to maintain to an astonishing degree in the reverse direction when holding responsibility at headquarters himself.

These were the two institutional bodies in the background. In the foreground was a man of commanding presence and influence, Dr. Walter Miller, who had first entered the city of Kano in Northern Nigeria on Good Friday in the year 1900. A Devonian, brought up in a Plymouth Brethren family, Miller had become an Anglican during his medical course at St. Bartholomew's Hospital. At the end of his second year he attended the Convention at Keswick and there, having pledged himself to serve God overseas, enrolled as a member of the Student Volunteer Missionary Union. This brought him into close relationship with a group of men famous in the

missionary life of the Church before the First World War – Temple
Gairdner, Willie Holland, J. H. Oldham, Alec Fraser – and their
friendship continued to support him in the often lonely experiences
of his pioneer mission to Northern Nigeria. Before his arrival there
he had spent a year of service in a Sierra Leone Hospital and some
months in Cairo, where he met a few Hausa tribesmen and showed
himself unusually adept at picking up their language. Finally he
landed in Nigeria with two fellow recruits and proceeded to make
the journey from Lagos to Jebba and then north-eastwards for four
hundred miles into territory where no Europeans were to be found.

The story of his heroic adventures, leading ultimately to the
establishment of a missionary compound within the Muslim city of
Zaria, is one of the epics of missionary history. Max summarised it
in his felicitous way at the memorial service for Dr. Miller in 1952:

"On Good Friday 1900 a procession of five white men and their
African porters filed through one of the great gates into the city of
Kano. They represented the vanguard of the twentieth century
pressing in upon what was still the almost untouched medieval
culture and civilisation of the western Sudan. The invaders of that
old walled city came, as men had come for centuries, on their feet.
They had walked, literally and painfully, the whole long way up
from the coast. And within a matter of weeks three of those white
men were dead or invalided home. One, their leader Bishop
Tugwell, had returned to his duties at the coast. And one remained,
Dr. Walter Miller, there to stay and fulfil a life-work of 52 years."
A similar tribute appeared in an article in the *Nigerian Review* after
Miller's death. The Hon. Eyo Ita, Principal of the People's Institute
in Calabar, spoke of him as one of the greatest sons of Nigeria. "In
our perplexities with 'expatriates' the type of Dr. Miller comes
forward to clear our sky and qualify our attitudes." No one, as Max
declared, ever overmatched his understanding of the inner thoughts
and racial idioms of the people he loved. He translated the Bible
into Hausa and lived to speak the language so well as to fulfil his
ambition not to be recognised as a foreigner when speaking in the
dark!

Here was a lay doctor of towering personality who, when Max
arrived in Zaria in 1927, had already spent twenty-seven years there
in a position of undisputed leadership and had established an
institution to which he was deeply attached – not a hospital but a
school. There, in the midst of a Muslim city, he reigned over his
boys and devoted his energies to preparing them to take up posts in
the new Nigeria which was then coming into being. There was also a
small dispensary dealing with mild complaints but his interests were

focussed in the school and in translation work for which he was so well equipped.

The second actor in the foreground was Guy Bullen who had gone out as an ordained missionary in November 1926. The fact that he was ordained was not altogether welcome to Miller, but Guy's open and even radiant personality could not fail to commend him to the older man. But a certain tension was bound to arise from the fact that the Hausa Band, of which Guy was a member, was dedicated to evangelistic work out in the Hausa Emirates. Miller on the other hand was firmly entrenched in Zaria and believed that the essence of missionary strategy was to maintain a strong base at the very heart of a Muslim stronghold. Guy had become fully aware of the situation before Max arrived, aware that the Government was anxious to prevent trouble by removing the Christian institution from its place within the city, yet equally aware that Miller could not be moved against his will and that he was, in fact, entirely opposed to any change. How could the new recruits fulfil their ambition if the senior man, possessed of so lengthy an experience, was out of sympathy with what they wanted to do?

II

Into this situation Max entered on December 10, 1927. The voyage out had been uneventful though, as Miller had been returning from furlough, there had been opportunities for many talks with him. The older man had given the younger his confidence and in their general outlook they found much in common. But once arrived in Zaria, with Miller in full control of the familiar surroundings, things became more difficult. Only two days after arrival Max was writing:

> My word I've had some eye-openers. This mission is in a perfect tangle and it will need an amazing amount of grace to help to untangle it. The Bishop is quite in the wrong place but the real difficulties are going to be in the School. As far as I can see Miller is an old dear and a saint but I don't see much prospect of any changes ever being possible and he keeps such a hand on the boys that one has very little look in. However love is the really big thing, Lord I want to reflect Thy life.

Here at once were the elements of tragedy which must have helped to bring about the final breakdown. Max was soon to be torn between his affection and admiration for this pioneering hero and his all too clear recognition that the affairs of the school were far from satisfactory, and that it was in any case obstructing the task of wider evangelism amongst the Hausa tribes whom he and his Band were pledged to serve. For the time being he could pour out his feelings with complete confidence to Guy, and while the latter remained on the station this was the great solace. But Guy's time for furlough was not far off and when he had gone Max could only express his feelings through letters to the one who seemed so far away.

Not unnaturally Miller felt the tension and wrote about it in his book *Reflections of a Pioneer* some years later.

"It was difficult for men and women new to the work, knowing little of the language or the people and their religion to realise how much *was* being done, how invaluable was the site, though small, in the heart of a big Muslim city, in which many a man, wanting a talk on spiritual things, had been able to come quite easily, sometimes entirely disguised and stay long hours talking till late at night with me on spiritual matters and how easily contacts *made* might be lost! They scarcely realised with what difficulty and hard work had been built up a big school of Muslim boys, most of them boarders" (pp. 215 f).

With so much of this Max would have sympathised entirely, and yet he already knew how great were the perils associated with property and institutions and specialisation along a single line. For him the call of the wider world and the challenge of the future together constituted a divine imperative.

However, in spite of some early disillusionments, he lost none of the excitement of actually being in the place which he had prayed about and longed to see. He was soon taking classes of boys who knew some English and working away at the Hausa language himself. Guy, who had already won the hearts of the Europeans stationed near by, was introducing Max to those who could help his boys get jobs. Two days before Christmas he was down with his first attack of fever but managed to share in some of the season's festivities. As the New Year dawned, little knowing what it held in store for him, he chose as his motto: "That in all things, whether by life or by death, Christ may be glorified in me."

After a month of sharing in the school-teaching and struggling with Hausa, he began work in the dispensary. This, added to three hours a day on language and teaching responsibilities, made life almost impossibly full and led him to the conclusion that new recruits should at all costs be given freedom in their first six months to concentrate all their energies on language study. One day he was spending seven hours at accounts, having been asked to take over the mess. Yet in the midst of all this and letter writing he was avid to read Bergson and Kant!

The last two days of January brought welcome relief in the shape of a visit with Guy to a consultation with the Lieutenant Governor at Kaduna. This gave Max the first opportunity to embark on the travel diary, a literary form which he was to use to such advantage some twenty years later. I quote some extracts to give a taste of his vivid style.

"The sun rose according to schedule. My boys, as I wanted them specially punctual, were later than usual. Breakfast followed the same old groove. Then came packing. Staying with Lieutenant Governors not having previously been a hobby of mine this needed considerable forethought as I could very well arrive and when dressing for dinner slip round and say 'Palmer (the L-G) old dear I've omitted my cuff-links!'" (In an earlier letter he had written: "I take about 2 hours dressing into those ghastly evening clothes.") "Finally, however, everything, including my black silk socks (3/6) and an enormous quantity of spare clothing, was packed, a brief race to the Dispensary resulted in the manufacture of some Potassium Iodide and then I flew up to Dr. Miller for instruction if he had any. Finally at 12.30 Guy took charge of the wheel and with Kity (his boy) and Bayaro (mine) amongst the baggage at the back we set off in the mission charabanc for our 55 mile trip.

"As we got near Guy said, 'Now we're coming to Hampstead.' Certainly Kaduna is a beautiful place. It is the Headquarters of Government in the North and was chosen for its ideal situation and climate. It is beautifully laid out with large areas round each house and the houses have had much money lavished upon them. You really might not be in Africa it is all so different to anywhere else. As we had a lot of spare time we went down to the public gardens by the river. The river falls in terraces and with lovely red, yellow and purple flowers against the background of Mango green.

"We motored round the native town and at last sailed up to the government house, not without gracefully acknowledging the salute at the gate. We were met by Mac Michael, the Governor's Secretary, a nice fellow late of Magdalene College, Cambridge. At the same moment the L.G. came up and took us both off to watch the tennis on their lawn. They've got a grass court which is as lovely as it is rare in Africa. I found myself sitting next to Mrs. Palmer, a very charming person. Generally I should be tongue tied but I must have been inspired as although the subject was essentially botanical

39

I kept my end up for over ½ an hour discussing flowers, no whit terrified by the fact that she only used the Latin names of them!

"My word it was a good dinner. I'm not used to high society but it was quite enjoyable, and as a change much to be welcomed. By the way I had my real opportunity of making a mutt of myself. The Port was handed round for the toast of the King. The Secretary who sat next to me whispered 'We always have The King' and then had the sense to suggest water! I'm glad that in College Dinners I never gave way as one can just drink water and toast in water quite calmly now! The ladies went to bed about 9.45. The talk soon drifted to our business and we rose to go to bed at 12.45 a.m."

Next morning they called on the Surveyor General and a senior officer who, they found, rose every morning while it was still dark to read his Hausa New Testament. Max comments:

"There's much that might be better in Government but my word there's tons that might be worse. More and more am I coming round to feel that there is a better way to treat and meet Government than has been employed in the past. I want to take the new line. Co-operation *is* possible and I want to say how much I regret much that I have said against Government. I've been learning more and more of Government's task out here and I've come to the conclusion, sudden though the change may seem, that really Government are largely right and missions are wrong. I think that on the whole the wrong method of trying to work has been tried and in good Medical and Educational work, with later on literature, we have a means of tackling the job up here that is quite independent of any need for being in big cities like Zaria. I'm wondering if being in a city is really a strategic gain. I think good Medical and Educational work will attract people to it. There's no room inside cities for expansion or industrial work. Literature can get anywhere and does not need a city or a centre."

Characteristically, Max went on to surmise that history might have been made in the past twenty-four fours! Guy and he, who were absolutely united, would shut themselves up *in camera* and prepare a draft which would go first to Dr. Miller and then to England. In substance it was to the effect that the time had come to fall in with the wishes of the Government, to move out from Zaria, to set up a new mission station on a site outside the city which the Government would make available, and so to reverse the whole conception of mission in Northern Nigeria from that of clinging to a stockade at the heart of a Muslim city to that of establishing a new outpost on virgin soil, which could be both a centre of attraction and a beacon of radiation. Their concern was for the untouched tribes of

40

the Hausa peoples who, they felt, would never come in to the small compound immured in Zaria City. "We're in a deep rut here and we must get out."

It is not hard to imagine the critical tensions which all this created in the Zaria camp. Max felt that Miller had in many ways given false impressions to the Government and that statements of his, made in good faith, were exaggerated and could not be trusted. Miller, on his side, was faced by the prospect of seeing his life's work pulled up by the roots and an attempt made to transplant it elsewhere. Could it then survive? What would happen to his boys to whom he was devoted? Was all this upheaval necessary? He believed he knew the real situation better than government officials and certainly better than these young missionaries, one of whom had been in Nigeria less than two months! And naturally Max was aware of this and deeply troubled for he had an enormous regard and much affection for Miller and had no desire to hurt him. But with other members of the Hausa Band preparing to come out and join him and Guy, it seemed that the nature of the whole enterprise was at stake. He felt that he had talked too much in the past too idealistically. The call now was for *action* even if it meant exposure to some mud-slinging (the mud of Northern Nigeria had already entered deeply into his imagination as the title of his first publication *Seeing Visions in Mud* so amply reveals).

III

So the months wore on. All the time there was the longing to have Mary at his side to share the joys and sorrows of his life in Zaria. There were many happy days. His work in the dispensary occupied increasing amounts of his time and brought the satisfaction of knowing that he was really reaching individuals and ministering to their needs. He enjoyed his activities with the boys, though his heart was not really in the formal teaching. His friendship with Guy Bullen was a constant enrichment, not least because Guy was not inhibited from telling him when his dealings with others were either resented or misunderstood. Guy was more inclined to apply psychological theorising than Max was but in a heart-searching passage of his diary he admitted that Guy had helped him as none other could have done. "It seems that the force of my life is a driving spirit which is not leadership. I try to force people to my own conclusions

41

when I ought to lead them. It is all the cursed lack of humility which I know so well I have got. In the process I've alienated ever so many folks. I put causes and ideas above individuals and just because of that I lack the love without which nothing can be done."

But in mid-April Guy left for England on furlough and now the only one on the station to whom Max could talk with a sense of sympathetic understanding was a woman teacher who had herself suffered from the almost vindictive treatment she had received from a senior colleague. He found constant refreshment in his books and his carefully guarded devotions but he was a lonely man, bubbling over with ideas which he longed to put into effect, but constantly frustrated by the "rottenness" of the whole administration and by the unbelievable "pettiness" which poisoned personal relationships. Repeatedly there comes an explosion in the diary about jealousies and favouritism and scrupulosity until in a measured summing-up he exclaims: "If asked to write to C.M.S. my annual report I should be tempted to write thus:

From point of view of People and Possibilities I am Entranced, Enthusiastic, Expectant.

From point of view of C.M.S. in Zaria I am Disappointed, Disillusioned, Disgusted!"

So he sought refuge in never-ceasing activity. Language study, dispensary service, games with the boys, endless writing (twenty-seven letters in one day) and reading in every spare moment. And he found some relief from the pettinesses of Zaria by comparing them with the controversies going on in England over the revision of the Prayer Book with "fanatics trying to get rid of everything in the Revised Book that does not fit in with fundamentalist teaching". To Mary he wrote: "I'm longing to rescue you from England with its petty preoccupation on side issues." He tried as always to keep the really big things before his imagination – God's love, Christ's commission, the Holy Spirit's leading, the Bible as the never-failing source of inspiration and direction – but it was far from easy in the midst of heat and dust and appalling smells and a body which was only beginning to adjust itself to new climatic conditions.

In August "the storm burst at last". Miller sent an entirely unacceptable letter to the Lieutenant-Governor who replied tartly and reported the matter to higher authority. Max's convictions were wholly on the side of the Government. "All this trouble is on my mind – I've not been able to pray or think or read. God understands." Next day found him in hospital where he spent two weeks. Lung trouble was suspected but not identified. Then for the whole of September he was taken away to higher ground and

42

another mission area where he should have been resting. Instead he seized the opportunity to make long treks accompanied by his devoted house-boy and become acquainted with what had already been accomplished on the Bauchi Plateau. Yet he could not shake off the oppressive burden of the problem of Zaria and its future. He wrestled with it in prayer, seeking desperately for guidance and courage to do God's will. Back in his lodging early in October he spent "a very happy quiet Sunday, comforted by the thought of the Vine sustaining the servant branch". But on October 9 the one word Indigestion appears in large capital letters and there the diary ends. In a letter to Mary, written two days after, he still could not fail to see the funny side of things: "the most incredible indigestion coupled with a rotten cough hasn't helped matters. Tell it not to Miss F., and publish it not in the pulpit at Holy Trinity, but the only thing that has helped my indigestion has been Port! And I loathe that so much that I've just had a glass of lemonade to take away the taste and within ten minutes was thoroughly sick! Heigh ho! Anyway I hope it will soon be over."

Alas, it was not soon over. He still was convinced that he was suffering from nervous strain and that all would be right again when Guy Bullen returned from furlough in two months' time. But as is well known today, two of the greatest enemies to health are malnutrition and fatigue and both of these had played all too sinister a part in the past few months. So came the crisis. Recording it many years later he wrote: "Shortly after getting back to Zaria I was playing hockey with the boys. Dr. Miller had taught them the game magnificently and shortly before this we had taken on a European team, captained by an Irish international, and had easily beaten them. But this particular afternoon I wasn't feeling too good. Back in my room, just before taking my bath, I took my temperature and found it was 104°. Dr. Miller came over at once and got me driven over to the European hospital on the other side of the city. There the doctor took a very grim view of the situation and said that both my lungs were seriously affected and that I must go back to England at once." Down to Lagos by train, transported to the ship in which throughout the voyage he lay critically ill, brought ashore at Plymouth to find Mary waiting for him and then to the sanatorium at Linford in the New Forest where many weary months were to be spent.

So, as it seemed, the dashing young centre-forward leading his Hausa Band towards the goal of their ambitions, had met the knock-out blow which was to end it all. He had, in less than a year, passed through an experience of the ambiguities of the missionary life such as few can have undergone. How much the spiritual and mental and personal struggles contributed to his breakdown none can tell. The glorious result is not in doubt. He who seemed to have been defeated on the field, returned from the darkness to become the leading light in the Church of England's missionary outreach in the mid-twentieth century.

4

"Baffled to fight better"

MANY HAVE FOUND the section on his illness in Max's autobiography the most moving and most significant in the whole book. It is a story quickly told but it represents literally years of bodily affliction and mental strain. It was as if a hurricane had destroyed all his and Mary's hopes and plans when they had scarcely begun to build. As he expressed it in a deeply-felt interpretation which he gave to Mary in 1932:

> For very dark they were those days. How dark for you
> I think I'll never know, for you were bearing me
> And your ownself, whilst keeping Mother free
> From her dark doubts.

Mother Warren had lost her son Jack soon after he had been invalided home with T.B. in January of 1929. Max was lying dangerously ill at the same time. Mary was thus given the responsibility of sustaining and encouraging both Mother and son while at the same time carrying on her own duties, first as teacher, then on the staff of one of the C.M.S. training colleges.

Max has paid a wonderful tribute to the doctors and nurses who cared for him and brought him back to a large measure of health at a time when the remarkable advances in the treatment of tuberculosis had not yet been made. The whole exercise demanded almost unbelievable patience. Progress seemed snail-like to one whose pattern of life had been that of the deer. Worst of all the utter exhaustion had plunged him into a darkness of the soul from which there seemed to be no escape. Even Mary's visits brought only a glimmer of light. She would come down at the weekend, in hope and expectancy, only to be met by long periods of stony silence. He was utterly exhausted in body and mind and in the early months of the sickness all the efforts of the doctors seemed to be in vain. And then came the shattering blow of the removal of his right eye.

Humanly speaking two men saved him. One was Sir Henry Gauvain of the Treloar Homes who diagnosed the full nature of his complaint and finally sent him out after two years and nine months of sickness and disability suffering only from some reduction of movement in one elbow and one wrist. So often, as all who knew him intimately were well aware, he had troubles with "brother ass" as he called his recalcitrant body, but he never complained and rarely even referred to it. To the majority of his friends and acquaintances it came as a revelation to read of the fearful nature of his ordeal in sanatorium and hospital.

The other man was little known to the world at large and few had any idea of the part he had played in Max's recovery. This was George Lyward, a man who had poured out his own energies to such a degree at Glenalmond School, where he had been teaching, that he suffered a breakdown and came to be a fellow-patient at Morland Hall. He was not a trained psychiatrist but had acquired a great deal of knowledge in what was then only a developing practice and combined it with such wise methods of approach to individuals in need that he eventually became one of the most successful healers and educators of boys who seemed to present insoluble problems in their behaviour at school.

His methods were those of completely *accepting* the person in need, patiently, by questioning, drawing out the implications of the person's impulsive statements and leading him to forget all self-pity and go forward to maturity of feeling in relation to his particular circumstances. In a fine tribute, a writer who spent a period at Finchden Manor in Kent where Lyward later worked, said: "To homeless boys he gave the warmth of home, and more, to the friendless, the trustfulness of friendship and more, to the despaired of, a future and more, to the self-pitying, clarity, humour, courage and more." And in a letter after he died Max wrote of him: "He brought me up against barriers and helped me over them – or not so much helped me as helped me to help myself over them. He gave me an entirely new idea of the love of God, in the strength of which I have lived ever since" (*Crowded Canvas*, p. 69).

The story of his meeting with Lyward and the results that followed from it is surely one of the unforgettable descriptions of spiritual experience of modern times. I propose to give it in his own words.

II

"One morning early in my stay at Morland Hall I was lying in my bed, outside the chalet, at peace with the world. One of the patients, George Lyward, came to visit me. After we had introduced ourselves he asked me what I had been doing before being taken ill. I told him that I had been a missionary in Nigeria. 'What made you want to be a missionary?' That kind of question always flummoxes me. There is no simple answer. One cannot embark on a life-story. So normally I make a more or less stupid answer. In this case I said something lame about 'a sense of adventure'. It was a ridiculous answer, yet one of the best things I ever said, for back came the question, 'Do you know the derivation of the word "adventure", the two Latin words ad and venio, "to come up against".' I confessed to having enough Latin for that. Then came the devastating remark, 'I wonder if you have ever really come up against anything.' Put thus baldly it does not sound much of a remark, though a bit startling after less than five minutes acquaintance. But the conversation was so unexpected, the challenge so sharp, that I was silenced. He talked on for a few minutes and then left me with my 'moment of truth'. How true could Browning be:

> Just when we are safest, there's a sunset touch,
> A fancy from a flower-bell, some one's death,
> A chorus-ending from Euripides, –
> And that's enough for fifty hopes and fears, . . .
> The grand Perhaps!

It was certainly something of a sunset touch, something of a dying within myself that happened that morning, for as by a flash of lightning I had seen something of my inner self exposed. God works in strange ways. That odd, almost inconsequential conversation, as it may have seemed to that stranger, compelled me to begin asking myself some real questions about myself.

"Next day George Lyward came back, I told him I thought he had put his finger on the spot and would he please continue probing. Satisfied that I meant it, he began. For week after week (during the period the consultant had cheerfully prognosticated as perhaps six weeks of life!) George proceeded to strip me down to essentials. He had taken some training in psycho-analysis and I had no shadow of doubt that he knew what he was doing with me, and that he had been sent to do something no one else could do.

47

"There were often times when I wondered if there were any more essentials left to be discovered. What was devastating was that everything that came up from 'the depths' was clearly seen to be what the Bible, without mincing matters, calls 'filthy rags'. All my past, all my relationships were under scrutiny. If I was to go through with this dimension of healing then no holds could be barred.

"One unforgettable morning he told me that my real trouble was that while I was my age intellectually, emotionally I was at most eight years old. 'That gap has to be bridged,' he said. 'How do I do that?' I asked, and, 'How long will it take?' I had now committed myself to him for healing at another level, the one Sir Henry hinted at with his words 'sunshine inside'. Curiously I remained quite detached from the physical healing that was also in progress. For me it was obvious that the physical healing by itself would be fruitless, unless the other was accomplished as well.

"To my query about bridging the gap George replied, 'Oh, it needn't take very long if you are really prepared to be completely honest with yourself, and will trust me.' How difficult and painful it is to be completely honest with myself I was to discover – indeed the discovery has had to be life-long – but already I had learnt enough to know that this was the most important encounter of my life – that I was really face to face with God for the first time. George Lyward was God's instrument – the man in the gap – but the real business had to be done between myself and God. And at one stage, as I went down into the abyss, I lost God altogether. Early on in the 'analysis' to which I was submitting myself I had come to face the fact that for too long I had been living on a 'second-hand' religious experience, something sheltered because inherited. In saying this I am in no way repudiating my religious heritage. To deny one's earlier 'intimations of immortality' is a form of blasphemy. As the earlier pages of this narrative will have made abundantly clear I was already, in a multitude of ways, a debtor to the grace of God through family and teachers and friends. But I could not build on this heritage because I was sheltering behind it.

"What my Father had meant by way of inspiration, the window-opening friendship of Pat O'Regan, the leadership of my brother Jack, the sharing in a vision with Guy Bullen, Mother's patient devotion, Mary's persevering love at this time of the apparent failure of all our hopes – all this was real, splendidly real. Nevertheless I knew that I had never been confronted with the totality of the divine demand upon myself. I had never yet 'come up against God'. And that 'adventure' is terrifying. 'How awe-ful is this place.'

"I can remember vividly a night some little while later when, in my despair with myself, I thought I was going madn. The phrase from Francis Thompson's *The Hound of Heaven,* a poem greatly beloved by Guy Bullen, haunted me – 'the labyrinthine paths of mine own mind'. I could not hear the relentless footsteps 'hurrying after'. All that I seemed conscious of was the labyrinth. The further I wandered the murkier it became, and it appeared to be spiralling downwards. I suppose I did fall asleep at the last. But I was a rag next morning. How this did not become apparent to doctor and nurse I do not know. It was just as well it didn't. Had my para-medical treatment been discovered I suspect that George Lyward would have been packed off by the next train!

"When he came round later that morning I told him that I had been in hell, that there seemed to be no bottom to the well I was descending. 'Oh, yes there is,' he said. 'Do you know what you'll find at the bottom?' Wearily I replied, 'No, what?' 'You will discover God and his name is Love.'

"That reads very prosaically. But to a very sick man, physically, mentally and spiritually sick, to hear that said by the one to whom I had committed myself body and soul, it was a revelation of hope. From that moment I never looked back. Very gently, partly through the therapy of dream interpretation, George drew me up out of the abyss. He taught me then the priceless lesson that having seen myself as I really was I must learn to love that self precisely because it was that self that God loved. There is a whole gospel in that lesson. That is how I found my way slowly back to Galatians 2:20, or to put it more truly, how the Christ of St. Paul, of my Father, of Pat O'Regan, of Guy Bullen, of Mother and Mary, and of how many other friends, became truly mine.

"Was this a conversion experience? In the commonly used sense of the word the answer must surely be 'no'. It was rather a personal encounter of a kind which meant that someone I had always known had revealed himself to me as being of necessity 'the Great Unknown' and only then to be for ever afterwards in a quite indefinable way 'well-known'."

To which I would only add, because Max so loved the Old Testament and constantly found in its stories insight applicable to his own experience, some words of Anthony Phillips about the effect of the Exile on Israel.

Now even the assurance of the presence of God given to Israel through the temple had been removed. She was forced to enter the dark abyss, the ancient unknown. Israel as she had been was dead. But one must die to live: it is in the dark abyss, the silent unknown, that the real issues of life are decided.

(God B.C. p. 34)

III

1932 was an *annus mirabilis*. On May 7, almost five years after their engagement, Max and Mary were married at Tunbridge Wells. On May 22 he was made a deacon in Winchester Cathedral. Through the inspired imagination of one of his most loyal friends who was then a curate in Southampton, a post had been created for him as Youth Organiser of the Diocese, this to be combined with a curacy at St. John's, Boscombe, where he gained his first experience of a steady parochial ministry. St. John's was the leading evangelical parish in the Bournemouth area and was at the time under the charge of the Rev. G. Foster Carter, a man with an early record of high academic attainment who subsequently devoted himself untiringly to the work of the pastoral ministry. Max admired and trusted him completely and residence in the parish brought rich personal rewards.

As far as the Diocese was concerned, he had to start from scratch and discover new ways of giving young people a distinctive place within the life of the Church. This was a mission after his own heart for it was in so many ways comparable to the work which he and Mary had shared together in the C.S.S.M. There was a flavour of pioneer missionary experience in visiting parishes and trying to transmit his own vision of youth for Christ. Groups were formed for prayer and Bible-study and these were strengthened by the participation of members in summer holiday camps. There they gained a wider outlook and found common cause with those who might come from differing traditions of churchmanship.

This new possibility of joining together in the one mission of evangelism gained striking expression in the campaign at Bournemouth which Max was largely responsible for organising in 1933. This brought him into close touch with an old friend whom he had first come to know at Christ Church, Gipsy Hill, the Rev. Bryan Green. Bryan was then Chaplain to the Oxford Pastorate and his proposal was to bring down a large party of undergraduates from Oxford and Cambridge (some one hundred and twenty ultimately descended on Bournemouth), together with assistant missioners under whom they would work. This was the first time, it appears, that those belonging to all types of churchmanship were prepared to co-operate in a united mission. Max and Bryan worked in the closest harmony on the basis of the preparations which Max had so carefully and so wisely made and by general consent a profound impression was made on the church life of the whole area.

But this was not simply an isolated local event. It was the precursor of a new emphasis on evangelism in the Church of England by those belonging to differing schools of thought, and of the establishment of the Archbishops' Commission on Evangelism in which Bryan Green played so prominent a part. Under the chairmanship of Bishop Christopher Chavasse of Rochester, a widely circulated report was published and a regular *Bulletin on Evangelism* (to which Max contributed) made available. He did not in the least surrender his own evangelical convictions but, as always, he was ready and eager to join with anyone in bearing witness to Christ and his saving power.

The period in the Winchester diocese provided an excellent means of finding his feet back in the life of the community and of getting to know the patterns of parochial life in the Church of England. But after four years he was ready for a position of greater challenge and responsibility. This came to him utterly unexpectedly but none the less compellingly: it was to Cambridge, the place of so many wonderful memories, and therein to Holy Trinity, the church where one of his heroes, Charles Simeon, ministered for over fifty years, the church which he had so often attended as an under-graduate and where he had first set eyes on Mary, the church set in so strategic a position in the very heart of the city and whose Vicar in his own day had been Edward Woods, a man he so greatly admired. He took counsel with others but there could have been little doubt in his own mind. In February 1936 Max was inducted to the incumbency while Mary, with Rosemary aged two (Pat was born in October), set to work to make the Vicarage a centre of hospitality for the years to come.

Besides being Vicar of Holy Trinity he was Secretary of the Cambridge Pastorate, an evangelical organisation which, like its counterpart at Oxford, sought to supplement the pastoral work of college chaplains by helping to pay the salaries of two or three ordained men of evangelical persuasion who would carry out pastoral duties in ways consistent with that tradition. The Chairman of the Oxford Council at that time was Christopher Chavasse, Master of St. Peter's Hall, and he had doubtless heard the praises of Max from his brother-in-law, Foster Carter. He wrote to him in the following terms:

My dear Warren,

I heard with the liveliest pleasure and thankfulness that you had been offered, and had accepted, Holy Trinity, Cambridge. I do not suppose there is a man in England who can enter more into your feelings and fears at this time than myself. It was thirteen years ago that I was ordered to St. Aldate's, and I shall never forget my despair as I travelled down from the North. But God's calling is God's enabling; and you are far more qualified in every way, than I ever was, to undertake what may be the greatest position of importance and influence in the Church of England. The terror of the post is that it can be as big as you make it. Thirteen years ago, Oxford had its peculiar difficulties; but by the grace of God we have surmounted them, and can now offer through St. Aldate's a real contribution to religion in Oxford that has its influence all over the country. Cambridge, in the past, was more favoured; but at the present time it has other problems which are almost more daunting than those we had to encounter after the War. The great thing is that you know Cambridge through and through; and you also possess a marvellous sense of values as regards religion. We shall back you with unceasing prayer; and I believe that your going to Cambridge may mean a co-operation between the two Universities such as ought to have existed long ago, and might be most fruitful for both places. I blush to remember that we had the impertinence to ask one marked out to be the leader in Cambridge actually to come to Oxford in a subordinate position. At any rate, it shows how right we were to make an effort to obtain you, and how right you were to refuse. Green's Mission next February will be a wonderful start for your work; though I could wish, for your sake, that you had been given a term to settle down and find your bearings.

As Max looked forward to the new work he saw unlimited opportunities arising for personal friendships with undergraduates and for "missionary" work comparable to that which he had hoped to do overseas. With this *evangelistic* responsibility pressing upon him, it is perhaps surprising that he was also keenly aware of his duty to give his most careful attention to the regular public *worship* in Holy Trinity. Evangelicals, though often men of prayer and deep personal devotion, have not been noted for their conduct of public worship. In many cases it has seemed that other details of the service can be quite subordinate to the one central exercise – the preaching of the Word.

But as the log-books which Max wrote up with meticulous regularity reveal, every service, however routine its character, was planned down to the last detail, the aim always being to construct *an ordered whole* in which some major theme could be recognised as in control of all the parts. He had no wish to introduce novelties simply to cause excitement or create superficial interest. He believed that the Prayer Book services, if carried through reverently and intelligently, could still provide a worthy vehicle for public worship and an adequate preparation of hearts for the more direct listening to the Word of God mediated through the sermon. He was determined that Holy Trinity should be a centre not only of evangelical *witness* but also of evangelical *worship* and there is ample reason for believing that he did not fail.

In a revealing address given to the students at Ridley Hall after he had served for a period at Holy Trinity, he spoke frankly about his own experience.

One of my most vivid recollections of the time I spent at Ridley is that of the night before the C.O.C. paper on Worship. Three of us were convinced that we were going to fail. No one had succeeded in making the subject in the least bit alive and we were bored to tears by it and in our ignorance could not see where it fitted in. With elaborate care however we worked out charts about eight to ten feet long giving every detail of the various services from the Didache down to the Deposited Book. We made an all-night sitting before the exam in order to memorise the subtle distinctions between the Apostolical Constitutions and the Orthodox Liturgies. At 2 a.m. we walked round Cambridge in our dressing gowns and were marched back to Ridley by a policeman who not unnaturally considered our behaviour and appearance irregular. In due course we reached the examination hall. One of us just got enough marks to pass, one just got enough marks to fail and the third went to sleep and was unable to show up a paper at all!

That brief history contains a good deal of material for the moralist. My purpose however in telling it is simply to try and explain to you how I have changed from a person who was bored to tears by the whole subject into an enthusiast for it. Indeed my only justification for standing here at all is that I am such an enthusiast, for my past record, as I've briefly etched it, does not suggest that I'm a Liturgical Scholar.

Now this has been my experience. I found, as every man must find, that services occupy a very considerable portion of the time of a clergyman. I was forced up against the fact that either these exercises were to be real or I should lose my soul. I began then to try and understand them.

At the same time I began to find on all hands how decisive was the influence of worship on those who came to church. I found that apart altogether from the doctrinal emphasis of any particular church, worship as such either appealed or repelled and that the key to the attraction or repulsion was in every case the reality or sincerity of the service.

I began to learn my own colossal responsibility. At the same time it was borne in on me that real Christian Worship is a corporate achievement. That the Choir and congregation must share the sincerity of the Minister.

I began to see from this that Worship in church can be a real means of building up the Christian life. At the same time there came also the discovery that Worship can really be a means of Evangelism. A God-centred worship brings people to God.

I realised now that Worship was to be one of the great adventures of my life and demanded from me all the thought and care and prayer I could put into it.

While recognising the importance of adoration in the presence of divine mystery, he yet believed that the greater emphasis should lie on worship as preparation for ethical obedience. He concluded his talk in these words:

To me the enjoyment of the presence of God can never be the end of worship, as it were the last term in a series of experiences. That to me involves a static conception of the being of God and the nature of Life which is the reverse of Truth. Rather, as I see communion, the enjoyment of the presence of God must ever be a stimulus to more adequate response by myself to the Love of God which I apprehend when I enjoy His presence. The Love of God is Charity – an active will and purpose for Good towards the Universe of which Man is a part. Only in obedience shall we be perfected and so able to join in the full worship of the Heavenly Host.

In regard to preaching he was more dependent upon outsiders. He set about planning courses of sermons in term-time to be given by men whom he knew had something to say about Christ and could say it intelligibly. One whom he often invited to preach was Charles

Raven, the Regius Professor of Divinity. It would be hard to imagine a man more different from Max in appearance, in intellectual interests, in temperament, in pulpit-style. Yet he passed the test of preaching Christ and being devoted to Christ. He used no notes, he gripped the congregation by his intense, almost hypnotic look, and by his particularly resonant voice.

In contrast Max was precise, quiet, reliant upon the sheer arresting power of the theme which he had pondered over so carefully and written out so painstakingly. There was something extraordinarily distinctive and attractive about his voice and demeanour when speaking in public. There was always a deep *seriousness* – the hall-mark it has been claimed of early nineteenth-century evangelicals – even though humour was not far away and prevented any trace of pomposity. Words written about a fellow Irishman of his time seem to me to come very near to describing Max: "His voice was low and pleasant . . . there was a calm in him like that of someone who was as much a witness as a doer. His dignity was that of a man who respected all men, and himself among them, not like the irritable dignity of . . . people who fear that their authority is greater than their presence and must continually be re-asserted." (Don Davie writing about W. R. Rodgers in *Closing Time* p. 27.)

The tradition of Scriptural preaching at Holy Trinity stretched back to the notable days of Charles Simeon, and Max gladly followed it. This was specially the case as he saw war approaching and tried, like an Old Testament prophet, to be a watchman and an interpreter. There were no fireworks, but through his thoughtful sermons in which he was always endeavouring to relate the Bible to contemporary problems and experiences, he made Holy Trinity a centre both for truly corporate worship and for a deepening understanding of the Christian revelation.

But although his leadership in worship and teaching was outstanding, it was in pastoral relationships that his genius found its supreme expression. This was the case not only among regular members of the congregation and undergraduates but also amongst the many evacuees and refugees who came to Cambridge after the outbreak of war. In addition, his long concern for literary evangelism showed itself as he made available for his people and for visitors some of the best Christian thinking of his time on war-issues. The parish magazine was transformed into a monthly bulletin with a supplement included: Max was already on his way to the News-Letter technique which was to constitute one of his most significant contributions to the missionary enterprise in this century.

To give but one example of his personal influence in Cambridge let me quote from a letter written to Mary at a time of Max's illness in the sixties:

> I really must make an attempt to write a letter which is so long overdue – not easy because it comes from the very depth of my heart in gratitude to Canon Warren for what he did for me long years ago in Cambridge. I was just one of the many he must have prepared for Confirmation at that time but I was 21 and had been out in the wilderness for a long time, rejecting the heresies of the sect I had been brought up in and fumbling for a Faith which made sense against the background of life in 1940. When I was finally jerked into a realisation that once I had committed myself to a belief in Christ, it could no longer be a private and individual matter but was the beginning of a growth in relationships with other people, not a cosy static end to my wanderings, I found myself pushed and hurried towards the vestry door at Holy Trinity. How grateful I was that he never poked to find out by what process I had arrived but just took it for granted that the Holy Spirit had blown me there. I don't suppose I was much help; thinking back on myself I was probably completely taciturn during every session we had, which was mostly a desperate shyness and partly an inability to formulate the thinking process which was going on in my mind.
>
> But now, after 11 years in the mission field with my husband and 10 back in England, I find myself drawn more and more into Diocesan activities, into lay training and conference work with young people, and what he taught me about prayer and worship comes back over and over again. It is like a deep well from which I can draw repeatedly, sometimes in the things he said and the words he used but mostly, of course, just himself and his own witness in everything he did. You see, I never had any difficulty in believing in God Almighty, a careful Judge and Provider, but tremendous difficulty in realising that He cared about the details of my everyday life, my hopes and failures and stumblings; this was the stumbling block which Max helped me over and of course from that point I was able to start growing. Worship and prayer and life itself became a whole thing and the love of God in Christ began to be part of me, not just something I said I believed in.

IV

Such were Max's activities in worship, preaching and pastoral guidance. But he did not confine himself to Holy Trinity or even to Cambridge. The missionary imperative was still a constant concern and he was soon invited to become a member of the important C.M.S. Executive Committee. Perhaps equally important to him at this stage was his sense of responsibility towards the cause of evangelicalism by reason of the very fact that he was vicar of the church where a man had given such leadership in the early nineteenth century that its influence was still in evidence more than a century later. Nothing could have been more congenial to Max than the planning and preparation of the commemoration of the centenary of Charles Simeon's death, in November 1936. He was not content with the promise of a single sermon by the Archbishop of Canterbury on the Sunday nearest the actual date. Rather he set to work, as soon as possible after his appointment, to organise a whole week of addresses, designed to interpret Simeon and his significance for Cambridge and the Church at large in the twentieth century. He was successful in gaining the enthusiastic help of a panel of distinguished speakers and in a very real sense put evangelicalism once again "on the map".

This was his first effort but it was soon to be followed by an even more significant project in the realm of literature. (The Simeon addresses were published soon after delivery.) It was the bringing into existence in 1942 of the Evangelical Fellowship for Theological Literature. Max was not solely responsible but there can be little doubt that it was his brain-child and that no one did more than he, through the thirty years of its existence, to support it actively and to guide it along fruitful lines of development.

The need for such a Fellowship was (to quote from the founding document) "the dearth of theological writing inspired by evangelical insights, and the consequent failure of evangelicalism to make its proper contribution to the Church of England as one of the schools of thought within the Church". This dearth can be accounted for in various ways. In an illuminating chapter of his book *Truth to Life*, A. O. J. Cockshutt points out that in the nineteenth century there was a three-fold division in the Church of England generally described as High Church, Broad Church and evangelicals. Whereas the first two busied themselves with intellectual problems – the nature of the Church, authority, relation to the State, loyalty to the Fathers – the evangelicals concerned themselves with morals and above all with *action*. They were perhaps deficient in ideas and in intellectual research but gave themselves unstintingly to philanthropic and missionary activities. Moreover much of this activity owed its inspiration to laymen such as Wilberforce and Shaftesbury though, as Max believed, the towering figure of Simeon, more concerned with preaching and doctrine, should be set alongside them.

This concentration on action, derived from their devoted and regular reading of the Bible, left them ill prepared for the storms aroused by the Oxford Movement, with its emphasis on the authority of the Church, or the movement of Biblical criticism, with its apparent loosening of the authority of Scripture. As Ian Bradley has shown in his fine book *The Call to Seriousness*, it was only after 1860 that the "anti" complex developed amongst evangelicals. They continued their good works but were thrown on the defensive intellectually, becoming anti-Rome, anti-ritual, anti-biblical criticism, anti-Darwin and anti-worldliness. To a degree this promoted unity, for there are few things that so unite as opposition to common foes. But it tended to obscure the unity which is to be found in devotion to Christ alone.

In general – at least until the vast extensions of higher education and not always then – the layman has been indifferent to academic subtleties and historical ambiguities. Being concerned with practical matters and the need for action, he has sought a clear-cut manual of faith and discipline. Evangelicals found this supremely in the Bible and in the worship book which was so clearly based upon it, namely the Book of Common Prayer. To tamper with these, to suggest inaccuracies or to propound varieties of interpretation, was to remove the sure and certain foundation on which their own spiritual security and evangelistic motivation were based. If the handbook could not be relied on, who could go forward with any confidence?

These were the kinds of stirrings of mind and conscience which brought about splits amongst evangelicals, first in the C.M.S. in 1922, and then in attitudes to the revision of the Prayer Book in 1928. The vague term "liberal" was attached to those who were anxious to welcome the results of historical criticism and of scientific research. In reaction, the term "conservative" was applied to those who clung to the literal interpretation of the Bible and, in a lesser degree, to the 1662 Prayer Book and the 39 Articles. This meant that in the universities, and in many parishes, the period between the wars was one of suspicion and controversy amongst evangelicals, of attempted consolidation of old traditions rather than of advance into new discoveries, and of the "dearth" of constructive theological writing to which reference has already been made. The danger was that evangelicals would cut themselves off from the new culture which had come into being through the patient work of those engaged in historical and scientific research.

Max had passed through times of acute distress while an undergraduate and later in residence at Ridley Hall because so often friends whom he loved and worked with in evangelistic activity regarded him as "unsound", "too intellectual", or as too ready to compromise on fundamentals. No man loved the Bible more devotedly or lived with it more expectantly. But when it came to the Book of Jonah, for example, he could not accept that it was other than a valuable story, not a literal account of events culminating in the reformation of Nineveh. When he listened to men like the Vicar of Holy Trinity in his undergraduate days, or the Principal of Ridley Hall while he was in residence there, he could not write them off as other than devoted followers of Christ because they would not subscribe to particular doctrines of Revelation and the Atonement. He was convinced that the evangelical tradition, stemming from such a man as Simeon, had a valid and valuable part to play within the totality of the Church of England. But he believed also that it had a real contribution to make *theologically*. His genius was to see that this could best be done, not by leaving it to lonely individuals to stumble upon some piece of useful research, but rather by gathering together a group of his own contemporaries for mutual illumination and encouragement and by stimulating individuals to prepare for publication historical or doctrinal manuscripts on subjects which had captured their interest.

As soon as he became established at the C.M.S. headquarters in Salisbury Square, he was near the heart of publishing and gained the influential support of the Editor of *The Record* newspaper. He began to write himself. But with complete unselfishness he was always on the lookout for a young man of scholarly promise who could devote himself to the study of some worth while subject which could add to the evangelical contribution to the Church at large. It was a propitious time. The evangelical theological Colleges had recruited able younger men on their staffs, St. Peter's Hall at Oxford was beginning to make its mark and men of evangelical background were being appointed to college chaplaincies. The E.F.T.L. proved to be an admirable means of drawing together and holding together a community of research and writing which, by 1952, had a hundred and fifty members consisting of parochial clergy, missionaries, and university or college teachers. Amidst his many achievements this, of which he was the inspiring genius, stands out as one of his greatest.

In 1944 he wrote thus about it to Alexander C. Zabriskie, Dean of the Seminary in Alexandria, Virginia, which at that time maintained the most distinctively evangelical and missionary emphasis of any of the colleges training clergy for the Episcopal Church.

"As regards theological position, we determined to resist any temptation to hyphenate the word 'evangelical'. We believe that word can stand on its own merits as enshrining a great tradition within Anglicanism and wide enough to embrace theologically conservative and liberal elements. The original company who met at Cambridge represented every wing of evangelical thought and our group, now grown much larger, still does so . . . From the start we saw the need to be in close touch with others of similar persuasion overseas. We have already got a number of missionary members. And my visit to Canada has been fruitful in establishing a firm link with a group there. I very much hope that through you and your company we may be able to have a link with you in the U.S.A." Though nothing substantial developed in America, Max did everything in his power to foster relations between evangelicals in England and those in sympathy with them in the Episcopal Church of the U.S.A.

In 1971 E.F.T.L. ceased to exist as a formal body. This may have been a disappointment to Max for he had attended its annual conferences with astonishing regularity considering his other commitments and had given immense encouragement to scores of younger scholars. But he was never a man to attempt to prolong the life-span of an organisation whose work had been largely accomplished. In a letter to Leonard Hickin, an old friend, in 1977, shortly before his death, he wrote:

> Strictly speaking my retirement had nothing to do with the E.F.T.L. packing up. Its job really was done. Its ablest members were by now so heavily involved in major international conferences that they could rarely, if ever, attend. This, plus cost of travel, meant that fewer felt able to attend conferences, and this involved a financial crisis . . . What I do think is that there could be a place for a revived E.F.T.L. on a quite different basis, consisting of a group of evangelicals specifically concerned with wrestling together over some of the great issues of today: race, other religions, the working of the Holy Spirit etc. – *not* a big group like E.F.T.L. perhaps a

dozen at most, an evangelical "think-tank". I believe this could be very valuable.

Those who shared in any way in E.F.T.L. will always regard Max as author, and, in a measure, the finisher of an influential and eminently worth-while enterprise.

V

Max took his full share in two other constructive evangelical manifestoes produced soon after the War. One was the document entitled *Evangelicals Affirm* in the year of the Lambeth Conference 1948, the other *The Fulness of Christ,* (1950) the statement put out by a group of evangelicals invited by Dr. Fisher, then Archbishop of Canterbury, to summarise their distinctive and particular contribution within the Church of England. These were joint efforts. In addition he produced two notable booklets *What is an Evangelical?* (1944) and *The Sevenfold Secret* (1962), each designed to set out as clearly as possible his own understanding of the term evangelical within the context of the Church of England.

The two accounts are very similar, showing little sign of change in his views over the eighteen years. His vision is that of a "catholic evangelicalism", not as an end in itself but as a constitutive part of a larger whole, making within that whole its own distinctive contribution. He glories in the fact that the Anglican Communion holds within its embrace "a greater variety of insights and interpretations than any other communion can match". So evangelicals do not seek to dominate or absorb but rather to strive for the continuing recognition of certain cardinal principles or ideas which characterise their own tradition. He tries to hold them in proper balance and above all seeks to apply his principles to life.

How then does he define these "cardinal principles"? In the earlier booklet evangelism is given an absolute priority, in the second it is simply taken for granted: "an evangelical ministry or activity which is not in some real sense evangelistic is most certainly not evangelical, whatever else it may be." Evangelicals regard the Church not primarily as a worshipping community, important as that aspect of its life undoubtedly is. They cannot help viewing the Church as primarily a *redeeming* community, called to share in the divine purpose of salvation for the world. The corollary of this gives Max his second principle: it is an emphasis on the need for conversion. "Here indeed we have the very heart of the evangelical approach, the citadel of its doctrine, the key to its pastoralia, the method of its evangelism." What it implies is personal encounter with Jesus Christ issuing in personal commitment to him. He does not dwell on the question of *how* this may happen, though he quotes with full approval Douglas Webster's appeal to the conversion of Paul who, through his conversion experience, recognised that "Jesus was real for him, that he was alive for him and this came to imply (when he had thought it through) that Jesus had actually died for him". Whatever word is used – encounter, recognition, realisation – the all-important matter is the meeting with Jesus Christ and the full commitment to him.

The third principle he defines as trusting the Holy Spirit. "Our aim with all our converts is to make them independent of us and dependent wholly on the continuing presence of the Holy Spirit." And nothing is more important for maintaining this continuing dependence than a constant colloquy with Holy Scripture, in the construction of which the Holy Spirit operated through men of old and in the interpretation of which the Spirit still operates today. Max pleads for a wide perspective on the Bible, cosmic and historical, not literal and propositional, and for a reverent approach to that Book "whose true understanding is the main purpose of divinity and obedience to which is the way of salvation".

The fourth principle (which comes sixth in the *Sevenfold Secret*) is defined in one case as the priesthood of all believers and then, more emphatically in the other, as a conviction about the priesthood of the laity. This was a matter on which he felt a sense almost of outrage. Why were the laity so little called upon and entrusted with responsibility in the worship and witness of the Church of England? In the history of evangelicalism, lay men and women had played outstanding parts. Nowhere was this more evident than in the mission field. But why again were layfolk allowed to do things abroad which they were excluded from doing at home?

There were few matters on which he felt more impatient, thereby, incidentally, showing himself to be a quarter of a century ahead of the time when the role of the laity has at last begun to receive due recognition in Anglican and Roman Catholic circles. He insisted that the "holy priesthood" includes clerical and lay functionaries alike. There is differentiation of function within the total *Laos* but not a hierarchy of status. "The whole *Laos* exists to be God's priest for the world, God's witness in the world, God's Messenger to the world . . . I believe that in our particular witness to the nature of the Church we have the key to open the door to a new evangelistic enterprise. We are not afraid of the ordinary man. We are not separated from him by exaggerated doctrines of the significance of an earthly priesthood. Indeed we hold firmly to the belief that in the solemn activity of introducing men and women to God as to their Creator, Judge and Saviour, the layman can play as direct a part as any ordained priest."

In his 1962 lecture, given, it may be noted, after nearly twenty years of working closely with laymen in the fellowship of C.M.S. he wrote even more passionately:

> The supreme priestly act is, at whatever cost to oneself, to be ready to serve as a midwife of the soul, to be ready to become the point at which a sinner is enabled to enjoy the assurance that by the self-offering of Jesus he is "at-one" with God. That ministry, that supremely priestly ministry, with all the "spiritual sacrifices" involved, can be discharged as effectively by a layman as by any ordained priest. We who have been ordained have been ordained to be the servants of Christ. No priest ever ceases to be a deacon. Washing the feet of the holy priesthood is our highest vocation. [He was speaking to clergy.] That, when we are not busy magnifying our clerical office, or being little evangelical popes, is something we know to be among the most glorious of the traditions of our own school of thought in our beloved Church, one of the most significant contributions we have to offer to its work of evangelism in the world today.

This did not mean any denigration of the place of the Holy Communion in the life of God's people. In fact he named the proper use of the sacrament as one of the distinctive contributions of evangelicals, going back to Simeon's time. He welcomed the Liturgical Movement. "Almost every development of it so far is away from the medieval misconceptions of the sacrament and towards a view of it which is essentially expressive of real scriptural and evangelical insights." Then, with a characteristic needling, he continued: "And let us escape from the tyranny of a static view of the Holy Communion which imagines that its scriptural validity depends on the point of the compass faced by the celebrant. We can with 'the more readiness and decency break the Bread before the people', showing the manual acts, from any point of the compass we like. *What matters supremely is that there is a communion of the people.*" (My italics.)

"Everything about the service should be so designed as to promote the activity of the people, their share in the common action, and play down the dominant and exclusive role which the clergy have arrogated to themselves over the centuries."

In summary it would not, I think, be unfair to suggest that the title of his 1944 Lectures in Rochester might equally well have been What is an *Evangelist*? Life, action, devotion to Christ, dependence on the Spirit, constant nourishment from the Bible, service to the limit – these were his passionate concerns. And this made him so acceptable to those who would have differed from him on many aspects of biblical interpretation or of ecclesiastical form. He never pretended to be a philosopher, probing into the foundations of knowledge and the mysteries of language. History, in which he delighted, was concerned with men of action and he wanted to continue to make history by carrying on the evangelistic work and the missionary outreach of the evangelical forefathers. These he regarded as having played a worthy *part* in the Church of England, not as a party seeking to dominate or absorb. It was a narrow distinction. What is certain is that Max bent all his energies to do the work of an evangelist himself and to renew in his fellow evangelicals the vision of the essential task which they had been called to fulfil.

PART II

The Missionary Leader

5

Taking stock

AMIDST ALL THE pressures of his Cambridge activities as Vicar of
Holy Trinity and leader of the Pastorate in the University, Max
never allowed his sense of responsibility towards the overseas work
of the Church to diminish. In particular he remained devoted to
C.M.S. He fully supported the local organisation in the town and
kept watch for possible recruits in the university. The authorities in
London, recognising his abilities and the value of his service already
rendered to the Society, invited him to join its important Executive
Committee and subsequently to become a member of the Appointments Sub-Committee. When therefore in 1942 Wilson Cash, the
General Secretary, was appointed Bishop of Worcester, Max
became actively involved in the search for a successor.

In his autobiography he has told the story of the successive stages
in this search: how when the initial list of suggested names appeared
he was startled to find his own included and how he promptly
asked for it to be deleted: how the man first chosen by the
Committee declined the offer of nomination: how then the Committee, from whose meeting he was absent because of sickness,
decided to put his name forward in spite of his original request to be
excluded from the list: and how, therefore, he found himself
confronted with the utterly unexpected invitation to assume the
office of major responsibility in the Church of England's largest
missionary society. In his usual way, Max consulted men whose
judgment he had come to value; but there could have been little
doubt in his own mind, after he and Mary had considered the call
which had never in any way been sought, that this was indeed a call
from God which he could not possibly refuse.

So it came about that one who had dedicated his life without
reserve to the missionary cause some twenty years earlier and had
then almost lost his life on the mission field: who had during a long

and weary period of struggle for survival re-dedicated himself to God's service in whatever form it might take: who, though still bearing marks of bodily weakness, proved himself able to give effective leadership first to young people in a diocese and then to the variegated congregation of a busy parish within a University city: now found himself entrusted with the leadership of one of the most far-reaching enterprises of the whole Christian Church. Two diocesan Bishops in writing to him about his appointment used almost the same description of his new office: "One of the most important in the whole of the Church of England", "one of the most vital in the whole Church". In his thirty-eighth year he began to sit in the chair, at the famous office in Salisbury Square, which he was to regard as his own for the next twenty-one years.

II

Max began his new work with the enormous advantage of having been in intimate touch with the life of the Society through virtually the whole of the difficult period between the two Wars. He had known on the one hand the outburst of enthusiasm within the Church of England in the early 1920's when there came a new realisation that the whole Church had been entrusted with missionary responsibility towards the world. On the other hand, he had been well aware of the crisis within C.M.S. itself as many of its earnest supporters felt unable to continue their membership within the Society because of differences concerning the nature of the authority and the methods of interpretation of the Bible. He had experienced at first hand tensions amongst missionaries as a result of differing convictions about priorities in actual missionary work and at the same time had seen how inevitably political considerations affected missionary strategy. Moreover, through his involvement in missionary organisations in diocese and parish in England, he had at least begun to appreciate the problems to be faced if home support for missions was to be maintained. Finally, through serving on Committees at the Society's headquarters, he had become familiar with the structure of the large organisation which he had now been called to lead.

So far as the general missionary situation was concerned he could hardly have assumed responsibility at a more critical time. From many points of view the beginning of the decade preceding his appointment can now be seen to have been a kind of watershed: the ever widening penetration and growing domination by Europe in world affairs, which had been characteristic of the historical period from the sixteenth century onwards, had now reached their climax. From this point onwards the story becomes one of hesitation, compromise, and retreat.

Max Warren was one of the first to recognise the cultural influence on world mission, so strikingly described by William Barrett:

> The idea of world history was born of the European mind at a time when Europe itself was spreading its power to the four quarters of the globe. We, who are so used to it, forget how novel this idea was and how late in its appearance. The voyages of the fifteenth century, and the continued explorations and settlements that followed, opened the whole world to European civilisation. Hitherto history had been local or tribal, limited to particular peoples or empires. By the eighteenth century, the age of enlightenment could envisage all humanity as the subject of one history and the whole earth as the theatre of a single drama.
>
> The exuberant and positive mood of the Enlightenment overflowed into the beginning of the nineteenth century. The younger Hegel may be taken as an exemplary spokesman; he was the first major philosopher to take world history as his explicit theme . . . The modern age, as he saw it, was the flowering of enlightenment out of the narrow other-worldliness of the Middle Ages. Three great events had combined to usher in this period – the Renaissance, the Reformation, and the development of science. Each of these represented a broadening and a liberalisation of the mind. This new era of mankind, then, seemed everywhere destined for the confident expansion of human liberty and the heightening of human self-consciousness.*

But, as Barrett goes on to show, no longer can the religious concerns of the Reformation nor the humanistic ideals of the Renaissance be regarded as central or determinative for world history. The only one of the three events which at present holds the whole world's attention is the emergence of modern science and technology. "Technology . . . creates one world out of our planet for the first time since humans appeared upon it. In so doing, it

---

* William Barrett *The Illusion of Technique* p. 177f.

transforms world history itself from an abstract and daring idea in the minds of philosophers and historians two centuries ago into an actual and pressing reality, full of promise but also freighted with catastrophic possibilities."*

Two great branches of missionary work had stemmed from the Reformation and the Renaissance respectively. In the expanding world, Christian leaders had gradually come to recognise their responsibility for ensuring that within this expansion the revealed truths of their faith should be proclaimed. Though Protestants were comparatively slow in taking up the challenge, by the end of the eighteenth century enthusiasm had been generated and the urge to make known to all the world's inhabitants the message of salvation had come to be increasingly felt. In Europe, and amongst the North American settlers, evangelists had called men and women to repent and believe the gospel. Was it not now a plain Christian duty to proclaim this same gospel to the whole of mankind?

Again, medieval Europe had enjoyed the benefits of a civilisation in which all human life found its fulfilment within the sanctification which Christian culture supplied. As colonists proceeded to establish themselves in other parts of the world, was it not the responsibility of their mother churches to provide the means by which that sanctification could be established even on foreign soil? And if daughter churches could be planted in the colonies, could it not then be the object of hope that the peoples of the world would bring their gifts and aspirations into this same area of sanctification?

Thus the nineteenth century witnessed a vast expansion of the missionary enterprise. On the one hand the Roman Catholic Church and the Church of England sought first to establish churches, with attendant ministries, wherever colonies of their own adherents had been planted outside Europe and in course of time gathered non-Christian peoples within the same sanctifying structures. On the other hand the churches and sects belonging to the Reformed tradition sought to send missionaries overseas who would preach the gospel both to emigrants and to the indigenous peoples of foreign lands. The Church of England was unusual, even perhaps unique, in that it contained within its comprehensiveness both a more catholic and a more evangelical missionary outreach. The first expressed itself pre-eminently through the Society for the Propagation of the Gospel, the second through the Church Missionary Society. Thus, until the beginning of the twentieth century, missionary work generally had been closely related both to

* Ibid. p. 179.

colonisation and to commerce: wherever a particular European nation held sway, either politically or economically, there its particular expression or expressions of the Christian faith were promulgated.

III

It was at the turn of the century that missionary enthusiasm reached its peak. The whole world was opening up and travellers could proceed in relative safety by land or by sea. Slogans such as "the evangelisation of the world in this generation" or "the earth shall be filled with the glory of God as the waters cover the sea" gained an eager response. With increasing opportunities for movement and meeting it was natural that the leaders of the varying missionary enterprises should wish to take counsel together and work towards a common strategy. So it came about that the first great missionary conference assembled in Edinburgh in 1910 and although there were hesitations and uncertainties about official representation from within the Church of England, and in spite of the fact that the Roman Catholic Church did not participate at all, Edinburgh was beyond doubt a landmark in missionary co-operation and forged invaluable links just before the devastating rupture of European unity in the 1914–18 War.

For roughly a decade after the Armistice the mood in Britain in particular was one of relief and renewed hope. The hideous nightmare had passed, the war to end wars had been fought and won, Britain's role in the world to maintain peace and to establish good government was still unimpaired. Its Prime Minister could still assert that "the British Empire is a saving fact in a very distracted world. It is the most hopeful experiment in human organisation which the world has yet seen". Moreover, just as it seemed that the British people had been called to exercise a stewardship on behalf of the unity and welfare of mankind, so within the Church of England there arose a new sense of the responsibility of the whole Church, not only of the members of the missionary societies, to make disciples of all nations. One of the most notable events of the Twenties was the launching of the World Call to the Church at a great missionary convention in 1925 when representatives from all over the country gathered in London. Student missionary campaigns took the challenge to leading cities. It almost seemed that the need for reconstruction after the War had generated a new sense of responsibility for the spiritual welfare of the world at large.

So valuable had the interchange of experiences and ideas at Edinburgh proved to be that there remained every hope that a similar gathering would be arranged after a suitable interval. Significantly this took place in Jerusalem in 1928, just before the sinister succession of events which culminated in the Second World War. This time there was no hesitation on the part of the Church of England. An impressive delegation was led by William Temple, who was at that time Bishop of Manchester, and hope was still bright that the Christian Churches could sound forth to the nations a message of salvation at a time when all religions were under threat from the rising tide of secularism. In fact, as a modern commentator has written, the unified statement of the Message which was unanimously adopted by the members of the Conference "remains a most remarkable, even great, document, full of strength and great inspiration and stirring truth". In spite of the appearance on the international scene of signs of an approaching time of troubles, the delegates could view the future of the whole missionary cause with confidence and hope.

How different was the atmosphere at Tambaram ten years later! The report from the first section which dealt with *The Faith by which the Church lives* declared:

"The Christian Church today is called to live, and to give life, in a world shaken to its foundations. When the International Missionary Council met at Jerusalem ten years ago, the faith was strong that a new and better world had been born amidst the destruction of the Great War, and that the Church might lead in building it up. Today that faith is shattered."

So great had been the change in the international situation during the Thirties that many had doubted whether the projected Conference could ever take place. It was cause for deep thanksgiving that so representative a gathering of Christians from all parts of the world should have assembled on Indian soil just before the terrible antagonisms between the nations erupted into open conflict.

Perhaps the most valuable emphases to emerge from Tambaram were those concerned first with the unfinished evangelistic task demanding the urgent attention of all the Churches and secondly with the honoured place of the younger Churches as autonomous members of the total Christian community. But the feature of the Conference which gained greatest publicity, and by which it has chiefly been remembered, was the *theological* debate engendered by a notable book prepared in advance: Hendrik Kraemer's volume, *The Christian Message in a Non-Christian World*. Only six years had passed since a controversial report by a distinguished body of American laymen, under the leadership of the philosopher William Hocking, had appeared with the title *Rethinking Missions*. This had advocated a strongly liberal approach, that of "sharing spiritual experiences in a common search for truth". Now, however, Kraemer responded equally strongly, advocating a return to what he called biblical realism and an uncompromising testimony to the revelation of the living God therein contained. Not sharing experience but bearing witness to revealed truth – this, he believed, was the task of the Christian Church. But there was no final agreement at the Conference. There was indeed little support for the Laymen's proposed programme. On the other hand many hesitated to adopt Kraemer's judgment of other religions. In the final report it was simply stated:

> As to whether the non-Christian religions as total systems of thought and life may be regarded as in some sense or to some degree manifesting God's revelation, Christians are not agreed.

Had war been averted, the debate might have been carried on constructively as delegates returned to their home churches. As it was, they had scarcely arrived back and reported when the world was once again plunged into a devastating war.

IV

I have tried to sketch the world-situation and the missionary task within the world-situation as they confronted Max when he began his new work in June 1942. It is interesting to recall that only a few weeks earlier William Temple's enthronement at Canterbury had brought encouragement and hope to vast numbers who believed that he could give a statesman-like leadership in Church and Nation both during the anxious days of war and in the coming new era of the post-war world. Few, I think, imagined that the young man walking along Fleet Street to an office in Salisbury Square was destined to exert a world-wide influence in the next twenty years comparable even to that which Temple had exercised over the previous twenty.

Shortly after he had accepted the call to leadership in the C.M.S.

an article appeared in *The Times*, out of which Max clipped a section and pasted it in his diary. It read:

> It is the business of a statesman to lead: and with his ear perpetually to the ground he is in no posture of leadership. The honest leader determines his course by the light of his own conscience and the special knowledge available to him: not by ascertaining the views of his necessarily less well-informed followers, in order that he may meekly conform. Having decided for himself what is right, he has then to convince the rank and file, knowing that if he fails to win or hold their support they will dismiss him and transfer their trust to another. That and that only is the sanction for the ultimate control of public opinion over policy.

Beside the clipping is Max's own comment:

> This seems to me challengingly relevant to other kinds of leadership besides politics. Leadership involves discovering what is right, laying a course, and convincing the rank and file of its rightness or making way for some other leader.
> Here is the fearful burden of responsibility, however much one may have colleagues for 99% of the way. There will remain the last 1% when one must be ahead and alone.
> May the leadership of Jesus and the guidance of His Spirit be the rule day by day. Then in the crisis His will shall be done.

To become well-informed himself and then to convince the rank and file of the rightness of any proposed course of action: these were to be his constant concerns during all his years of leadership in the Society's affairs. But he never interpreted these concerns narrowly or tried to fulfil them in any individualistic way. He was always on the lookout for those who could assist him, either by supplying him with information which they already possessed or by going in search of whatever information he needed of a particular kind. He read omnivorously to enrich his own mind but was always ready to receive the even more valuable information that could be gained by personal contacts. Then in the matter of convincing the rank and file he recognised that this was a task far beyond his own unaided efforts. Everything would depend on the assistance of helpers sympathetic with his ideas and policies but, still more important, equipped to communicate them both to the rank and file of members of the Society at home and to the vast company of those within the area of C.M.S. responsibility abroad. To gather and transmit information himself and to build up a team of skilled assistants able to reach out to the interests and experiences of ordinary men and women – this became the dual task to which he now bent all his energies.

But at first, war-time conditions added enormously to the difficulties of this task. For the time being it seemed best for the family home to remain in Cambridge, though this involved moving out of the Holy Trinity Vicarage. Day after day Max travelled on the 6.41 a.m. train from Cambridge to Liverpool St. and was often not home again until six or seven p.m. Then there was fire-watching to be done and the handicap of an arm which had to be supported by a splint. Before he had completed his first month in office he was struck by a serious illness which kept him away from London for two whole months. Had it not been for the fairly recent discovery of the M and B drugs he might never have returned at all.

Characteristically he regarded this illness as a blessing "without any disguise".

> Without it I would never have been able to sort out any impressions or see the work at C.M.S. in any kind of focus. Further I think by the grace of God I've been shown something of the secret of how to live. "To live well is to live slowly." And I think I see also that it is not sufficient to know one can't master the job for a long while. One has got to feel this inability and accept it gladly. Only so is there peace and strength.

Happily, from this time onwards, in spite of frequent periods of exhaustion and the disabilities of a body which was never functioning, as he would have said, on every cylinder, he succeeded in carrying out his duties without any break because of illness throughout his years at C.M.S. He was constantly on the move to different parts of the British Isles and made long travel journeys overseas. Moreover he shared the life of commuters to and fro to the London office. Yet, supported as he was by the whole-hearted partnership of Mary in the home, by the ever-increasing understanding and devotion of the staff in C.M.S. House, and controlled in the organisation of his own programmes of work by a wise economy of time, his weakened body took the strain.

V

As he contemplated the world issues with which he would be compelled to deal and the complexities of the leadership of a great Society, he determined that nothing should divert his attention from what had already for many years been a guiding principle: the absolute priority of personal relationships and the supreme value of personal contacts. After less than four months of learning his job he wrote in his diary:

> Reflecting on my work I find myself at the moment with one fixed point only. I have no sort of doubt that a primary obligation laid upon me is to make and keep the work of the Society *personalised* and to count the achievement of real personal contacts with the Missionaries a first call on my time. I believe under God's guidance this will make for something vital in the days to come. It is the only way that "Membership" will have any meaning for our missionaries.
>
> I believe that "Membership" in meaning and implication represents one of the lines along which I've got to work hard because it is so decisive for the preservation of the Voluntary Association principle in our Church's life not least in order to enable the Church to make an effective impact on secular society. I believe Martin Buber's "Thou and I" [*sic*] must be translated into a philosophy of society and it can only be done in terms of voluntary associations.

Three years passed and he was re-affirming his conviction:

> I believe that if one can give unhurried time to missionaries we shall do more than any other single thing to get the Society on to a more even keel in the difficult days ahead. But there is a deep resentment, not altogether articulate, at the preoccupation of Secretaries with Committees.

To provide suitable conditions for the establishment of easy personal relationships Max and Mary committed themselves to one of the most extended programmes of hospitality that a married pair can ever have undertaken. With little domestic help Mary organised a dinner-bed-and-breakfast service which brought visitor after visitor to the three homes – first in Blackheath, then in Little Cloister at Westminster and finally at Waymarks in East Dean. It might be a bishop, it might be a missionary, it might be a recruit or it might be a friend. After dinner Max would take the visitor to his study for talk around the fire. Always he prepared for the occasion by reminding himself of his visitor's concerns and so making him or her feel at the centre of the evening's conversation. This might happen twice a week or at a weekend or alternatively Max might arrange to dine in London with someone whom he wished particularly to consult. To a vast number of people, drawn from many nations and many walks of life, an evening with Max stands out as an unforgettable experience during which bonds were established of an intensely personal, even of a sacred kind.

But he was eager not only to share interests of a missionary or theological nature but also to foster good relations within the large family of which he was titular head at Salisbury Square. For this purpose he made constant use of the facilities of the retreat or conference house called St. Julian's in Sussex. He became Chairman of its Governing Committee and more will be said of his relationship with it later. So far as the promotion of good team work was concerned, he regarded St. Julian's as an ideal setting for withdrawal from the bustle and tensions of office life in London. For example, he records taking down a party of six laymen on the staff of the house for a weekend in December 1945 and outlines the aims he hoped to achieve by such retreats. He wanted them to get to know each other better, to see their work in perspective, to understand the particular contribution of each within the team and above all to dedicate themselves afresh to God for the fulfilment of his purpose. Many a small group, gathered at St. Julian's under his leadership, gained a new vision of their relationship to God and to one another within the great missionary cause.

Yet his concern for personal contacts was not confined to clerical friends or to missionary staffs. His early morning journeys from Cambridge to London in the war years brought him into daily touch with a group of fellow commuters whose confidence he won and who soon were prepared to discuss some of the deepest questions about man and society and God. Out of his conversations in such unlikely conditions came one of his earliest booklets, *But – suppose He was right*. It is dedicated to the Good Company on the 6.41 train and provides an early example of Max's willingness to submit whatever he wrote to the scrutiny and criticism of others. In this case he tried to make sure that his language and arguments were intelligible to the informed layman before he let the book go out in published form.

The title led in to four propositions which were expanded with the help of illustrations from the life and witness of Christians overseas – a method which Max was to use with increasing effect as he developed his voluminous correspondence with missionaries in Asia and Africa. The main purpose of the book was to focus attention on the nature of Jesus' own ministry: he never exploited people but rather believed in them and drew the best out of them: he penetrated behind superficial appearances and exposed real situations: he went all lengths to snatch victory out of defeat. The way of love, of imagination, of courageous faith was the way which Max himself intended to follow as his own ministry opened out before him.

The other remarkable early example of his capacity to win the confidence and friendship of those with very different backgrounds of experience from his own is to be found in his account of his first crossing of the Atlantic. As this was in 1943, passengers were allowed no choices in regard to cabins – they accepted whatever places were allotted to them. Max found himself in the company of four trade Unionists who were on their way to the U.S.A. as a fraternal delegation. For three days he listened to their discussions and arguments about social and economic conditions in the post war world. Then the question of religion was raised and Max wrestled with the problem, which was to be with him constantly, of how to relate the Christian faith to every aspect of human life. Finally, on the last evening, a wider audience gathered to hear his views on colonial questions. How often this was to be his theme in speaking and writing during the next twenty-one years! "Crossing the Atlantic in the third [sic] winter of the war was the unexpected setting for my first attempt to look into the future and to think aloud about race relations, burgeoning nationalism, and the gospel."

So love for people, and a concentration of desire and effort upon the establishment of truly personal relationships with individuals, were set in the very forefront of the new General Secretary's programme. His modesty and eagerness to learn, coupled with his delicate humour, quickly loosened barriers and inspired confidence. He never indulged in gossip, he never betrayed a confidence (the title of the first book he ever wrote was *Loyalty*). However distinguished his career came to be as scholar, administrator, writer, prophet, nothing, I think, will be judged to have been more important than his never-flagging eagerness to know and be known by individual men and women.

6

The new age

UNDER NORMAL CONDITIONS a new General Secretary would have made plans to journey overseas to make contact with missionaries as soon as seemed conveniently possible. But five years were to pass before Max could set out on such a tour. (The journey to North America in 1943–4 was on a mission of a different kind.) This he came to regard as a blessing rather than a deprivation for these five years at headquarters, with frequent journeys to different parts of Britain, enabled him to gain an intimate knowledge of the home side of the work and of the problems of the post war world before embarking on voyages of exploration which inevitably involved temporary breakaways from the complex organisation at Salisbury Square. In certain respects the large Headquarters House was comparable to one of the Newspaper Houses on Fleet Street or to one of the Business Headquarters in the vicinity and Max's first task was to make himself familiar with every aspect of the Society's work. In a letter to his successor in 1964 he wrote:

> I had the great good fortune to come in in 1942 when there was no possibility of travel (except to the U.S.A.). I had five years in which to build a whole heap of things including understanding and confidence. And even that was not long enough. Now there is a different world and you are not allowed five years or even one!

First of all he sought to obtain a true picture of the *history* of the Society and of its significance within the ongoing history of the mid-twentieth century. His training as a historian led him always to look first at the past when trying to sketch out a policy for the future.

"I am deeply convinced," he wrote in 1957, "that only a right attitude to the past provides me with any possibility whatever of a right attitude to the future. And by a right attitude to the past I mean a genuine conviction that the Holy Spirit was operating in the past, that he guided our fathers before us, and that he was all the while at work taking up the cross-threads of human ignorance and failure and sin and using them to weave a pattern whose full revealing awaits the future. This does not mean that we treat the past as sacred, that we must not pass judgment upon it. Far from that I believe we only do justice to the past when we lift it up into our belief that God was in it both creatively and redemptively, creating all that was good in it and redeeming all that was evil and mistaken. A belief in the God of history is a positive invitation to the passing of judgments upon history. But our judgments will be passed with due humility for we will remember that we are ourselves in history and that God is at work today, the creative agent in anything good that we do and the Redeemer of that which is wrong. In such humility we can even sometimes see clearly enough to judge ourselves or at least prepare ourselves for judgment.

"From this standpoint, from this understanding of history, we can see tomorrow and tomorrow and tomorrow not as a merely successive movement but as a pathway continuous from the past and effulgent with the divine glory. We can go out not knowing whither we go but knowing with whom we go, our prayer the simple one – 'Lead us, O God'.

"I believe that history matters tremendously and that we must take the past as seriously as we hope the future will take us. There is an attitude of mind involved which is not easy to compass. I am not advocating the approach of the traditionalist. I do not idolise the past. I am not a conservative in the common meaning of that term. I am deeply convinced that we sometimes keep faith with the past best by making some new departure which will, in fact, fulfil what in the past was being attempted in other ways. But I make this departure in fellowship-with-the-past and not in any sort of contemptuous antagonism for it. As it were, I try and enter into conversation with the past, make it my contemporary, argue with it and treat it as a living companion. I do not believe we can understand the present and plan for the future unless we see clearly how continuous the present is with the past and how all-pervading is the influence of past patterns upon present behaviour."

Thus for better, for worse, the Society had chosen as its leader a man who was passionately interested in history, who believed that history was still in the making under the controlling hand of God, and that he himself had been called to play a part in the creating and redeeming of history in which God Himself was engaged. He never ceased to be thankful for the inspiring guidance of the teachers who had helped him to think imaginatively about the past: they "gave me a passion for history which is the drive behind anything I write. History is such a living dynamic thing and a theology which is not of the living stuff of events seems to me to be unreal".

This theology, he firmly believed, was essentially that of the Bible. He constantly kept company with the great prophets of the Old Testament – Amos, Isaiah, Jeremiah – and accepted their interpretation of the events of their own day. But none of the prophets seems to have made so direct an appeal to him as did the prophet Habakkuk. In many sermons and addresses he reminded his hearers of the daring way in which this prophet had identified the advancing Chaldeans as the divinely-sent executors of judgment upon God's people. When giving Bible readings at Meadville in 1954 to a large group of Americans about to go overseas to their mission stations, he startled them by suggesting that Habakkuk's word about the Chaldeans might equally be applied to the Chinese Communists under Chairman Mao. And in the last of his books published in 1976 he returned to the ancient prophecy. "A careful student of political events, baffled at the prospect of the impending destruction of the Covenant people at the hands of a brutal enemy, he (i.e. Habakkuk) heard a staggering word from God: 'I am raising up the Chaldeans that savage and impetuous nation.'"

Yet this appeal to the actions of the living God in history was not confined to the prophets of the Old Testament. Clearly such an appeal was at the very heart of Paul's Gospel. In his diary at the Whitby, Ontario, Conference in 1947, he recorded his sudden deeper appreciation of Paul's references to Mystery in the economy of God. "Nation may rise against nation but there is someone at work in the world. I think I've got a glimpse into what Paul meant by *Mystery* in writing to the Ephesians. The mystery of the gospel, whatever else it means, surely includes the element of the unpredictable, that quality of 'happening' which human reason cannot anticipate, cannot command and cannot frustrate."

This element of unpredictability Max loved to celebrate through an aphorism which he enunciated more than once. "We must recover our faith", he declared, "that God is in control of history, with the corollary that the God who is in control of history is himself uncontrollable." However, although it would be sheer folly for man to attempt to control God, two strategies were available for his active pursuit. One was to accept the challenge of Jesus to his contemporaries that they should discern the "signs of the times".

81

The other was to take heed to Jesus' exhortation that men ought always to *pray* and not to faint. Max set himself with great determination to collect the best possible information about significant current events so that, like the prophet of old, he could assist his contemporaries in the task of discernment and interpretation. At the same time he called upon his fellow-workers to join with him in a renewed discipline of prayer for the spread of God's Kingdom of righteousness and love among the nations of the world.

II

First of all then he tried to assess the present position of the Society within the unfolding purpose of God. To do this he reminded himself of its history, the details of which were to him a constant source of inspiration. Again and again in his writing he looked back to the birth of C.M.S. under the inspired leadership of John Venn in the early months of 1799. He never ceased to acknowledge with deepest admiration and gratitude the contribution made by Charles Simeon to the development of the Society in the early decades of the nineteenth century. He regarded Henry Venn, the General Secretary in the mid-nineteenth century, as a man of outstanding wisdom and far-sighted statesmanship who had inaugurated a new era in the Society's affairs by encouraging in every way the upbuilding of native churches under native leadership. A third era had roughly coincided with the half-century from 1900 onwards, an era which had seen a remarkable development of institutional life in mission areas – diocesan organisations, hospitals, and particularly colleges and schools, some of which were already attaining the status of self-government. Max began at once to look ahead to the celebration of the Society's Third Jubilee in 1949. To what new ventures was God calling the Society within the working out of his purpose in world-history?

In order to become aware of the "signs of the times" in the contemporary world Max turned daily to *The Times* and weekly to *The Economist*. He regarded the latter as the regular medium of the best-informed survey of world-movements, political and economic, and he remained one of its devoted readers to the end of his life. In addition he contrived somehow to read widely in history, in biography and in international affairs, besides remaining faithful to a sustained study of biblical and historical theology. Nothing seems to have relaxed him more than "a good read". This was the joy of a long railway journey: a whole book could be devoured. This too was the refreshment of a holiday or of a day off – that he could, as it were, enter into conversation with writers known or unknown to him and so enrich his own mind and imagination with their discoveries.

One of the most remarkable examples of his delight in reading, first for his own enjoyment and then for the pleasure of sharing his newly-acquired reflections with a friend, is to be found in a letter written to Michael Hennell at the conclusion of a family holiday in Yorkshire in the summer of 1950. He "inflicted" this letter of fourteen closely-typed pages on his friend, he wrote, because "the exercise helps to focus something of what I've learnt in that queerly adjusted apparatus for forgetfulness which I call my mind". He had clearly been in his element, keeping company with some of the great figures of the nineteenth century and looking for further light on a subject which was of perennial interest to him – the contribution which evangelicals made to thought and action in that period. He had rejoiced in Kitson Clark's *The English Inheritance* particularly because "so rarely do you find an Anglican approach to the Free Church tradition which is not subtly patronising. But here set forth with detachment and yet enthusiasm there is a magnificent presentation of the share of the Free Church and dissenting tradition in the working out of our National tradition of liberty, something far larger than the issue of religious liberty". About Archbishop Garbett's *Church and State in England* he had some reservations, particularly about his attitude to disestablishment. "My own hope is that the establishment may remain but be greatly strengthened by the Union in this country of all the main Protestant Churches. To me therefore the whole argument of the Archbishop's book makes towards the reduction of the Anglican Church to a sect, and a not unduly impressive sect at that, in which the English contribution to the Christianising of the world is going to play a much smaller part than in the past."

Next he began to enthuse about G. M. Trevelyan's *Grey of Fallodon*, Philip Guedalla's *Palmerston*, and John Morley's two-volume *Life of Gladstone*. In each of these he had been on the look-out for references to evangelical influences and was able to suggest numerous questions which could well be followed up by research students e.g. "How much of Gladstone's background was really low-Church and not evangelical at all?" What might Gladstone's development have been if he had gone to Cambridge instead of to Oxford? "However he went to Oxford. That melancholy fact remains and explains, alas, how much!" And then in a more serious reflection: "One has to face frankly the fact that Gladstone, Manning and Newman all started from an evangelical background, and so did the Wilberforces. What was the weakness of the evangelicalism of that day? What may be its weakness still in the light of that past? And when one has allowed for all the weakness how comes it that as a school of thought it not only persists but has shown again and again powers of recuperation and in our own day is not by any means without vigour. This at least seems indisputable that the real strength of evangelicalism lies in the truths which have gripped evangelicals and hardly at all in the Evangelicals who have been gripped by these truths."

Such was his holiday reading and such were some of his reflections. The best holiday for him was not so much to be transported in *space* to some secluded spot for the enjoyment of natural beauty (though on his travels he wrote impressive descriptions of places he visited): rather it was to be transported in *time* and to live for a while with great characters of the past, particularly those of the nineteenth century. He recognised how vitally important an understanding of the nineteenth century was for an intelligent approach to the problems of the twentieth. A holiday gave him the chance to deepen his own perception of the intellectual and spiritual forces which had been operative within the life of Nation and Church during the period since C.M.S. was founded at the end of the eighteenth century.

III

After he had been in office for some two years and so had found opportunity to acquaint himself with the many aspects of the Society's work, he felt ready to set out in extended form his own conception of the distinctive role which the Society was being called upon to play in the period after the close of the war. He submitted his memorandum first to his fellow Secretaries, then after revision to the Executive Committee, and finally in printed form to the Society as a whole. It is a revealing document, characteristic both of the man himself and of his method of working.

He begins with a brief meditation, anchoring his wider considerations to Romans 9–11, to what he calls an "inspiring but disconcerting rock of Scripture". "From this vantage point," he urges (echoing his favourite prophet), "let us watch and see what

God will say to us. He does not speak in the same way to every generation . . . We have to be ready for that. But our hope remains that God still has work for the C.M.S. to do, for a C.M.S. recognisably continuous with the past, whatever new things may be shown to us. I hope that something of the deep profundity of St. Paul's argument in Romans 9–11 may be the background of all our thinking in these coming days as we consider the policy of our Society."

He then went on to sketch the new context within which the Society must now do its work. The memorandum is full of prophetic insights. First he tried to stress the significance of the emergence of the *social service state*, not only in Britain but increasingly on other parts of the world. The underlying theory might be Marxist or democratic or tribal but one effect was common to all state-ordered societies: "a progressive development of state interference in every department of human life." This would become increasingly evident in all countries of the world as modern techniques became more widely available. It followed that "the permanent tension in our life as Christians is that we have always to seek to make society more Christian and so can and must co-operate with the state when it is doing right, the while we protest against and do our best to sabotage every effort of human society to find its end in itself. An awareness of this tension, and the acceptance of the suffering and misunderstanding it will involve, is absolutely essential if the missionary work of the Church is to be maintained in our time."

Secondly, and rather naturally, Max drew attention to what he called a burgeoning *nationalism* the world over. It might have been expected that he would have laid emphasis upon the reaction in Asia and Africa against colonialism and the political ambitions of Western powers. He was well aware of this and drew attention to it on many occasions. But he had the insight to recognise how great a part *economic* considerations played and how nationalism could be regarded as "a self-protective mechanism against the but half understood, but obviously powerful economic forces making for standardisation all over the world". Much of this passionate resistance to a monochrome internationalism he felt to be good, for his whole instinct was towards the preservation of a rich variety whether in the political or the ecclesiastical world. He was anxious that missionaries should assess the phenomenon of nationalism fairly and "seek the difficult end of harmonising the maximum of variety and not imposing a minimum of uniformity".

The third factor in the world situation which seemed at first sight much closer to the missionary concern was the emergence of *indigenous churches*. He gave reasons for putting it in third place on his list and thereby bore witness to an important theological principle which was to govern much of his own activity. "I have set the growing churches overseas as the third fact deliberately," he wrote, "because I believe it is urgently necessary to see those churches within the given historical context of today, a context defined by the fact of the 'omnicompetent' modern State and the powerful forces of Nationalism. The Church is, of course, never only within a given historical context. It is always at the same time part of the Eternal Word breaking into history. This fact upon which our faith is grounded remains the incalculable factor in every human situation. By this faith, very literally, we Christians live and move and have that disturbing power in the world to which recorded history abundantly testifies. But at the same time there remains a continual temptation to romanticise the Eternal and to forget that in all incarnations there is the fact of limitation. We have tended to do so much of this of late in missionary circles that a revolt against romanticism of this rather easy sentimental sort is long overdue."

I have quoted this reflection of his at length because it seems to me to set forth in a short space the essence of the theology which constituted the framework of his own life and work. He believed passionately that God was in control of history and that in certain ways the 'Eternal Word' had broken into history. But this 'breaking in' was always limited by the actual conditions existing in history.

> It is by no breath,
> Turn of eye, wave of hand, that salvation
> joins issue with death.

There could be no romanticising of the Eternal. There could be no escape from the limitations imposed by the context within which the "breaking in" occurred. And what had been the case whenever the Eternal Word had become incarnate in the past, must likewise be true as the Word becomes incarnate in the life of the Church to-day. There are limitations and it is incumbent upon Christians to face them honestly and to recognise their implications both for the developing churches themselves and for the Western missionaries' attitudes towards them. It became Max's constant concern, both in spoken addresses and still more in writings such as his News-Letter, to make clear what was the nature of the "limitations" and at the same time to renew faith in the ceaseless activity of the Eternal Word in the world.

At that stage he singled out what appeared to be three dominant characteristics of the indigenous churches. They were a nationalist temper, a sensitiveness such as may be seen in a growing adolescent, and a consciousness of being economically underdeveloped. Towards all of these manifestations he showed a lively sympathy, deploring, for example, "the enervating paternalism and irrational pride of their elder brethren". Everything possible must be done to encourage the development of autonomous churches and to ease their way forward to self-support. But this should not be done at the expense of sentimental acceptance of every move towards autonomy as being necessarily right or of the abrupt withdrawal of all missionary assistance educationally or economically. Max saw further ahead than most of his Anglican contemporaries as to what was likely to be the trend of events in Asia and Africa but he was not prepared to panic and leave the indigenous churches to shoulder their burdens alone. The gradual handing over of *institutions* he believed to be inevitable but of the continuing need for *personal* offers of assistance and co-operation he had no shadow of doubt.

Yet this was the fourth factor which deeply concerned him for he was conscious of "the inadequacy in point of numbers, training and quality of the missionary personnel". He compared the situation just before the First World War when C.M.S. had 1385 missionaries on the active list with that in 1938 when the number had dropped to 1085. Moreover there had been a marked increase in the proportion of those engaged in educational and medical work as over against those giving pastoral and evangelistic leadership. While never underestimating the importance of schools and hospitals, he knew how easy it was to be turned aside from the unfinished *evangelistic* task of the Church. He was determined to keep in the forefront, for himself and for others, the call of God to go beyond the settled and established, out into those areas of life where Christ was not already named. "The assurance by which a Christian lives," he claimed, "has nothing in common with what the world calls security. We are committed to a belief that in every situation there is an incalculable factor, which is comprised of God's particular intention at that time and place, and His resources. This incalculable factor can be apprehended by faith alone." Nevertheless, it was incumbent upon his servants to look carefully at the resources available (a) in men and women and (b) in money: this Max proceeded with careful analysis to do.

In conclusion he referred again to the "incalculable" factor which is outside the range of all human considerations. He never lost sight of the possibility of *Revival*, a new movement of the Spirit of God which would lead his servants to launch out in wholly unprecedented ways. He looked back on the history of Revivals in the Church and never lost hope that somewhere within the world-wide fellowship of Christians new energies and even new forms would manifest themselves. He had in fact hoped, as had many others, that the experiences of the war years might have issued in a revival of religious life in Britain itself. Stephen Spender recalls what he describes as "the religious mood of the war. There was a feeling of incandescent faith which never quite took fire". (*The Thirties and After*, p. 96.) Similarly Max wrote on Jan 1, 1946: "It really looked (in the winter of 1940–1941) as if a new world was swimming into our ken. The comradeship of the trenches in the 1914–1918 war was the comradeship of the queue and the underground shelter, the comradeship of A.R.P. and W.V.S. in 1940–1941. The country trembled on the brink of a religious revival. It only just did not happen." But he never ceased to hope. He rejoiced for example in the Revival in Uganda even though some of its features could only be regarded as extravagant and divisive. Meanwhile he pleaded urgently with all the members of the Society to pray for a new movement of the Spirit and to be ready to fashion new means to new ends in the midst of the challenging events of the post-war world.

IV

Such was Max's submission to the members of the Society at large concerning the policy to be pursued in the days lying ahead. But general principles are not enough. They need to be supplemented by steady and continuing provision of up-to-date news of particular needs and of actual events on the mission field. To achieve this he needed the help of experts in new modes of communication; he also needed a suitable medium to convey his own impressions and reflections gained while standing on his watch-tower at C.M.S. Headquarters. For the first of these needs he built up a Home Secretariat whose competence was probably equal to, or even better than, any comparable organisation of the day. For the second he found time to write a succession of small books and pamphlets dealing with such topics of current interest as the use of time, church and state, partnership, church union and Holy Communion. Above all he laid hold of a recent innovation in C.M.S. circles, a monthly News-Letter, and made it the means of such successful communication that his name, and his contribution to the missionary policy of the whole Church, became known throughout the Christian world. I shall speak later about the way in which he built up his staff. For the moment something must be said about the expansion of the News-Letter.

This form of communication may have had its origin in the remarkably influential Christian News-Letter edited by Dr. J. H. Oldham in the days of war stringency. It was at any rate adopted by Dr. Cash, Max's predecessor, early in the war as an economical way of keeping C.M.S. supporters, in particular layfolk, in touch with significant developments in the life of the Society. Max took it over when only thirty-one issues had so far appeared. The next 232 News-Letters proved to be his own undisputed pulpit from which he addressed missionaries, home supporters and, before long, a widely varied audience dispersed all over the world. They were, as he affirmed, "a genuine attempt to come to terms with the real context within which the Christian Mission had to operate" and they remained always the General Secretary's distinctive responsibility: he did not commit his colleagues or the Society at large to the views he expressed but was given freedom to send them out with the title C.M.S. News-Letter attached.

A revealing exchange of letters took place in 1966 between him and his successor John Taylor when the latter was firmly established in his new office. He wrote asking Max to consider writing an article on the Nigerian situation which he would incorporate in a future News-Letter. But Max felt bound to decline.

"Four or five years before I left 6 Salisbury Square," he wrote, "I felt so much under pressure that I did for a time consider the News-Letter only coming out six times a year. But on further consideration I became quite clear that this would be a major blunder . . . Your News-Letters are making a terrific impact. I remain impenitently of the conviction that taking the longest and broadest views, the C.M.S. News-Letter represents one of the most important things that the Society is doing. It probably does more to create an image of the Society as regards its thinking than anything else the Society produces – and as you well know its wide circulation exercises an influence amongst many people who know virtually nothing about C.M.S.

"This leads me to the next point. I do really doubt whether it ought ever to pass out of your hands as General Secretary.

"Precisely the same suggestion was made to me when I was feeling the pressure of things that you now have in mind. I thought about this a lot and it was not immodesty which led me to reject the idea.

"The character of the News-Letter lies precisely in the fact that it is a personal communication from the General Secretary. On countless occasions I was able to say, when people challenged me, that the News-Letter was an expression of personal opinion and was in no sense of the word an official document representing either the Society, or anyone else's opinion besides my own."

We possess then in the News-Letter a fascinating record of Max's own interpretation of world events and their significance for the Christian cause over a period of more than twenty years. He received help from two invaluable research assistants, first Elizabeth France and then Greta Preston, who collected and collated material for him. They might present extracts from books but he never recommended a book to his readers which he had not actually read himself. He would plan a theme as far as a year ahead for his assistants' guidance and often when he had made a first draft he would have it sent out to three or four informed persons for criticism which, however stringent, he was always prepared to consider with the greatest care. On some subjects he felt relative confidence e.g. Islam and West Africa. On others, particularly on philosophical aspects of Hinduism, he felt his weakness: in fact he confessed to Greta that the News-Letter on Hinduism caused him more difficulty than any other that he wrote.

Year after year he wove patterns of appropriate length and attractiveness of presentation out of his own informed reflections and the material assembled by the members of his team. Although he never finally bequeathed a large book to posterity, in a very real sense the approximately four hundred thousand words of the News-Letters can be regarded as his most distinctive contribution to the religious literature of the twentieth century.

V

What then were the qualities and chief characteristics of Max's News-Letters which caused them to be so welcome to so large a circle of readers? A perusal of the earlier letters before he took control reveals a largely domestic scene with news of the movements of missionaries, the financial outlook, the effect of the war in China, exhortations to carry on in spite of difficulties such as the damage caused at Salisbury Square by incendiary bombs. The outlook is optimistic and there are numerous references to triumphs of the gospel: the war period, it is said "may be the prelude to the greatest era in the history of the Church".

But from the beginning Max tried to lift his readers' thoughts to the large issues confronting heralds of the gospel. In his very first Letter he raised the subject of the costly task of *translation*, "perhaps the biggest single task facing the Church of this generation" and one which, in days to come, was never far from his thoughts. This was not just a matter of translating the Christian verities into foreign languages but rather the gaining of a far deeper understanding of the actual situations in, for example, China and India in order that the word of God might be applied to these situations and not to simplicities of our own imagining. "As yet very few people in this country are really alive to the revolutionary effects that the war with Japan is having on China."

In his second Letter he raised the whole question of the relationship between Church and State (the theme of Archbishop Temple's speech at his first Canterbury diocesan conference) and its bearing on missionary activity. He saw that the issue was most likely to become critical in the field of education and gave as an illustration the development of schools and colleges in Sierra Leone. At first the Church enjoyed a monopoly of education in the colony but that day was past. Could the Christian Church, and Christian missions in particular, resist pressures which were tending more and more towards the total control of education by the Social Service State?

The third turned to a wholly different aspect of missionary activity which might at first sight have seemed remote from the interests of C.M.S. supporters. It was the part being played and likely in the future to be played by American missions in general and by the Episcopal Church in America in particular. Here was his opportunity to introduce the theme of historical movement which always fascinated him. He saw the history of the United States hitherto as the history of her "frontier". But that period had in a certain sense come to an end. (Though Max could hardly have foreseen the immense migration westwards which was to take place within the next decade.) So today, he claimed, "we are watching what may still prove to be one of the most decisive events in world history: We might call it 'the return of Columbus' or the rediscovery by America of the world." He pointed out that America was evincing a wholly new interest in Africa, and recognising in a new way its responsibility for the peace of the world. What then would this mean for new possibilities of co-operation between the C.M.S.

91

and the missionary leaders within the Episcopal Church? He was destined in due course to make numerous trips to the U.S.A., to assist, for example, in the development there of the Overseas Mission Society, and to learn incidentally of the wide distribution of his own News-Letter amongst American missionaries. (An American friend of mine, who worked as a missionary in Japan, told me that, for him, the most important missionary reading during his time there was the C.M.S. News-Letter.)

Max could well have become an outstanding journalist. He seemed to spot instinctively the places in the world where important events were taking place, and by the help of books and newspapers and correspondence with missionaries in those places he was able to ring the changes and sustain the interest of his readers. Now it was the South Indian scheme of Church Union: now it was the effect on the future of Africa that the enlistment of black troops in the war effort was likely to have: now the influence of economic considerations on evangelism: now the nature of true community: now the possibility that "the Holy Spirit may desire Indian forms to enshrine the gospel in Indian life". On all these topics he wrote with obvious knowledge and insight and it is no wonder that within a year, in spite of the pressing exigencies of war, the circulation of the News-Letter was increasing rapidly and Max's name was becoming widely known.

The astonishing thing is that the fecundity of his mind and the sense of his continuing responsibility were such that it is impossible to detect any decline of relevance or any staleness of presentation over the long period of twenty-one years. Thirteen of the Letters which appeared during his last three years in office were published in book form and they were amongst his best. In the preface he summarises the purpose of the Letters in terms which go far towards encompassing the whole sweep of his labours as General Secretary. After referring to the sheer mass of information to which people are exposed today he writes: "This being so, and because Christians are very much 'in' the world, some attempt must be made to try to see the inner meaning of what is happening around us, and particularly the meaning of events in parts of the world which are unfamiliar to us, but which are bound up with us in the bundle of life to-day.

"The C.M.S. News-Letter has been *primarily* concerned with events in Asia and Africa. But always these events, and their meaning, are understood as having a direct relevance for those who do not live in those continents. 'No man is an island.' Insularity is still what it has always been, a demonic curse with power to enfeeble. For Christians, indeed, the implication of the New Testament understanding of 'the Body of Christ' positively demands our active involvement in thought and prayer and action with those who are also of that Body in other parts of the world. Only so can we be responsible citizens both of our own countries and of the Kingdom of God."

As he went on to tell his readers, he was always looking for the signs of God's presence: whatever the immediate appearances might be, he believed that it was possible to discern, however imperfectly, the working out of God's purposes. He claimed no monopoly in the ability to read such signs but gladly recognised that writers about other kinds of experience than his own could wittingly or unwittingly bear witness to the divine factor operative in the world's history. "I have often discovered more truth, more genuine, if unconscious, theological insight in books by economists, sociologists, politicians, travellers, historians and scientists, than I have discerned in much so-called theological writing." He had the right to say this for he did keep abreast of the theological writing of his own time. It was in the holding together of theology (Biblical theology in particular) with the movements of ideas and aspirations and policies and events in the world around that Max excelled.

A future historian will be able to find invaluable material for the interpretation of world history during the years 1942–63 in these Letters. Their range is extraordinary. Land development in Africa, literature and literacy, the revolt against imperialism in its many forms, Egypt's relations with the Arab world, ministerial training, the crisis in the world's affairs after the explosion of the atom bomb, educational policies, the place of women in the new Africa, the significance of Afghanistan ("a mountain range and a river have shaped the destinies of mighty nations and may yet again decisively affect the peace of the world" – this in January 1952); the importance of land, soil and water in the Middle East, the nature of power, the political situation in Ceylon, foreign students in England, the Ugandan crisis, the race problem, the preparation of missionaries, the resurgence of ancient religions, the crucial importance of learning the language of a particular area, Christ and Culture. He never repeated himself except insofar as he might return to a problem which had been discussed before but now had taken on some new aspect. He never tackled a subject without having first equipped himself with the best possible information. He never lost sight of his main concern: to illustrate by first-hand examples the way in which the purposes of God were being worked out in the movements of individuals and of societies.

One who was in close touch with Max over many years recently commented:

"I've just had to skim quickly through the News-Letters for the 1950's. Their impact was almost overwhelming. It was devastating to be reminded of the themes and subject-matter Max brought to attention then and to realise to how large an extent they have been neglected or have come newly to attention now. I was also left with an appalling sense of my own failure to play adequately my part in the terrific educational process that needed to be built up consequent on the News-Letters." I myself would find it hard to specify instances where his judgments or prophecies proved to be wrong in the light of subsequent events. He was courageous (he was quick to pierce through to the heart of the matter at the time of the Suez crisis), and at the same time cautious (he would not commit himself to hasty impressions in public). He and his assistants enjoyed their work to the full. It is likely that he will be remembered by the great series of News-Letters more than by any others of his not inconsiderable achievements.

VI

I suggested that whereas Max always had a profound sense of God's over-ruling control of historic events, he also believed that it was incumbent upon his servants to direct their activities first by discerning the signs of the times and then by renewing their strength for those activities by regular and persistent prayer. He confessed more than once his own sense of inadequacy in prayer and yet few men can have sought more earnestly than he to preserve regular times for quiet and reflection and intercession. However tired he might be, he would seek new inspiration from the Bible and, in remembrance and petition, would stretch out towards those who were his fellow-workers in the service of the Kingdom.

One of his earliest appeals to these fellow-workers was contained in a small booklet with the striking title *The Master of Time*. He dedicated it to those who had known the pressure of time and had joined in the quest for its mastery: it was by contemplating him who was indeed the Master of Time by living in complete dependence upon God, whatever the character of the here and now might be, that this mastery could at least in a measure be achieved. "How do we acquire this attitude which welcomes the *Now* with all its limitations? We do it by the practice of the presence of Christ, in whom the Eternal became NOW with all the limitations of the NOW. That is the meaning of the Incarnation in terms of Time."

Yet, while recognising the need to discern the presence of Eternity in any momentary Now, he also knew the importance of discipline in reserving times for intercession. Every two months, beginning in July–August 1942, he addressed a "prayer-paper" to his "fellow-intercessors" and these are full of freshness of illustration and depth of spiritual understanding. Bunyan's armour of All Prayer, the mountaineer's time to contemplate, Nehemiah the practical man of affairs but also the man of constant prayer, the garden lover in Nigeria planting trees for posterity, the question whether the sense of "belongingness" created in wartime would continue afterwards, the connection between prayer and money – money only being "fruitful spiritually as it remains a token of personal relationship" – many of these letters may be regarded as classics of devotion for they always remain in touch with the real world and its needs, while seeking to relate all these needs to the self-giving of God himself.

He delighted to share with his readers treasures derived from his own reading. It might be a devastating sentence from C. S. Lewis: "There have been some who were so occupied in spreading Christianity that they never gave a thought to Christ." It might be a perceptive comment by Herbert Farmer: "You cannot move forward without giving up. Nothing is more important than to know when we must surrender things valuable for things more valuable." Or at the beginning of a new year a lovely thought from the autobiography of Katharine Hathaway: "The next new dawn that breaks upon the ruin of today's world will surely begin to shine . . . at the moment when some future wanderer lifts up his head and sees something as if for the first time, and pauses to admire, then feels in his breast a kindling fire of gratitude and wonder and then, instinctively following the sequence, falls on his knees to worship the mystery and so gives himself to God." Always he seemed to have some new aspect of the prayer-life to celebrate.

But the note which recurs again and again, and which was central in his own prayer experience, was that of the necessity to maintain the *personal* reference and the *personal* relationship in every approach to God and in every stretching out to our contemporaries. "Only what is personal, what is spiritual, remains." It is in the context of the family, of the bonds of friendship, of the association of those engaged in a common cause, that prayer becomes most vital and most real. One of his most deeply-felt papers was that written as commentary on the text: "If two of you shall agree on earth as touching any thing that they shall ask, it shall be done for them of my Father which is in heaven." (A.V.) He focussed attention on the word *agree* and interpreted the Greek original as that of the symphony, as harmony. "Agreement is a much deeper thing than uniformity of outlook. The two who pray may see many things from quite different points of view. Far from that making agreement difficult, it is the essential condition without which harmony is impossible." But "harmony of relationship is possible only through friendship" and "prevailing prayer" can only be experienced when there is genuine fellowship. Moreover the following verse is the key to everything else. Prayer must be *in his Name.*

> To be gathered in his Name implies harmony of intention and a deep fellowship of obedience. Personal relationships are thus perfected by THE PERSON and prayer prevails.

So Max called upon his prayer partners within the C.M.S. Fellowship not to attempt to be workers *for* God but to be workers *with* Him, to dedicate themselves to be "agents of His initiative". At any moment Eternity might be touching time in a special, a sacramental way. "Our aspiration will be to treat Time sacramentally – to live, that is, sacramentally in Time, conscious that in the Nowness of every day God is directly coming into human life through the things that happen to us and the things we do and above all, through all the personal relationships involved in the work to which we have been called."

7

Building a team

I

MAX ASSUMED HIS new office at what may have been the most critical
juncture in the whole history of C.M.S. By its very nature the
Society was an association, a fellowship, a world-wide family, in
which some members were at Headquarters in London, some were
banded together in parochial groups in Britain, Ireland, Australia,
New Zealand and South Africa, some were working as missionaries
in Asia and Africa. But because of war conditions parochial
organisations had been disrupted, while those serving abroad had
great difficulty in returning to their home bases on furlough; in
London the General Secretary and the Home Secretary had
recently left for other work, and the acting General Secretary was a
man nearing the age of retirement. Communications were difficult
in the extreme and good communications are essential if a community is to retain its vitality. Recruitment was almost at a
standstill.

The new leader set to work at once to restore confidence and to
inspire hope for the future. This he proceeded to do in three main
ways: through unwearying attention to possibilities of making
personal contact and establishing personal relationships, through
the use of every available means of communicating with the
Society's home supporters and with missionaries on the field, and
through reconstructing the staff at Headquarters in such a way that
it would function as an efficient team. He never tired of affirming
that his own position was essentially that of *primus inter pares* but if
he was *primus* he could not escape the responsibility of team
formation and team leadership. He knew in his inmost heart that he
must constantly be one step ahead, and once expressed it in this
way:

> The secret of any leadership he [i.e. The General Secretary]
> can achieve lies in his having a wider knowledge of the Church,

the world and the Society than any of his fellow-Secretaries, and in thinking a very long way ahead, and working towards his goal patiently, if necessary going round two sides of the square rather than forcing a passage down the diagonal!

I have already referred to the supreme importance he attached to unhurried sessions with individuals. These demanded preparation, attention, listening. I have also noted his use of booklets and the News-Letter as a means of communicating with widely scattered readers. In addition he was concerned for the inner circle of members and prepared with great care statements about the history, nature and function of the Society for distribution, and then letters of information and interpretation which could be printed and sent out to missionaries together with other inspirational material. *Our Society in the Calling of God* was laid before the Executive Committee and then forwarded to members at home and abroad; *A Letter of Interpretation* followed by *Invitation to Danger* and *The Will to Go On* was sent out to all missionaries; a pamphlet entitled *The Miracle of Midian* and a remarkable printed letter on the faith and order of the Church of England entitled *Decent Order and Godly Discipline* were also sent to missionaries. All these gave a clear indication, at the beginning of his régime, of what manner of man he was, what were the realities of the world-situation as he saw them and what were the lines of advance along which he was calling his fellow-workers to go.

Certain key-notes are struck which were to characterise his whole period in office. Loyalty, trust, friendship, interdependence: without these qualities members of the Society could never fulfil their calling. The primacy of the gospel: this had been entrusted to all who dared to call themselves missionaries and it was their bounden duty to *translate* that gospel into their own situations whatever they might be. The gospel will remain hid and meaningless "if we do not accept the arduous responsibility of translating it into the vernacular of life as well as of speech". A glad acceptance of the ordered framework of the Anglican tradition was coupled with a readiness to work in fellowship and harmony with other Christian communities wherever this was possible.

These were the positive notes. At the same time, he was determined to sound a note of warning concerning the realities of the world-situation as he saw them. "If you ask me the question, 'Watchman, what of the night?' I must in all candour reply, 'The night is very dark indeed, an icy rain is falling, and the wind is rising'" – this in 1948. He believed that even as recently as 1942, people in Britain "were still living to some extent in the mental attitude of the 1920's. We still thought that it might be possible to rescue some of the patterns of that old world from the deluge." But now it had become clear that "our present organisation and our traditional method of approach are totally inadequate to grapple with the contemporary situation." In particular, the Second World War had delivered lethal blows to Britain's financial credit, its political prestige and its colonial powers. Realignment of the Society's resources had become inevitable. Reconsideration of strategy was essential. This must not mean retreat. Indeed there would be constant need for new experiments. But to imagine that missionary work in Asia and Africa in the post-war world could be carried on according to the pattern of the first half of the century was sheer delusion.

One other note in his stirring letters to missionaries is interesting. It is the note of the *warrior*. Perhaps the memories of his own naval-forebears remained with him. He certainly loved the stories of John Buchan with their heroic adventurers. Most of all, of course, he admired the first great missionary who wrote about the conflict with principalities and powers and the need to be equipped with the whole armour of God. Consciously or unconsciously, he often returned to the image of missionaries being in the forefront of the struggle with the forces of evil. Memories of the war were still vivid. They could regard themselves as commandos or shock troops called now to fresh ventures for the sake of the Kingdom of God.

So, as the leader of a task-force, he wrote about "tactics of concentration", of "effective spiritual attack against those forces of evil which are the constant enemy of the Church of God". He likened missionaries on the field to Gideon's three hundred guerillas, alert, ready to move quickly, equipped to deal with any surprising new situation. He recalled the words of a foreign commander referring to English soldiers under his command in the Low Countries: "They possess one singular virtue beyond any other nation, for they are always willing to go on." And then: "We missionaries are part of an international army of which that testimony is far more certainly true than of the sons of any particular race or nation. We march with those who many times 'might have had the opportunity to have returned' but who, by the grace of God were 'willing to go on'. The trumpets have sounded for multitudes of such already. With them and in their company we look for the triumph of God."

Still in the aftermath of war, this was the challenge which he tried to communicate to his comrades in the field in the early days of his leadership. He called for re-alignment, for new adventures in evangelism. And from this concentration on the task of evangelism he never deviated. Only, as we shall see, his imagery regarding the "strategy" and "tactics" to be employed underwent a marked change some ten years later.

II

Personal conversations and personal communications through letters held pride of place amidst his many activities throughout his career. He had an aversion to the telephone and rarely used it. But in the words of a friend: "Letters, most often in his own hand, flowed in on every conceivable subject, including quotations he had come across that were in my field of research, copy of a lecture or sermon he had given somewhere, a draft of a paper he was going to give, asking for my opinion." And scores of others of his friends could bear a similar testimony.

This did not mean, however, that he was indifferent to the task of administration to which he had been called at Headquarters. It was, in fact, a most complex organisation with its large staff and its many agents at home and overseas. Nothing could be more important than the creation of a team-spirit in Salisbury Square amongst those who would be sensitive to his own visions and dedicated to the task of bringing them into effect. Not that he wanted "Yes men" but rather men and women of strength who were prepared to criticise when necessary but always in the spirit of loyalty and devotion to the common cause.

Almost immediately the question of a new President arose. Sir Robert Williams was ill at the time of Max's appointment and died soon afterwards. By the rules of the Society the President must be a layman and the choice might have fallen upon some distinguished figure able to play little part in the day-to-day affairs of the Society. Instead Max put forward the name of a man whom he had known as a friend since boyhood days, a man very different from himself in experience and temperament but one who was entirely familiar with the business life of the city of London and with government circles in Whitehall. In course of time this man, Kenneth Grubb, was to become Chairman both of the House of Laity in the Church Assembly of the Church of England and of the Churches' Commission on International Affairs within the World Council of

Churches. Thus Max secured a close ally inside organisations whose activities often had a bearing on the work of C.M.S. but in which he (Max) had no official standing.

The partnership which continued throughout his period of office proved to be a very remarkable one. Max made it a rule to treat all correspondence with the President as taking priority over anything else that he might be doing. He kept him informed about all major matters, had regular meetings with him to discuss impending business and normally had dinner with him, together with the Treasurer of the Society and the Chairman of the Executive Committee, on the evening before that Committee was due to meet. The President gave of his time ungrudgingly and, as Max wrote, no previous President had held office through any comparable period of change.

Yet the two men were by no means mirror images of one another. The President gave an impression of distance whereas Max was always approachable. The President was essentially a man of businesslike action whereas Max was the man who, in carefully guarded periods of withdrawal, saw visions and dreamed dreams. The President had wide experience of formulating laws of procedure (and gave invaluable aid in the revising of the laws and bye-laws of the Society) whereas Max was always allergic to institutions and to all forms of bureaucracy. The President accepted major responsibilities on committees within ecclesiastical and ecumenical circles whereas Max confined himself almost entirely to the domestic organisations within C.M.S. Yet they respected one another and complemented one another to the immense benefit of the Society as a whole.

The fruitful combination of such differences was only possible because of their deep agreement on the basic principles of Christian life and thought and their common devotion to the missionary cause. The President had himself been a lay missionary in Brazil and had played a considerable part in improving missionary media of communication. He had experienced the "feel" of the Society's work and of the evangelical tradition long before he became President. He was able to engage in theological discussions and gave confidence to other laymen who might be less well versed on these matters than himself.

In due course of time each man wrote an autobiography and each paid tribute to the other. Here is Max's to the President:

> There is no possible accounting of the debt the Society owes to his wisdom, his statesmanship and unremitting attention to its

affairs. When his knighthood was to be gazetted he was asked under what heading he would wish the recognition to be made. He had a wide variety of choice. It was characteristic of Sir Kenneth that he asked for the heading "President of the Church Missionary Society".

Here is the President's to Max:

> No man of my acquaintance, in successive post-war governments or in business or public affairs, made a more accurate and realistic estimate of the courses which the newly independent countries would take in politics or in religious attitudes and in the event have mostly taken.

Max was also fortunate in the extreme in having as Treasurer of the Society a chartered accountant, a man of faith and courage who guided its financial affairs through stormy seas of overdrafts and retrenchments and special appeals in the period of economic readjustment after the war. In addition he enjoyed to the full his relations with successive Chairmen of the Executive Committee, men again who were willing to contribute to the Society's counsels the harvest of their own experiences often in other lands. He constantly alluded to the essentially *lay* character of the Society. He enjoyed the sessions with his lay advisers for, as one of his episcopal friends wrote, Max was convinced that laymen were more able than clergy in doing most things!

III

After the President, the colleague with whom the General Secretary needed to keep most closely in touch was the Home Secretary, the man responsible for the exacting task of informing and encouraging those at the home base who were called upon to support the Society by prayer, study and regular giving. As already suggested, this task was made the more difficult by the exigencies of war-time which affected transport and communications in particular. It needed a tough and imaginative man who could get around the country and could begin to envisage new ways of promoting vital membership within the Society.

Possibly the first appointment to the post, for which Max himself was responsible, was not the best that could have been made. It is true that many who might otherwise have been considered were serving as chaplains to the Forces and the time may not have been ripe for experiments in new ways of communication. Tom Isherwood, who was chosen, had a fine record behind him as preacher and theological teacher and withal was a warm-hearted and completely loyal colleague. But physically he was not the man to journey hither and thither in war-time England and though he was eloquent as a preacher to regular congregations he was not equipped to experiment with new methods to meet new situations. His personal support and sympathy were invaluable to Max during his first four years but then Tom resigned to return to Canada. Thus a second opportunity arose for Max to make a recommendation to the Appointments Committee. This time he made no mistake.

Having watched Leslie Fisher, Rector of Bermondsey, in operation as a member of the Home Committee, he called him in one day to ask if he would consider filling the vacant post of Home Secretary. Such an idea had never entered Leslie's head. He had stayed with his people through the horrors of the blitz and had imagined that if he survived to the end of the war he would continue to stay with them in the period of reconstruction. But as Max told him of the needs for pastoral care and for imaginative developments first in C.M.S. House, then amongst the Organising Secretaries, and in the parishes supporting the Society, he caught a sense of mission to the wider Church and to the world overseas. So there began a partnership which must have been one of the most creative of modern times. Again, however, the two men were very different in temperament and outlook: one was the man of vision who surveyed the world and painted word-pictures on a wide canvas: the other was a man of action, down to earth, a brilliant organiser, alive to new developments of a technical kind, full of enthusiasm which he managed to impart to his staff at the House and to his corps of organising secretaries in the dioceses. Max did not drive a car: Leslie was continually in the car and enabled Max to make the regular journey to and fro from Blackheath not only a time of physical relaxation, but also an invaluable occasion for the sharing of mutual concerns. Leslie trusted Max completely and did everything in his power to transform vision into actual living experience. Their deepest bonds were an unquenchable sense of humour and an unswerving devotion to Christ. No combination could have been happier or more fruitful.

After the Home Secretary, the member of the team with whom Max needed to be in constant consultation was the Woman Secretary. No organisation in the Church of England had provided such a place for the ministry of women as had the C.M.S. Some among its missionaries were nurses and teachers but the larger number were engaged in evangelistic and pastoral work in ways hardly distinguishable from those of their male colleagues, except that they were excluded from the performance of those functions specifically reserved for a bishop or a priest. The selection and training and care of this large body of women were tasks of the highest responsibility and the General Secretary needed to have complete confidence in the one charged with their oversight. Again he could hardly have been happier than he was destined to be in his association with Ena Price, who, like himself of Irish descent, served with him almost from the beginning to the end of his time in Salisbury Square.

Not only was Ena a constant source of information about the various aspects of the women's work: she was also the provider of that feminine presence and touch in the inner councils of the Society which Max seemed to need. Inevitably occasions arose when he felt the strain of things, especially when, after a long committee or meeting of Secretaries, he felt that his hopes and aspirations for future developments had either been misunderstood or actively opposed. He could be depressed and sometimes near to despair. It was at such times that it became of supreme importance to him to have the sympathy and support of one who had actually been present in the committee or meeting and who was able to share the experience of it with him from a woman's point of view. In the light of all the recent talk about women's liberation and women's ordination it is noteworthy that for years past the C.M.S. has accorded women a place of major responsibility in its Secretariat and in its work overseas.

Another Secretary who worked with him through most of his years in office was Harry Wittenbach, a China missionary, who with his wife was interned by the Japanese in Stanley Camp, Hong Kong. Max met him soon after his return to England and quickly decided that this was the man he wanted as Secretary for the Far East. "He was able," Harry comments, "to build up a Secretarial team and to hold together a group of people, trusting each of us to get on with his particular job without interference and backing us up, yet making it clear that we were a team and that we shared responsibility. Nothing was ever taken to Committee unless all the Secretaries approved. And if the Executive Committee were unhappy about some proposed course of action Max, however disappointed, would never press the motion, respecting that the final decision must be the Committee's. He never gave instructions: it was always advice or suggestions."

With this complete respect for his colleagues there went a deep concern for their welfare. Every Christmas, and on the anniversary of each Secretary's appointment, a letter was sent commenting on what he had accomplished in his work and conveying encouragement for the future. Max seemed to miss nothing in the skill and patience needed to preserve loyalty and harmony within a team.

So strong was his concern for the maintenance of the team spirit that he may at times have underestimated the importance of independent thought and action. His attitude was in a measure ambivalent. He did not want yes-men but at the same time, as one of his colleagues has commented, he was frightened of "lone wolves", however able. He was deeply influenced by the ideas of Florence Allshorn about the psychology of co-operative enterprises and yet he was constantly on the lookout for the individual, with the courage of his or her convictions, who was ready to take a distinctive line or to carry a lonely responsibility.

Perhaps the ablest of his colleagues *theologically* was Campbell Milford who, after theological studies at Oxford, came to grips with Indian thought during his period of service in that country. He could enter into debate with Max on theoretical issues (and this was an exercise which Max tremendously enjoyed) and also, at times, on matters of policy. For example, after the war the question of short term service by key men and women became increasingly problematical. Max had a deep conviction about, and had himself made a firm commitment to, service *for life* in the missionary cause. He was always generous in his attitude towards those who, for one reason or another, felt compelled to return from overseas and resume work at home. But still he was reluctant to encourage any limited commitment, either to a particular place or for a particular time. Campbell differed from him and, at least in a few cases, succeeded in winning his point. On other major issues such as the devolution of property, where differences existed within the Executive Committee, he stood firmly on Max's side. The company of Secretaries was never in the least monochrome. Max's delight was ever in a richness of variety within an overarching unity of trust and loyalty, a unity which had no need of a rigid framework of a constitutional or dogmatic kind. Such an ideal could hardly have been attained without persistent and perceptive attention on the part of the leader to varieties of gifts and temperaments and potentialities.

The consentient testimony is that Max's Secretariat was consistently "a happy team".

105

IV

The Secretaries constituted a kind of governing body within C.M.S. House. But there were many assistants, and Max set to work at once to make every one of them aware of his or her significance within the total scheme of things. In the pre-war years the hierarchical structure of the Society had been accepted without question. The General Secretary was a massive figure, steady as a rock, regarded with admiration but hardly known as a personal presence to any except his closest colleagues. Max's whole instinct was to strive for more democratic relationships and, where desirable, to create new posts of responsibility. The Secretariat still directed policies but there were "under Secretaries" who were encouraged to develop new methods of working.

For example, in 1944 Max gained permission to appoint Elizabeth France as his research assistant. The help he so urgently needed was in the task of collecting accurate and up-to-date information. So he encouraged Elizabeth to have long talks with as many missionaries as possible, as and when they returned to England on furlough. In addition, as she remembers, his aim was "to help missionary societies to work less in a vacuum and to be not only more in touch with one another but also with other organisations involved in similar fields. Max used to send me off to attend meetings and follow the programmes of such varied bodies as the Fabian Colonial Bureau, the Victoria League, the Peckham Experiment, the Groundnut Scheme for East Africa, and the post-war reconstruction group which led to the formation of Inter-Church Aid." Then he asked her to start a Book Club to stimulate missionaries to read more, arranged for her to become secretary of the newly-formed Committee on Religious Liberty, and constantly sought her reactions (she having come in from outside the Society) to the aims and methods of the Society for which she was now working. "It all seemed part of the move to keep C.M.S. from becoming parochial and to be ready to make use of the skills and experience of people from outside" – all this without in the least diminishing the cultivation of the family spirit within the Society itself.

Elizabeth's comments on her early association with Max throw a vivid light upon the new enthusiasm which he succeeded in communicating to his assistants.

Max would use younger members of staff as sounding boards for his ideas in such a way that we were never made to feel "small fry" but rather that it really helped him to have our views. He led but never drove us, and when he wanted me to work on some new project we would settle down to an uninterrupted evening at the Royal Empire Society while he outlined what was in his mind. He never dictated how it should be developed but would throw out ideas in such a way that they became part of me. His enthusiasm would keep me going for some time with an unnatural (for me) degree of optimism until the momentum waned in the face of mounting practical problems. Then, if I could get it, another hour with Max would enable me to see a way through the difficulties so that exasperation and frustration gave way to renewed inspiration. An experience of that creative tension about which he wrote.

Inevitably a massive amount of material was constantly piling up which it seemed important that Max should look through but which it was humanly not possible for him to tackle with only twenty-four hours in the day. He used to tell me that provided he was not being lazy about it he believed he would be guided in his selection, and he certainly had an incredible way of picking out seemingly at random some of the very items which later events showed it was particularly important that he should have seen. And with his photographic memory he was capable of quickly reading through a page and quoting from it verbatim a few hours or days later.

After Elizabeth, Greta Preston became his research assistant and continued in the same role as collector of information from people, from books and from magazines. He always insisted that the success of the News-Letter was due to the team work of those who were his helpers: they engaged in the excitement of the search, chose items of potential significance and then gladly allowed him freedom to organise the material as he deemed best. So far as the printed word was concerned, especially for those actively engaged in missionary or evangelistic work, the News-Letter provided just what was needed. But there was also the wider public to be considered, those more familiar with modern methods of publicity, films, charts, photographs, striking lay-outs, and, increasingly, radio and television.

Max recognised the importance of these media but was content to leave developments in this area to the "home" team. In 1946 a man of outstanding gifts was recruited who was not only one of the foremost professionals of the time in advertising and publicity, but also a person of deep and sensitive spirituality. He and Max "clicked" at once, and within a matter of weeks Leslie Stubbings produced a post-war publicity plan for C.M.S. (subsequently published as *Invitation to Adventure*) which, after acceptance by committees, became the framework within which C.M.S. transformed its public relations and became one of the most effective communicators of events happening in the world and interpreters of their significance for Christians. In his autobiography Max claims that Leslie's introduction to the ranks of the Society's staff was "not the least significant event for the Church of England in the mid-twentieth century of Anglican affairs". What he does not say is that it was he who had the foresight to recognise the need of the church for the expertise of gifted laypeople, and made it possible for the skills of Leslie Stubbings and others to be used in the communication of the Christian gospel from a base in the C.M.S. headquarters staff.

One other creation of a new post deserves mention. In 1953 Douglas Webster, who had served in parishes and on the staff of the London College of Divinity, was appointed Home Education Secretary of the Society. Instead of plunging him at once into routine work at Headquarters, Max arranged for him to be seconded to the distinguished Swedish Professor, Bengt Sundkler, who had asked for help in translating into English his *magnum opus* on the Church of South India. Douglas was thus able to gain invaluable knowledge about the Christian Mission from a man of wide experience and deep insight, before taking up his new duties. Soon afterwards Dr. Donald Coggan went to East Africa at the request of C.M.S. to conduct short lecture courses for clergy, and this proved to be such a useful experiment that one of the Ugandan bishops asked for a visitor to come for a similar but more extended visit. As a result Douglas went out for three months, part of which he spent in getting to know the situation, and part of it in conferring with groups.

It was after other similar journeys to Africa and Asia by Douglas that Max imaginatively conceived the possibility of releasing him from his duties as Education Secretary and setting him free for a peripatetic ministry. In 1961 he was given the title of Theologian Missioner, it being understood that he would be available to lecture on the Bible and Doctrine, to conduct retreats and to assist in any refresher courses for clergy or lay-workers that might be arranged. This ministry, it was also understood, would not be confined to C.M.S. areas of responsibility. Overseas bishops and other missionary societies could call on the help of the Theologian Missioner whenever tours could be planned.

This new initiative was welcomed wholeheartedly within the younger Churches. Characteristically, Max allowed Douglas to develop his own pattern, assisting him in every possible way by commending him to bishops in overseas dioceses. He imposed no stereotype but trusted him to discover the best way of helping pastors and evangelists who were often working in demanding and isolated situations. He was always eager to learn from him, on his return from tours, the impressions he had gained. He wanted Douglas to make a contribution to the whole Anglican Communion, bringing the evangelical message into areas where it was either misunderstood or even unknown. It was a unique kind of ministry, world-wide in its scope, exceedingly taxing on the Missioner, who reckoned to spend some six months of each year moving from place to place overseas, but abundantly fruitful in its results. Once again Max had the foresight to see how a man with special gifts of lucid exposition of biblical and theological themes could make his maximum contribution to the upbuilding of the whole Church of Christ.

V

Gradually Max imparted a spirit of revived confidence and hope both to those at the home base and to the Society's missionaries overseas. He was getting a grip of the conditions within which C.M.S. must operate and at the same time was gaining the personal friendship of a rapidly growing number of its members at home and abroad. But just when he could have begun to feel that he had completed the first stage in his new career, that of reconstructing the home organisation before undertaking journeys overseas, there came one day a wholly unexpected letter which for the moment threw everything into turmoil. It was from Mr. Attlee, the Prime Minister, dated May 7, 1946, saying that he intended to submit Max's name to the King for succession to the vacant see of Carlisle if he would be willing to accept.

Only a few months earlier, when a friend informed him of his appointment to a bishopric, Max had written in his diary: "I am not surprised . . . I only wish I could be glad. I'm afraid I'm only sorry for a man who is made a bishop. He immediately gets cut off from ordinary life and ordinary people and lives in such a false world of ecclesiastical unrealities – unless he is a very big man indeed." And now he was faced with the prospect himself.

When he had returned home and consulted Mary, he wrote that same evening: "I do not feel that there is any difficulty about my answer. Deeply as I appreciate the great honour done to me by the Prime Minister of the Crown yet I do not in any sense of the word feel that this is a call from God and without that the enterprise could not be taken in hand. In addition there is the indubitable fact that I'm still learning my job at C.M.S. and to pull out just when things are getting really difficult would be a betrayal of trust. Some of the missionaries are beginning to trust me and through them I can, I think, serve the extension of Christ's Kingdom in the world better from C.M.S. than from anywhere else at this time."

Then more generally: "The real burden of the whole business is to bring me face to face with the unpleasant fact that apparently there are some responsible people who think that I might be able to be a bishop. But with all my heart and soul and mind I say 'Nolo Episcopari'. I know I have visions of what the Episcopate could be but I also know that I am constituted in such fashion that I could not realise those ideals. This is not just faithlessness. I just do not believe that most of the things bishops do are what I've been trained to do. They may be the right thing for some men to do but my preparation by God has been along other lines. I feel most clear that for a long time to come my calling is to serve the missionary movement with all there is of me. God help me, there is little enough to offer for that service. But for it at least I've had some training. For the office of a bishop I lack almost every qualification that seems at all important. I do hope that the way ahead may be made clear. But at least on this particular challenge I have no sort of doubt as to what my course is and where my duty lies."

The next day a letter from Dr. Garbett, the Archbishop of York, was waiting for him at the office and it soon became clear that the Prime Minister's invitation had the full support of both Archbishops. It was a critical juncture in Max's career. In his forty-second year he had been chosen as a man fitted to assume the pastoral oversight of an ancient see in the Northern Province and (it was evident enough) to represent the younger evangelicals of the Church of England on the episcopal bench. If he refused now, it was altogether likely that another invitation would come later. It was far from easy to resist the obvious wish of both Archbishops that he should, as it were, join the highest counsels of the Church of England.

But Max never envisaged the Church of England, or indeed the Anglican Communion, as a body to be presided over, governed and controlled by bishops alone. He had a deep conviction about the priesthood of all believers and of the importance of the laity within the decision-making of the Church. Moreover he was convinced that the structure of the Church was to be regarded not only in terms of province – diocese – deanery – parish. Room must be found for extra–diocesan and extra–parochial societies, orders, communities, fellowships, which could combine a relative autonomy with loyal service within the episcopally ordered whole. His own C.M.S. international community was such an "order" and he had been chosen as its leader. That was his God-given function, he believed, and he felt no call to exchange it for the office of a bishop, however honoured a place such an office might occupy within the Church of which he was a member.

He stated his case to the Archbishop of York who, though disappointed, accepted it gracefully. Although Dr. Fisher, the Archbishop of Canterbury, made overtures on subsequent occasions and although an invitation to an Australian Archbishopric was also later extended to him, Max's decision remained firm. To strive for world evangelism and to do all in his power to ensure that evangelicals would continue to play a vital part within the comprehensiveness of the Church of England – these were to be his major concerns. And the very nature of his office as General Secretary of C.M.S. gave him an unparalleled vantage point from which to operate. He worked in the centre of London and so of the whole British Commonwealth: he was head of probably the most efficiently organised unit within the Anglican Communion – a closely-knit "Cabinet" of colleagues, departmental assistants and advisers, secretaries and typists: he was in easy touch with editors and publishers: he was free from the statutory duties that have to be performed by any holder of an episcopal or parochial charge. He remained firm in the conviction that his own particular call was to serve as leader of a great missionary band rather than as overseer of a great diocesan institution. He rejoiced in the splendour of this calling and stayed within it until, as he believed, the order came for him to step aside and allow another to take his place.

One somewhat paradoxical comment may be added. In spite of the fact that Max declined to be nominated to episcopal office, few men can have been responsible for more episcopal appointments than he himself was. At the time when he became General Secretary, the Archbishop of Canterbury still held metropolitical jurisdiction in what have since, in most cases, become autonomous provinces. His normal practice was to ask Max to advise on the appointment to vacant bishoprics in C.M.S. areas and this advice was, in fact, always taken. One of the most remarkable examples of this co-operation was the choice of Leslie Brown, who had made so distinguished a contribution to theology and liturgy in South India, to become Bishop of Uganda in 1953. Max had a wonderful power of discerning a man's potentialities and the idea in this case was entirely his. Yet once the appointment was made, he remarked characteristically to one of his fellow-Secretaries: "Much as I love him (Leslie) I know full well that after he is a bishop I shall have to fight him!" Perhaps the greatest paradox of all is that he, who was suspicious of bishops, often disagreed with them, sometimes "fought" them, should have been chosen, out of all the many possibilities, to give the memorial address in Westminster Abbey to Archbishop Fisher, a bishop of bishops, in 1972.

8

The voluntary principle

I

IN THE INTERNATIONAL society within which he carried on his work, Max discerned four tendencies which he came to regard as serious dangers. He feared centralisation and bureaucratisation and institutionalisation and standardisation! He saw these as insidious growths, both in Church and State. His whole soul cried out for flexibility, mobility, individual initiatives and personal relationships. All these, he believed, could best be preserved by the retention and fostering of *voluntary associations* within every large social complex whether that were a Nation or a Church. C.M.S. was just such a voluntary association and he was prepared to defend to the limit its right to continue so to be. This involved him in a sustained struggle on two fronts, first against the movement to centralise the missionary work of the Church of England under the guidance, and perhaps governance, of the Church Assembly: second against a parallel movement to convert the free association of missionary societies forming the International Missionary Council into a constitutive department of the World Council of Churches. He never weakened in his conviction that both of these movements were misguided and likely to lead to the impairment, rather than the strengthening, of the missionary cause.

The first of these struggles brought him into open conflict early in his career at C.M.S. In 1946 Canon J. Mc Leod Campbell, who had himself been a missionary in Ceylon, published a book entitled *Christian History in the Making* which Dr. Garbett, then Archbishop of York, described as likely to be "the most important which has yet been written on the missionary work of the Anglican Communion". Max set to work to review it at length and his review was later published as a pamphlet with the intriguing title *Iona and Rome*. The historian's heart stirred within him as he read Campbell's account of early Christianity in Britain, especially when he drew attention to the *two* streams which ultimately flowed together – that emanating from Ireland and Scotland, Celtic Christianity, and that flowing from the continent and from Kent, Roman Christianity. "If, later on, the author appears to become more and more impatient with the enduring persistence of the genes of Columba, if he seems inclined to demand the unconditional surrender of 'Iona' to 'Rome', we can nevertheless be deeply grateful for the vision of the introductory chapter."

Max then went on to express certain doubts about the interpretation of history contained in the next few chapters. Had Campbell rightly understood the significance of the emergence of religious societies in England towards the end of the seventeenth century? Had he rightly judged the implications of Lutheran missionaries being employed in Anglican Missions? Had he, in celebrating the establishment of episcopacy within vast areas overseas, considered whether the particular form of English episcopacy, with its feudal origins, could in fact be exported? It is so easy, he pointed out, to confuse a skeletal ecclesiastical organisation with evangelism. "Human nature being what it is, it is commonly more attractive to be organised by 'Rome' than to be disturbed by 'Iona'." For the later chapters of the book, dealing with Christianity's relation to other faiths and with the problem of the Church's acclimatisation in other lands, Max had nothing but praise. Yet about their main emphasis, which was on the achievement of diocesan organisation all over the world, he had serious misgivings.

However it was with the whole implied challenge to the continuing existence of missionary *societies* that he really joined issue. Ideally, in Campbell's view, the Church should be its own missionary society: it should no longer need to entrust its missions to the care of divers self-perpetuating groups. But Max's rejoinder was sharp. The Church of England had never in fact entrusted its missionary activities to societies. It was in fact because nothing was being done officially that societies had been formed, voluntary associations of men and women banding themselves together to preach the gospel. Historical investigation showed that they had emerged at times of spiritual *revival*, that they owed much to *lay* initiative and that always the *personal* emphasis in their structures and operations had been uppermost. He repudiated any suggestion that C.M.S. for example, was seeking to direct policies overseas by controlling the power of the purse or by clinging to properties established at an early stage of an indigenous Church's development. At the very heart of its own policy was the aim of building up autonomous churches controlling their own institutions.

114

But that did not mean that an "evangelistic spearhead" would no longer be needed. There would never be lacking those prepared to take care of "ecclesiastical tidiness". But full scope must still be allowed for the "questing spirit of initiative", symbolised by *Iona*, if the overseas work of the Church was not to be gravely crippled.

It is remarkable that at so early a stage in his career, when the tide in political and ecclesiastical affairs, as well as in the ideology of the State and the theology of the Church, was flowing so strongly in the direction of collectivism and central control, Max should have made such a determined and courageous stand in support of the need for "two-ness", tension, dialectic, complementarity, if a corporate body is to remain healthy and strong. He was never a fanatic seeking to advance a single cause. He always tried to maintain godly discipline and decent order. But he was desperately anxious that "order" should not crush spontaneity or stifle responsiveness to new spiritual impulses. So he pleaded for "the spontaneous over-flow of devotion on the one hand and disciplined organisation on the other" and he believed that the devotion should flow out not just through individuals but through voluntary associations of those seized with a common concern for the evangelisation of the world. *Iona and Rome* was, I incline to think, the most brilliant symbolic title that he ever coined.

In all this Max was playing the role of advocate not only for the continuing existence of the missionary society but also for that of evangelicals within the Church of England . . . "The disciplined fellowship of religious societies," he declared in his Cambridge Lectures in 1964–5, "is the real clue to evangelical religion." The evangelicals who founded C.M.S. established at the heart of Anglican missionary expansion the principle that "persons sharing a similar spiritual experience, a similar concern for proclaiming the gospel and a general agreement as to the best means of doing so, should form societies for that purpose." The societies were small enough to unite for study, for prayer and for mutual encourage-ment. There was always the danger that they would seek complete independence, breaking out from the ordered discipline within which they operated. But this danger could never justify their complete suppression. It was for the health of the whole body that evangelical and evangelistic societies should continue to express their devotion through praying, through giving, and through offers of lifelong missionary service. Before ever he assumed office he was writing in his diary in 1942: "While the whole Church is committed to Mission by its foundation – yet in practice such is the insularity of most men and so circumscribed their concern that the active missionary work of the Church can only be fostered by those with a passion for it . . . But on other grounds too I feel the Society perhaps is important. It preserves the idea of a voluntary association and in so doing, amongst other things, fosters the democratic principle which in these days is of so vital an importance in the face of totalitarian tendencies."

This principle was so determinative in shaping Max's policies and leadership that it is worth quoting his considered expression of it when in 1957 he produced a document setting forth his vision of the Society's future *Towards 1999*. These are his words:

> Of this I am certain, that only a Voluntary Association of committed men and women who share a body of conviction both as to what needs doing and how it needs doing will ever be able to function as a unit for specialised evangelism. In one sense of the word that is a pragmatic approach. But it is on grounds of deepest theological principle that I would insist that the greatest need of the Church is for decentralisation of effort, not centralisation of power. And decentralisation of effort means a proper autonomy for Voluntary Associations which at the same time see themselves as loyal parts of the great Church itself. The theological principles involved here derive from the doctrine of the Holy Spirit which sees him as ever seeking fresh initiatives in the life of mankind, and never confining himself or his activities to the institutional life of his Church. This further carries with it a high doctrine of the laity which sees the ordinary man and woman as being always potential means by which the Holy Spirit takes some of his initiatives. This understanding of the work of the Holy Spirit lies at the very heart of any theological appraisal of the significance of the Voluntary Association as a principle, whether in Church or State. Somewhere here is to be found the theological rationale for democracy as it has been developed in the West under the inspiration of the gospel. I do not think that this is all fancy. But that is certainly to understate my own conviction. There are not very many theological insights which have at once an appeal to my mind and to my heart. This is one of them. And for this one I am prepared to do battle anywhere and at any time. That conviction underlies everything in this memorandum.

II

This passionate concern for what Max called "Middle Term" communities, respecting fully the rights of the individual on the one side and the lawful demands of the larger collective on the other, led him to take what in the 1950's was a minority position in ecumenical circles. It would be hard to think of anyone more wholeheartedly devoted to ecumenical relationships than Max. He was one of the leading voices in the Church of England to welcome the coming into being of the united Church of South India and did all in his power to ensure that C.M.S. would support it through the offering of financial aid and the continuing co-operation of personal agents. He allied himself with those seeking to lower barriers to Intercommunion. He delighted in his associations with leaders of non-Anglican missionary societies and played a notable part in the International Missionary Council's Conferences at Whitby, Canada in 1947 and at Willingen, Germany in 1952. At the former he acted as Chaplain and was mainly instrumental in producing an agreed statement which contained the term by which Whitby may be best remembered – *expectant evangelism*. At the latter he was one of the leading speakers and the theme of his address proved to be one of the most memorable features of the Conference – Missions under the Cross.

There could be no doubt about his enthusiasm for partnership with other societies and for the great values to be gained by membership in the International Missionary Council. But already at Whitby the hope began to be entertained that with the formation of the World Council of Churches the time would soon come when the I.M.C. would cease to exist as a separate organisation and would become instead a specific department of the World Council. Consultations began to take place and plans began to be made for the establishment of a Commission on World Mission and Evangelism within the World Council of Churches.

Max, however, was less than certain that such a merger was desirable. There was as much danger from centralised bureaucracy in Geneva as in Church House, Westminster. He feared the gradual replacement of the spirit of expectant evangelism, characteristic of a relatively small autonomous society, by grandiose programmes and verbal directives characteristic of all too many large international organisations. The ethos of the I.M.C. was one of mutual consultation and the sharing of thoughts, not that of a hierarchical structure and centralised constraint.

In 1956 he attended a meeting of the Joint Committee of the W.C.C. and the I.M.C. held in Germany and there stated his considered case. It was that whereas co-operation between the two bodies was eminently desirable, the proposal to unite them within a single structure was premature. He was not able to convince a large proportion of those present and consequently the motion to unite seemed likely to be passed without much opposition when presented to the Conference of the I.M.C. in Ghana the following year. Max had made his protest in Committee and determined to remain silent at the Conference itself.

But surprisingly he found himself almost compelled to speak as representing those members of the Conference who, though opposed, were not sufficiently at home in the English language to be sure of presenting their case effectively. It was a historic, and in many respects a dramatic occasion in missionary history, for whereas on one day of the Conference the case for the merger had been set forth by persuasive speeches as being the united wish of the officers of the I.M.C., on the next day Max, like a modern Luther, was given the opportunity to voice a negative opinion. It was as difficult a task as he ever had to undertake in public. Missionary leaders from all over the world were present. He had little time to prepare. He was bound to stand in opposition to many who were his deeply-valued friends and it could so easily have appeared that he was out of sympathy with the ecumenical cause.

He has written graphically about his strategy and about the substance of his objection in *Crowded Canvas*: in fact the two pages 157–158 in that book contain what is probably the most carefully considered and formulated exposition of Max's understanding of the place and function of missionary societies in the life of the Church to be found anywhere in his writings. Nearly twenty years later he directed a correspondent who had enquired of him about this subject to these pages in his autobiography. There, he said, he had set out the "underlying critical issues" affecting "the relation between centralised structures and the voluntary principle". Basically, as the two pages reveal, he joyfully accepted *tension* but resisted complete *integration*: he delighted in the interplay of differences but shrank from monolithic structures. "Links can be effective without being constitutional. This is a fundamental principle of community. To see this and to make provision for it is one of the best ways of safeguarding the structure of society from being exploited by a power-drunk individual or a power-obsessed bureaucracy. This has been the discovery of democracy at its best."

His on-the-spot diary written at Ghana makes illuminating and

often entertaining reading. There was never a trace of supercilious-
ness or superiority in his attitudes to his opponents. His own
modesty and humour and readiness to see both sides in any issue
prevented this. Moreover the bonds of friendship meant so much to
him that he would never allow them to be disturbed by differences
of opinion even on important matters. But at the same time he had
a sharp critical mind, he loved debate, he was quite prepared to be
in a minority and he constantly tried to see immediate problems
within the perspective of past history and of probable future
developments. Above all, although he was always fascinated by
words, written and spoken, he was still more concerned for *action*.
His fear at Ghana was that out of all the discussion and the
proposals for integration and for establishing a unified organisation
at Geneva, little would actually be *done* to further the task of
preaching the gospel to every creature. Some extracts from his
diary will reveal the depth of his concern.

When asked point blank by Dougall if I had anything to say I
delivered a bath full of cold water, tried to call folk back to
taking the fact of sin seriously and to stop imagining that more
organisations were the answer to the needs of the world. I also
pleaded with folk to look at the term partnership and see what
it means and try and do something about it instead of frothing
about discovering some other term. There was more rot talked
about the inadequacy of the term "partnership" to denote our
relations in mission in those two hours than can easily be
imagined by anyone who was not there. It is just like the
aversion to the term missionary. It is an escape from mission
into semantics. It is escapism – escapism – escapism. I am
more than ever certain that Norman Goodall was right when,
ten years ago, he said, "We have no right to expect God to give
us fresh insights about the Missionary Movement until we do
something about the insights he has given us in the past twenty
years." The truth is we find it far easier to go on talking about
mission than engaging in it.

I am quite sure that for me the time has come to get on with
the jobs which have been so clearly set before us and to cease
participating in ecumenical gossip parties. The problem is how
to retire from the scene gracefully and avoid needlessly hurting
good sincere Christians who see things quite differently. I do
pray for the wisdom and the grace to see how this can be
achieved within the next week.

I felt it quite vital to take this opportunity, the first I have had

119

to challenge publicly the whole approach of those concerned with Integration, who insist on basing it upon theological premises which are at one and the same time *a priori* hypotheses and also do not correspond with the realities of history and experience. It is a fallacy to start from what you think ought to be and then to force the facts to fit that premise and demand that action be determined by it.

Nothing has exasperated me more over the last few years than the bland assumption, reiterated monotonously, that there is only one understanding of the unity of the Church, and the equally bland assumption that this must find expression in one kind of ecumenical structure. By all means let us argue that one kind of ecumenical structure is desirable. But do not base it on a false theology. If we could for a moment leave theology out of it we could see the issue as it is and determine it on practical grounds of convenience, arriving at a true and workable compromise.

Well, at last, and publicly, I have got my deep conviction about this out into the open. The internal ferment of the last few years has now found expression and I confess to a feeling of vast relief. I have "burst" and now can move on to other tasks!

So ends this Conference. It has been a very great disappointment in almost every way. Badly arranged to begin with, badly chaired throughout, it has never got to grips with any issue of importance. All this expense and energy has been expended on nothing more than fixing up an organisational structure, about which a considerable minority of the Conference are luke-warm, and to which a small minority are deeply and convincedly opposed. In the end the elaborate theological facade which had been built up has failed to win conviction as a determining factor, and the scheme has been exposed for what it is, a technical device for promoting certain activities in connection with the World Mission of the Church.

The pity of it is that so many really fine men and women have given up so much time and energy for so many years in order to achieve so little. Even now there are several years of negotiations on the subject to be concluded before the integration can take effect in 1961. Meanwhile, as far as the Missionary Movement is concerned, the I.M.C. can, at best, give an uncertain leadership.

"To your tents O Israel" – and there let us equip ourselves for the new tasks that are so urgently waiting to be tackled and

for which the primary necessity is vision and courage and determination. May God grant us in C.M.S. to play our part in this
enterprise in fellowship with all others who are determined
upon treating mission as the number one priority, and who
believe that in this way, incidentally, they will best serve God's
purpose for the Unity of His Church.

Fifteen years after the official integration of the I.M.C. within the
W.C.C. had taken place at New Delhi in 1961, Max wrote an essay
containing some retrospective thoughts on this fusion. He had by
then retired to his Sussex home but, as the essay reveals, his mind
was as active and orderly as ever it was and his passionate interest in
the world mission remained undiminished. The essay was one of his
best. (It was published in Holland in 1978 in a volume honoring
Professor Dr. J. Verkuyl who had for many years been in charge of
Missiology on the faculty of the Free University of Amsterdam.) As
always he was fair and generous in his assessment of the good things
that had happened as a result of the merger. The movement towards
closer unity after the Second World War was natural, for doubtless
it needed a unified Church to speak the word of reconciliation to an
utterly disintegrated world. Was it not then also natural that the
Church's mission to the world should be set at the very centre of the
pursuit for unity? So it might seem. Yet the plain testimony of
history was that from St. Paul's day onwards, "Mission has, in fact,
as often as not, been an activity posing acute challenges to the
pursuit of organisational unity."
He then proceeded to sketch four grounds of doubt about the
desirability of integration. First he returned to his conviction that
the move to integrate was premature: the W.C.C. in his judgment
had not had time to settle its own structure and to determine its own
particular functions. Secondly he reiterated his fear of "bureaucratic
paralysis" and how this might affect the flexibility of inspiration and
direction hitherto exercised by the I.M.C. "Unless the missionary
movement can be responsive to the unpredictability of the Holy
Spirit it will soon cease to be a movement." Thirdly he outlined the
risk that the I.M.C. might become increasingly concerned with
questions of Church *order* instead of with the task of evangelisation
in which it had over the years given such invaluable leadership.
Here he made a favourite distinction: he would have been happy
with *association* but not with *integration*. Fourthly he was apprehensive lest the marked degree of understanding which had been
fostered by the I.M.C. between the more "conservative" and the
more "liberal" elements within the missionary enterprise would be

dissipated because of the obvious suspicion in some quarters about the policies of the W.C.C.

Having outlined his doubts, Max proceeded to ask how far they had been justified by what had happened over the past fifteen years. He readily recognised certain positive achievements such as the promotion of more cordial relationships with Eastern Orthodoxy, with the Pentecostals of Latin America and with the leaders of indigenous churches in Africa. Yet the danger remained that, as an integral part of the W.C.C., the Commission might lose its distinctive "drive", its concern for the great unevangelised areas of the world, its sense of *mission*, that is of being *sent* to perform a particular task. If that came to be the case, then almost certainly another association would be set up to link together those societies whose concern for world evangelism was still paramount.

III

The essay which I have just outlined was an exceedingly impressive clarion call by the elder statesman who never lost his zest for the great cause to which he had committed himself more than half a century earlier. To the end he gloried in the term *missionary*. It was a noun which exactly expressed the concept of sent-ness: "'As my Father hath sent Me even so send I you', stands in all its grandeur and its grimness as the commission of the missionary." And this sent-ness was primarily related not to worthy efforts to foster or revive commitments within an already existing Christian community, admirable as they might be. Rather it was concerned with cross-cultural, cross-national, cross-ideological adventures with the purpose of making Christ known in circles hitherto ignorant of his Name. Amidst all his manifold activities Max never allowed the ringing challenge of St. Paul to be drowned by the noise of busy assemblies:

> How shall they call on Him
> in Whom they have not believed
> And how shall they believe in Him
> of Whom they have not heard
> And how shall they hear
> without a preacher
> And how shall they preach
> except they be sent?

To be sent, to be a missionary, was the highest honour and the noblest vocation open to man or woman. Not only could the missionary bear witness to Christ: he or she could be the *personal* link between Christians in one country and those in another, a link such as could never be forged by more formal, constitutional bonds such as episcopacy, liturgy or even the Lambeth Conference. A missionary is a witness not only to the gospel of Christ but also to the universal character of the Church of Jesus Christ.

Yet he became aware that whereas in the world at large, in secular literature for example, the term "missionary" was often used in a thoroughly approving, even honorific way, in Christian circles a tendency had arisen to play it down because of its imperial associations and even to treat it with hostility. Doubtless this was in part due to the growth of autonomous churches with their own episcopal or presbyteral structures and the consequent ambivalence regarding the missionary's standing: was he an agent of the "sending" society or a member of the local church, subject to its discipline? Tensions were bound to arise. But Max was unwilling to cut the knot and to affirm Either-Or. The notion of sent-ness was too near his own heart and too valuable in the preservation of *personal* links to be lightly abandoned. He was utterly committed to the ideal of establishing autonomous churches in all possible areas and had no inhibitions about handing over C.M.S. property to them as soon as they were ready to handle it responsibly. But he refused to advocate any easy resolution of the tension inherent in the *missionary* vocation. The missionary was sent by God as a representative of mission-concerned Christians in one country or culture or religious persuasion to another country or culture, there to join in the evangelistic task with fellow-Christians. Sensitive to the organisation and discipline of the local Church, the missionary must at the same time preserve the sense of loyalty to those by whom he or she had been 'sent'.

Probably the most famous occasion on which Max felt constrained to defend the continuance of missionary terminology was at the Anglican Congress in Toronto in 1963. He and Archbishop Ramsey were close friends and had a great respect and affection for one another. But the Archbishop touched a sensitive spot when he attempted to get rid of the word "missionary". This is Max's record of the incident.

There was a long pause after Gilbert had finished. Then suddenly the Archbishop of Canterbury made the astounding statement that he thought the time had come when we must get

123

rid of the words "missionary" and "mission" because they no longer had any value and only led to misunderstanding. Nobody went to missionary meetings, and the use of these terms was a disadvantage. He then went on to say that the words "mission" and "missionary" did not occur in the New Testament. He said he thought we ought to "debunk" the word "missionary"! This was followed by the staggering statement that while, of course, the New Testament spoke of people being "sent" it had no noun to express the idea!!

I think the dear Archbishop must have been feeling the heat. Anyway the moment he had finished I asked for permission to speak. A good many smiles appeared on primatial and other faces!

I think that, in the mercy of God, I was enabled to speak graciously, for I was hopping with excitement. I knew that this was a moment when a decisive contradiction had to be made. I knew that the audience was an especially influential one, but that on this issue it was hopelessly muddled. I knew that perhaps this was my last chance of saying a word in season on this subject. Michael Thwaites, in his poem "The Jervis Bay" has a phrase that describes what I felt!

In my statement I asked permission to state another point of view. I went straight into the attack by saying that I thought there was a noun in the New Testament which corresponded to the word "sent" – the word Apostle. I went on to say that I thought it was a word that had some considerable value for most of those present in the room at that moment! I said that I imagined that none of them would want to "debunk" the word "Apostle"! (Shades of "The Apostolic Ministry" and "Apostolic Succession".) I think that remark can be said to have got a majority on my side!

I went on to say that I was convinced that there was no other term which could succinctly express what we meant. I then added that it seemed to me that the Church was losing its nerve over the word "missionary" just at the time when the world was beginning to understand it and use it properly. I told the company of the file I have been collecting over the last ten years of the way in which the secular press in Britain is using the word "missionary" in precisely its proper meaning, showing a real understanding of its "religious" connotation, but applying it to "secular" affairs, of which I gave a few examples very much at random. I wish I had had the file by me!

I cited the N. American attempt to coin the word "fraternal

worker" and how Stephen Neill had discovered that it could not be translated into six major European languages.

I pleaded for us to redeem the word, in so far as it has acquired unhappy overtones of colonialism and paternalism, and reminded the company of its great history and significance.

Over certain things Max was jealous with a "godly jealousy"!

IV

Max's passionate advocacy of the voluntary principle and his consistent magnifying of the missionary vocation had their direct effects on his conception of the kind of *training* needed for those accepted for service overseas and of the *pastoral care* needed by all the Society's agents. He was indefatigable in paying visits to the training colleges, getting to know recruits, concerning himself about their continuing development through prayer and study, and then seizing every possible opportunity of renewing contacts with missionaries when they came on furlough. His ideal was to be the father of a great family, not lording it over his children but guiding and supporting them to the fullest extent in the carrying out of their appointed tasks.

The family image was an honoured one and encouraged the growth of personal relationships by which he set such store. At the same time his historical studies provided him with another image, that of the communities of the Middle Ages, the monastic orders, many of whose members went out from the mother house on missionary expeditions as adventurers for the Kingdom of God. In his writings he sometimes likened his band of C.M.S. agents to one of the *Roman* orders but a closer parallel, I think, was to be found in his preferred system of Iona and the *Celtic* Church. There the structures were less formally organised and the character of the discipline was less regimented on the military pattern. A community was established and often the bishop was simply a member of the community, living under its rule. This, it seems to me, was the kind of community that Max envisaged and the training colleges were designed, not only to give instruction in Bible and Doctrine, but also to give practical guidance in the maintenance of inter-personal relationships, both in the life of devotion and in the day to day tasks of the community.

As early as 1936 C.M.S. had appointed a Committee to investigate the whole question of the recruiting, selection and training of candidates for missionary service. In an address to the Committee, the distinguished missionary-statesman Dr. J. H. Oldham began by saying:

> The question of the training of missionaries has been before missionary societies in one way and another ever since the Edinburgh Conference of 1910. I am more and more convinced that the question of the right selection and the training of missionaries is beyond all comparison the major question in the whole missionary enterprise.

He went on to stress certain basic missionary requirements: a capacity to grow and to learn and to live in community with others so that *a way of life* could be communicated in a day when so little *knowledge* of the Christian gospel could be presumed to exist, either in Britain or in lands overseas. He concluded by declaring that

> The really critical period in a missionary's career is his first term of service, because it is only then that he learns what he really wants. A great deal of the instruction given before he sails is lost to him because he cannot relate it to anything in his life. The first furlough is therefore primarily important, and I would urge that close attention be given to this.

It would be no exaggeration to say that the questions raised by Dr. Oldham in 1936 have failed to receive any widely agreed solutions during the more than forty years that have elapsed since that time. The 1936 Committee made a large number of recommendations, such as that the training colleges should remain in or near London, that the period of training for every candidate should not be less than six months, that this training should include both theological and language study and that as a normal procedure all missionaries should be required by the Society to make use of their first furlough for further training. There was scarcely time even to begin implementing these recommendations before war broke out, and survival rather than new developments became the immediate concern. Yet almost within a week of his acceptance of the post of General Secretary Max found himself being consulted about women's training (candidates in training had moved from London to Ridley Hall, Cambridge) and expressed his concern at "the high emotional pressure at which the students seem to live". Was "such conventual training as at present obtains" really necessary?

From that time on, plans for the future of the colleges constantly occupied his thoughts. Training for men candidates would have to make a quite new beginning and he envisaged this as including four principal aims:

(a) a re-orientation of thinking towards life abroad
(b) a deepening of the devotional life
(c) a discovery of the significance of the fellowship of C.M.S.
(d) an understanding of the art of living together in true relationship.

There would be opportunities for practical work in neighbouring parishes but these four aims he regarded as of primary importance. A woman candidate's training might extend to a longer period and would include more instruction in Bible and theology, but its essential aims would remain the same.

As in other training-schemes a number of questions had to be considered. The location? The time required? The staff? The academic and devotional discipline? In regard to the first the alternatives were either to remain as a self-enclosed unit in the London neighbourhood or to move to a context where other colleges were also operating e.g. to Selly Oak in Birmingham. The decision to remain in London had his unqualified support and it was not until after his own resignation that a move to Selly Oak was made. This was a significant issue. Max felt deeply that it was desirable for the colleges to remain close to the Headquarters of the Society and in consequence easily accessible to the Secretaries and to himself in particular. He wished to facilitate every kind of personal contact and, in his own programme of regular commitments, made it an absolute priority to visit the colleges, give lectures there, and establish links with the students.

But was the model of the isolated college, with its enclosed community, concentrating upon its own specialisation, the appropriate one for the post-war world? Max himself lived at the very hub of the world's affairs and was always relating them to his missionary responsibilities. There was nothing insular about 6 Salisbury Square! Rather it was constantly engaged in receiving information from and transmitting messages to the outside world. A move of the colleges to a wider context would not, it is true, have necessarily ensured a better training but it would at least have exposed students to regular contacts with those coming from different backgrounds

127

and pursuing different interests. To strike a proper balance between depth and breadth has been one of the great dilemmas in all training schemes. In general the emphasis in Britain has been on the side of depth and to achieve this it has seemed desirable to withdraw, at least for specified periods, from the noise and bustle of the market-place. But again the question arises: for how long? How long can one afford to live in a rarified atmosphere, where all are sharing one central concern? No one could have pleaded more eloquently than Max did for a theology of variety and even differences. Yet an isolated training college, like so many of the isolated theological colleges of the Church of England, could easily produce zealous advocates of a particular interpretation of Christian faith and practice at the cost of making them insensitive to other interpretations of Christianity and still more to other philosophies of life.

No one has solved the problem of the ideal preparation for the minister of the gospel, whether he or she is to serve at home or overseas. Nor has agreement been reached about the best methods of post-ordination or furlough training. The fact is that men and women are very different from one another and, especially in missionary circles, provision needs to be made for those who differ in social and educational and religious experience. Moreover, in the case of the missionary, there are far greater differences between the varying cultures within which the students will ultimately operate than is the case for those in the home ministry where a relatively homogeneous culture exists. Max constantly and consistently pressed towards the goal of world evangelisation. He longed that all within the Society – which he designated "a Christian Frontier field force concerned with evangelism" – should share his commitment and his hope. He wanted the "field force" to be trained to work together for the realisation of this one aim. He was willing to be constantly alongside the recruits, encouraging them, teaching them, praying for them. The personal friendship which he extended to them was marvellous. It still remains an open question whether the structural model of the training establishment which he advocated was the most suitable and effective to prepare his commandos, as he sometimes called them, for the conditions of the twentieth-century world.

V

One further notable example of Max's enthusiasm for community life as a means of deepening devotion and strengthening purpose was his whole-hearted support of St. Julian's in Sussex of whose council he served as chairman for some twenty years. Probably no place on earth came to mean so much to him. It was his Iona, the spot to which he returned again and again for refreshment of his own mind and spirit and to which he directed countless others for the same purpose. He wrote about it glowingly in an article contributed to the periodical *Theology* in May 1962 and again in his autobiography twelve years later. A few extracts from these two accounts may reveal something of his feeling for what was for him, in a very real sense, a "gate of heaven".

Life for Mary and myself . . . was reasonably full. We had our own methods of relaxation but one key to our survival was a regular withdrawal to St. Julian's. For us, St. Julian's was an unfailing resort for the much-needed re-charging of our physical, mental and spiritual batteries. The beauty of the place breathed an immediate benediction to a tired spirit. To walk through the front door was to know you were come to a Palace Beautiful.

The front door will certainly be open or on the latch, for one is not expected to ring. Stepping into the hall, where if the weather is cold a fire is burning, is to step out of noise into quietness. For even though the house is full of people, it is even more full of peace. Indeed it is likely that only noises from the kitchen in the distance will provide evidence of human presences. But they are there, and very soon the visitor will be shown his room, almost certainly "a room with a view". It will look out on a wide stretch of lawn running down to a lake, with coots and duck and swans busily self-absorbed. Away in the distance beyond the fields runs the line of the South Downs with Chanctonbury Ring clearly visible.

Is this some English Shangri-La, a blessed escape from the noisy pressures of an exhausting world? So, by some, it has been misconceived. In point of fact it is a training centre for a special kind of spiritual encounter, the starting point of adventures which find their fulfilment in strange places all over the globe.

Here was a place where you could let quietness and peace do its healing work. No one would ever intrude upon your stillness. But always available was the little "Society", part of whose serious responsibility it was to keep mentally alert, widely read, in touch with the wider world, and to be ready to meet the troubled and the perplexed should they ask for guidance.

Then, commenting on the vision of the founder, Florence Allshorn:

There will be no understanding of St. Julian's without a real and sympathetic understanding of the contemporary world, an understanding which is quite without illusion and entirely without despair. For St. Julian's will only yield its secrets to those who are prepared to be totally and painfully involved in the mess of humanity, in the agonising travail of our times. That could be said to be over-writing and may, by some, be judged as such. I accept the risk.

Florence Allshorn saw that the contemporary world was doing something to the spirit of man which corresponded to a wasting disease. Perhaps her own once-threatened consumption gave a special penetration to her mind on this point. She felt on her pulses the increasing aimlessness, the purposelessness of life, as it afflicts so many, breeding angst and nihilism, or just devil-may-careness. She saw very clearly that God was the missing value without whom life does make nonsense.

From all this it will be seen that what is being aimed at in St. Julian's is the provision of an oasis in the waste land, an oasis which will not be a settlement but a stage on the road, which, if the idea is not too complicated, is meant to be continuously recreated in varying forms in diverse circumstances wherever men and women who know the peace of God are at work on God's ministry of reconciliation.

A hallowed place, regulated silence and a dedicated community – such were the constituent elements of Max's Iona. It was a place lovingly tended by a resident "Society": to it pilgrims, active in their service to the world, could come for refreshment and renewal. But it was never to be at "journey's end": it was always to be regarded as "a stage on the road".

9

Exploring and Reporting

I

MAX REGARDED HIMSELF as fortunate to have been allowed roughly five years to establish himself at his home base before setting out on his travels. As soon however as conditions of the post-war world allowed, he committed himself to a series of overseas visits which did not end even when he retired from the General Secretaryship in 1963 but continued until 1970. Simply from the point of view of physical endurance this was remarkable, for he was rarely exempt from some bodily disability. From the point of view of creating a network of world-relationships and world-communications it was a towering achievement. It found expression in nearly forty travel diaries (averaging at least two hundred pages each), never written in note form nor hurriedly put together, but composed in his characteristic style and often containing profound reflections on current issues. However exhausting his day might have been, he normally retained enough energy to write something, even if more leisure was needed to describe his experiences fully.

All this labour was expended not primarily for his own satisfaction but rather as a source of up-to-date information for his fellow-Secretaries and as material for future researchers. The diaries were typed and carefully indexed and in course of time attractively bound. His own general preface and list of countries visited are worth recording to give some indication of the far-reaching significance of this side of his work. (See Appendix I.)

Although he had to wait for a period before beginning his planned visits, one opportunity arose (already mentioned in Chapter 5) for him to go to America while the war was still on and this, I think, brought far reaching consequences for his future. Only eighteen months after he had assumed his new office, he was invited to be one of a delegation of three sent by the Conference of British Missionary Societies to attend the Jubilee of the Foreign Missions

Conference of North America in Chicago. There he got to know many of the leaders of the missionary enterprise in the United States, while in Toronto he established warm relationships with well-wishers in the Canadian Churches. He was immediately fascinated by North America and over the next twenty years was to spend in all roughly eighteen months on American soil. He made some of the richest friendships of his life there, revelled in the chances to gain first-hand knowledge of the history of the American peoples and probably did as much as anybody to draw together British experience and American resources in the task of world-evangelisation during the post-war era.

That which began at Chicago in 1944 was further developed and deepened at the Whitby (Ontario) Conference of the International Missionary Council in July 1947. Happily he was invited to serve as Chaplain, a responsibility which he exercised with his usual meticulous care. The other delegates became aware of the quality of his devotional life and, through his work on the Steering Committee, came to recognise his ability in the sphere of missionary policy. He had, as it were, made his name both in North America and amongst missionary leaders from other parts of the world. It was not surprising that he was chosen as one of the main speakers at the next Conference of the I.M.C. at Willingen, Germany in 1952 and that the title of his address, "The Christian Mission and the Cross" came to be regarded as expressing the dominant theme of the whole assembly. In contrast to the hope expressed at Whitby in 1947 that with the ending of the Second World War the most difficult days of the Christian mission at last lay behind, Max declared at Willingen "that the most testing days of the Christian mission in our generation lie just ahead". He had established himself not only as leader of the largest missionary society in Britain but also as one of the most knowledgeable and farseeing members of the International Missionary Council.

The diaries reveal how greatly Max loved to travel. He had some bad periods at the beginning of ocean voyages and there were times when he was simply exhausted physically. But he never lost his zest for meeting new friends, seeing new places, gaining new historical perspectives and capturing new political insights. He always kept steadily in view the central task of proclaiming the gospel in those regions where Christ was not already known and he seized every opportunity to co-operate with those who shared his vision. But this did not make him unworldly or withdrawn. He responded eagerly to those who offered him hospitality, rejoicing in the meals they provided and above all, when in North America, enthusing over the seemingly endless varieties of ice-cream which he could sample. When opportunity occurred he was glad to see a good movie and seemed always to have a novel or biography on hand for his brief periods of relaxation. The marvel is that he was able to write such voluminous diaries in the middle of being constantly engaged with conferences, personal discussions, endless correspondence, sermons and lectures and excursions here and there to see new sights and to meet new people.

On his travels nothing gave him greater joy than to find C.M.S. missionaries giving devoted and creative service and thereby helping to build up an indigenous church in some particular area. He was forever asking himself how missionaries could be more adequately trained and equipped for their varying ministries and made it one of his chief concerns in America both to learn of the methods in use there and to tell his friends about the C.M.S. programme and the value of such a retreat-centre as St. Julian's. He was particularly interested in the American Methodists training-centre at Meadville, Pennsylvania and indeed he probably had closer relations with the Methodist than with the Episcopal Church in the U.S.A. He found himelf entirely at home in the Episcopal Seminary in Virginia which possessed a fine missionary tradition, but felt that as a whole the Episcopal Church lacked missionary enthusiasm and suffered from regarding missions as just a department in its organisational structure.

The Rev. Theodore Eastman, who in 1956 became Executive Secretary of the Overseas Mission Society (formed in 1953 as a volunteer missionary organisation largely concerned with arousing interest in the Christian mission through meetings and publications), came to know Max well and has acknowledged his sense of deep indebtedness to him in the development of his own theology and professional work. Looking back on Max's many visits to the U.S.A. and on the influence he exerted upon missionary thought and action in that country he has written:

> He had something of a love affair with the United States, I believe, and saw this nation and the Churches of this nation as a crucial element in the future development of the world. He loved our enthusiasm, energy and naïveté. He felt, however, that we had much to learn from the experience of English Christianity and the development of Anglican missions elsewhere in the world. He saw our missionary enterprise as being quite parochial and colonial. He urged us to increase our interest in and investment in Anglican and ecumenical work in

Africa, Asia and the Pacific beyond our "own" missionary districts. Max, more than anyone else, helped to open the eyes of American Episcopalians to what was going on elsewhere in the world. He had a tremendous influence on those who were concerned with our mission to the world and broadened their thinking and their vision.

It would be impossible to give a summary of his travels in a limited space. Instead therefore I propose to give a few selections from his diaries which will, I hope, illustrate the breadth of his interests and the vivid style of his writing.

II

First of all I give examples of his deep sense of being involved in the movement of *history*, a movement directed and controlled by God in a way surpassing our full comprehension, and yet constantly demanding our attention so that we may discern the signs of the times and may act according to what seems to us to be His manifest purpose.

He was profoundly aware of the fact that the missionary movement has a place in world history and cannot elect to operate independently of its total social environment.

> In a sense the last sixty years represent a tremendous rear-guard action by Britain. The immensely important question both for ourselves, and for mankind, is whether we are going to be able to call a halt to the retreat and find a line on which to stand, from which we can go forward to make a new and creative contribution to the rest of the world.
>
> This sixty years of retreat finds its reflection in the missionary movement. I do not mean by that that the affairs of the Kingdom of God are determined by the course of human history. But those affairs do take place *within* history. I think that it is a failure to accept this truth which vitiates so much Christian thinking and acting whether its premises are "Catholic" or "pietist". Both the "Catholic" and the "pietist" fail to do justice to the genuine importance of history. The "Catholic" tends to find reality and significance only in the Church. All else is more or less unreal and can therefore be

exploited by the Church. The "pietist" tends to find reality and significance only in individual experience. Everything else is temporary and can very easily be ignored by the Christian. (1955)

To gain a proper view of history within the providence of God should therefore be a vital part of missionary training.

History and the development of political theory and the relation of religion and culture ought to be compulsory study both for the ministry at home and for all theological colleges abroad, and for all missionaries. So few seem to realise that when we say that God works in and through history, that does not mean that He works in and through history to some pre-ordained pattern, but that He allows *ideas* freedom to have their logical development, seeking only to match them with other *ideas*, pending the mystery of His own final consummation of all things after the Judgment. If more Christians would see this, they would be more ready to take their citizenship of this world seriously. (1954)

One of his remarkable gifts was that of linking some particular aspect of his travel-experience with important earlier developments in Christian history. Flying on one occasion over the western limits of the Sahara, he noticed trails in the desert, so straight that they might well have been constructed by French military commanders. His imagination then looked back over the centuries to the great period of Muslim expansion.

Down these trails Islam came from Morocco seven or eight centuries ago and began its slow conquest of West Africa, a conquest which is still going on. Christianity came by sea. I wonder what significance this has had for the history of the two religions in their competition for the soul of West Africa. The slow infiltration across the desert must have been much less intimidating than the sudden irruption from the sea. Has this been part of the strength of Islam in West Africa? Meanwhile it is sobering to think that by the middle of the sixteenth century the Temne-Bullom peoples of Sierra Leone had a Christian dynasty, and that this brief experience disappeared without leaving a trace. The more one reflects on Church history, and the record of the Christian Mission, the more one is driven to make the most sober assessment of the achievement of the

135

nineteenth and early twentieth centuries. No Church in Asia or Africa is as strong as the Church of Augustine, Tertullian and Cyprian, or has as long a history. But where is that Church? The Coptic survival in Egypt is certainly not Cyprianic. And Augustine and Tertullian left no trace. And this, at least, seems certain, that the disappearance of the North African Church was due to its being a Church of the two Roman overlords. It was never the Church of the people of the land. One is left with a "certain fearful looking for of judgment", but with the faith that even if our enterprises fail and die, God can from the very stones raise up children for Abraham. It is better to be sober, and to have that kind of faith than to be carried away by romantic nonsense about the "World Church" or "our worldwide Anglican Communion". (1962)

III

Max travelled as a priest of the Church of England, took part in specifically Anglican conferences and ceremonies, and encouraged missionaries to work loyally within their own particular diocesan framework. But he was constantly asking himself questions about the place of the Church of England in God's continuing purpose and, even more sharply, whether the Anglican Communion as such was destined to continue as a separate denomination outside England. Was it not in danger of becoming a sect in other parts of the world rather than a constituent part of whatever more comprehensive Church developed in any particular land?

> I'm afraid that this particular group of Anglicans here has shocked me to the core. I'm not sure whether I am more shocked by the intransigent ones or by those who just accept everything they are told without trying to check it.
>
> But if the spirit of some of these brothers represents what happens to Anglicanism when it gets outside the disciplined restraints of English history then it has no future except as a sect. And this is a real danger. For the genius of Anglicanism is that it is English. I am not in the least bit sure that it can be exported and remain recognisably the same. This is *one* of my own reasons for supporting Church Union in India and Africa. Anglicanism by itself when exported does not, and cannot,

136

take on its proper shape. To take one illustration. The position of the bishop as we have received it is part of English history. Episcopacy, with us, has evolved in a certain direction. It has done so precisely because in our history the Free Churchmen have had a profound influence. Furthermore, the parson's free-hold has checked episcopal excesses. But these developments are lacking overseas. For these reasons alone we need to have added to our exported Anglicanism the balancing factors of Presbyterian, Congregational and Methodist polities. This thought has come to me very clearly over here and I must try and develop it. Anglicanism is very much more than a certain ecclesiastical polity and a form of liturgical worship. It is a temper of mind itself tempered by history. I am sure that Anglicanism, otherwise than in England, can only fulfil itself and its destiny in united Churches in the various countries. In England, if it is wisely led, it can yet become the rallying centre for English Christianity. But its sectarian tendencies must be resisted if it is to realise its destiny. (1959)

His own wide reading had brought him immeasurable gains and made him "free of the commonwealth of the mind in which denomination is wholly without significance".

Where on earth would we be without P. T. Forsyth, Oman, Dodd, Vincent Taylor, Micklem, Maxwell, Minear, Baillie, Rowley, not to mention Visser't Hooft, Newbigin, and a host of others? But according to strict Anglican doctrine, I could not receive the sacrament at their hands, and only under very exceptional circumstances be able to welcome them to Holy Communion. What utter rubbish it all is! And how it must break the heart of our Lord, and make the angels weep.

This is not to ask for indiscriminate intercommunion. The men just mentioned would be as opposed to casual intercommunion as I am. But at least let us learn to recognise that the Table belongs to Christ. And when occasion is appropriate, let us meet there as the humble beneficiaries of His boundless grace. This is a religion I can understand. Anglican "fencing of the Table" is sheer sectarianism, and not the less sectarianism for claiming to be Catholic. (1962)

He learned so much from his own travels that he could not refrain from wishing that many more Anglicans might have the same

137

privilege. In particular he regarded some experience outside England as an essential preparation for holding any responsible position within the Church.

> No one ought to be permitted to hold any high office in the Church of England without being compelled to spend some time travelling right outside the Anglican pale, discovering the relative insignificance of Anglicanism almost everywhere, and actually living and moving amongst really devoted Christians of other allegiances. Such would return with their appreciation of Anglicanism greatly strengthened by being concentrated on the point where it has in fact a contribution to offer, much less certain about some of its vaunted excellencies, and humbly aware that the values of other Churches are not just "un-covenanted mercies", over-flowing of a grace too large to be contained in an Anglican chalice, but in fact glorious manifestations of that Grace of God which must always transcend in glory the encompassing capacity of little human minds cast in their insular moulds. There ought to be an equivalent of the eighteenth Century "Grand Tour" before anyone is allowed to graduate as a leader of the Church of England. But on the "Grand Tour" it would have to be forbidden that the traveller should stay continuously with Anglicans. Of course it is possible that he might come back hating the human race and utterly convinced that Anglicanism is the exclusive "cultus" of heaven. In that case he would have to be promoted to the ecclesiastical equivalent of "The Chiltern Hundreds". He would be too dangerous to be allowed at large in public life!
> (1954)

IV

Although he could be sharp in his critical comments in face of what seemed to him to be complacency or hubris or prejudice or exclusiveness, he was always enthusiastic in his appreciation of reverent worship and devoted service. He rejoiced to find evidence, in remote and lonely places, of proper care being taken to offer to God an ordered sacrifice of praise and thanksgiving, a duty and privilege not always adequately fulfilled by evangelicals within the Church of England!

In Arnhem Land, N. Australia.

We had a service of Holy Communion and the great privilege was given me of being the Celebrant, with John Hewett assisting. There we were in that simple little elephant grass church, right off the map, with a congregation consisting of six Whites, and ten Aborigines. There at the sacrament of unity, the Stone Age and the twentieth century A.D. met in Him who is the centre and meaning of history and of the whole long process of our human development. It was a wonderful experience and one thanks God for having been allowed to have it. (1949)

At a Consecration Service in Nigeria.

The Litany was chanted superbly. Indeed it was exciting to come to Bonny and hear the Litany in a consecration service sung as it should be sung. The African Archdeacon who sang it did not emulate those miserable clerks in English Cathedrals who go right through the Litany without any variation of expression. With real perception he modulated and regulated his voice appropriately to the petitions he was voicing. It was profoundly impressive and very moving.

Perhaps I have been fortunate on this trip but I must say that few things have impressed me more in Eastern Nigeria than the real sensitivity to worship that we have found wherever we have been. It is immensely enheartening. (1957)

In Nigeria.

At 9 p.m. we all went over to the chapel for the final service of term – the Holy Communion. The men were all going off next morning at 5 a.m. It was a beautiful service with Seth celebrating. He took the prayers with a meaningfulness and reverence that I have seldom, if ever, heard surpassed. It was a great act of worship led by one whose whole soul breathes reverence for God and man and all life. I have always thought of Seth as one of the rare spirits. I thought so more than ever during the service. Men like Seth make you realise the tremendous gifts which Africa has got to bring to God for the service of his Church. We are apt to think of the Indian as the man with a peculiar genius for worship and adoration. Well this tour has taught me to expect "something new out of Africa" in this respect. The Indian has a deep capacity for reverence and for stillness. At this service I felt the same but with this added – a deep sense of wonder, of astonishment before the goodness of God. Seth conveyed this sense of wonder in a way which for me is quite unforgettable. (1957)

In the Sudan.

Yet it was in this countryside that we came on an experience that was worth the whole visit to Sudan. At one point about eight miles short of Meridi, at a hamlet which we discovered was called Kwanga, we ran past a little glade of trees and there an open air church had been set up. The glade was flanked on one side by six mango trees and on the other by some five fine white barked trees which I did not recognise. At the east end was another tree, balanced by one at the west end. Immediately in front of the tree at the east end was a lectern, its reading desk formed out of an old army camp cooker.

Flanking it was a chair covered with a mat. The body of "the church" was filled with small tree trunks on simple cross pieces of wood to lift them from the ground and form seats.

Here was an open-air church. A passer-by told us it was built and run by a Christian living in a small hut which we could see in the distance. A little while later he turned up himself with a number of other folk from the hamlet. His name is Petro. Formerly in the Army, he is a keen Christian and he has started this little church on his own initiative. Here he gathers all the folk he can, teaches them what he knows, and on Sunday preaches to them out of a New Testament which he has got from his brother, his own having been destroyed in a fire a year ago.

He gets as many as seventy folk together on a Sunday. He is not a pastor or a teacher and he gets no payment. He just does it out of the love he has for Christ.

It was incredibly moving and exciting to come on this little outpost of the Christian Church, where on weekdays those who are reading for baptism come to study under their own evangelist-teacher, himself a volunteer on no pay roll, and where on Sundays more than three-score simple folk of the Baka tribe meet to hear about the gospel. (1949–50)

V

Max always managed to take books with him and to read them *en route* but he also loved to observe the wonders of the world of

140

nature. Bird-watching he enjoyed but he seems to have delighted still more in the unlimited wealth of *colour* variations which travel allowed him to see. He would have liked to paint but had to be content to sketch *word-pictures*. These seem to me to reveal an unusual sensitivity, both in observation and in vocabulary.

In Arnhem Land.

The view which I have attempted to describe was transfigured last night by a sunset which would be dismissed as grotesquely exaggerated if it was put on a canvas. But, of course, part of the indescribable beauty of a sunset is the changing of the colours which cannot be captured in any medium. The paling blue of the western sky was first of all lit up by streamers of pink cloud which rapidly changed through a whole spectrum of oranges and red to deep rose. The sun did not so much set as blaze out in a great sheet of flame coloured orange which stretched in fading sequences half across the horizon. With the setting sun the hills turned violet and then indigo but the sky above was just a riot. The rose red had become a deep rich velvety brick red with scarlet streamers with a hint of copper and gold in it, and the sky in between a soft blue green which shimmered like shot silk with hints of silver and gold. The glory of the sunset circled the entire horizon until away in the east the reds and pinks finally faded into the purple of the advancing night. The evening star blazed away above all this like a flashing diamond suspended in space. It was almost three dimensional as it hung there, outblazing the half moon which soon began to fill the night with its soft silvers and greys and blacks. The hot wind of the day disappeared at sunset and the night was delightfully cool and still. (1949)

In Japan.

One cannot take one's eyes off Fuji. It changes from minute to minute, now riding clear above the clouds, swimming in the air, now clearly earthbound but representing a sight of aspiration, all its lines as eloquent of the ambition to reach beyond this earth to heaven as any Gothic cathedral. But how utterly different is the way in which these two aspirations are expressed. What does it mean to the Japanese soul that there is this symbol of the ascent of the spirit? (1959)

In Tanzania.

The heavens were declaring the glory of God and the earth was but reflecting His handiwork.

141

The background was that amazing blue which is not like the soft blue of our temperate zone, nor the harsh almost metallic blue that one can sometimes see over the Mediterranean. There was a touch of satin about it as though it had depth. This blue was varying in shades, the more dramatic because it appeared again and again in the context of such varied colours provided by the cloudscapes. I do not think I have ever seen cloudscapes more amazing. There was a concentration of vivid colour on the flight from Sydney to Brisbane in 1949 with some dramatic moments and tremendous contrasts. But the palette was a strictly limited one. There was that unforgettable flight over the North Pacific in 1947 through the forest columns of cumulus in which the monsoon was coming to birth, and the white clouds turned to pink and then to grey. But that was a study in pastel shades only. But on this evening of 19th November, 1955, there was a banquet of colour I have never seen surpassed.

The "little rains" had brought a tremendous mass of clouds to concentrate round the various mountain massifs. The location of these mountains to left and right and ahead as we ran over the plain made possible the contrasts as the setting sun caught the clouds at different angles. The sunset was a blazing furnace of yellow and orange with a red glow at its heart, and merging through shades of lemon it caught the fringe of the blue and melted it to the palest green. All this lay behind us, to be glimpsed only occasionally over one's shoulder when there was a slight bend in the road.

I find it difficult to know where to begin in describing the cloud-vista on each side and ahead as we drove along. It is bound to sound fantastic. Straight before us rain was sweeping across the Pare Mountains with a soft silvery grey sheen against a deep grey background. This silvery grey turned to pink mist where it caught the sun. Above the rain there was an angry mass of cumulus of deep grey and grey-blue colour swirling upwards till it faded into a pearl grey – and then suddenly there was a mass of snow white, almost dazzling in its brightness. I think the clouds over the Arushachini Hills to the south must have obscured the sunset glow and these cumulus topsails were so high that for them the sun was not setting at all and they still enjoyed its undimmed brightness.

Looking away towards the Arushachini one saw an astonishing sight. Deeply banked grey clouds full of rain were broken open at one point where a mixture of cloud and falling rain wore a rich blood red, a most improbable colour for rain or cloud.

The glistening white above the Pare, the blood colour over the Arushachini, were solitary gems of colour in a formidable setting of varying shades of grey, grey blue and ice blue. But to the north, above the slopes of Kilimanjaro, the paint box had been used to the full. Some clouds were almost pure gold, others were a very pale pink edging on angry dirty white or grey, yet others were vivid flamingo pink, yet others were saffron of the purest shade. But these colours were not adjacent. Their vivid effect was achieved by being interlaced with every variety of grey from the lightest to a colour almost as dark as charcoal. But there was nothing at all monotonous in this symphony of grey. The greys were shot through with strips of mauve and violet. Picture all this between the vivid blue of the sky and the sun-washed green of the hills, and the burnt gold of the bush.

There, I've tried to catch twenty minutes of as vivid enjoyment of beauty as I've ever experienced. The task was impossible. But at least in the days ahead I may be able to recapture the memory because I've attempted the impossible. Words cannot express a beauty one has not experienced. But they can enshrine a memory of something one has seen. (1955)

During the long convalescence after being invalided home from Nigeria Max tried to express some of his reflections in poetic form. But this was not his authentic literary medium. Happily he came to realise that it was through the disciplined writing of a daily diary that he could find the greatest satisfaction, both in giving outward form to his own deeply-felt impressions and at the same time recording for the benefit of others the nature of the world which he had been privileged to explore. More vividly even than his autobiography, the diaries give us photographs or "tapes" of the experiences which he recorded immediately without considering their possible impact on future readers.

Steven Axelrod has written perceptively about the function of poems in the recording of Robert Lowell's "experiences".

" 'Experience' " he writes, "does not mean only what 'happened' to Lowell for that formulation would place too much emphasis on an active but unilateral environment, and would reduce the experiencer's mind to the passive role of a transmitting lens. The mind itself is active, trembling to 'caress the light'. 'Experience' more truly means the sum of the relations and interactions between psyche and environment . . . Just as experience mediates between self and world, partaking of both, so Lowell's poems mediate between himself and his world, and between his personal history and that of his readers." (Robert Lowell. *Life and Art* p. 4.)

This description of "experience" would, I think, have appealed to Max. "Relations and interactions" constituted the very stuff of true life for him. And through his diaries those relations and interactions took shape. Some might regard them as his rough sketches which he could later write up with fuller attention to the structure and rhythm of an ordered narrative as, for example, in his News-Letters. But I feel bound to regard them as more than rough sketches. Obviously many sections of the diaries record a day's events without any attention being paid to their significance or to structural form. Then, however, a moment comes when his active mind "caresses the light". He sees a situation or an event not just as a bare "happening" but as a focussing point for all sorts of "relations and interactions". His imagination tries constantly to find fitting words and metaphors to capture and draw out the significance of what he has experienced.

In this way he gradually amassed a rich treasury of impressions and reflections which are never just commonplace and pedantic but rather are lively and honest reactions to a world of people and places more extensive and more varied than most of us have ever dreamed of.

10

The "why" and "wherefore"

I

FOR MAX, CHRISTIAN faith involved two major obligations. One was self-commitment to responsible *action* in worship and in witness: the other was self-dedication to hard *thinking,* expressing itself through speech and through writing. Missionary action must be inspired by and checked by missionary theology. As we have seen, he never ceased to admire those who had obeyed the call to go out as missionaries in the nineteenth century, often at the risk of their lives. But he was convinced that the compelling urge to evangelise had led evangelicals, in particular, either to neglect theology or to concentrate their attention upon too narrow a range of theological principles. He wanted to bring not only all mankind but also the entire range of human thought into the kingdom of Christ. He believed therefore that it was his duty to encourage the best possible theological thinking and writing, whether in churches at home or in the developing churches overseas.

In 1952, when reflecting on the Willingen Conference to which he himself made such a notable contribution, he wrote in his diary:

> It is a fact that the missionary movement, as a whole, has not matched the abundance of its *activity* by a comparable degree of thoughtful attention as to the "why" and "wherefore" of being *active.* This may have been understandable in the days when an expanding economy marched with an expanding imperialism and a supremely self-confident extension of culture, in days when resources were readily available to match the needs of expansion. But with the retreat of the West, with the recession of imperialism and of cultural dominion, and in view of the growing suspicion with which economic power is everywhere viewed, the situation has changed radically. Smaller resources, greater restrictions, and the growing threat

145

of alien philosophies have combined to make it imperative for missions to define the why and wherefore of their actions. And this involves theology. The alternative is sheer opportunism of the kind that wastes resources, damps enthusiasm, and finally fails for lack of recruits. No small part of our present embarrassment lies in the unwillingness of so many concerned with the missionary task of the Church to think theologically.

Max never attempted to produce an extended treatise on any particular branch of Christian doctrine. Nevertheless, everything he wrote was informed by theological insights and undergirded by careful theological reading. He was always on the watch for books which he could recommend to missionaries in training or to those already on the field, and probably no department of overseas work gave him more concern than the ordering and staffing of theological colleges. In his judgment, those called to minister in the newly developing churches must be given every possible assistance to relate their Christian commitment to the thought and culture, as well as to the personal and practical needs, of those to whom they would be ministering.

In addition, he devoutly hoped that the theology of missions and the history of missions might be accorded a larger place within the curriculum of the average theological college in Britain, and even that they might come to be recognised as worthy subjects of study in university faculties of theology. In a powerful sermon preached before the University of Cambridge in February 1956 on the text "Strive to excel in building up the Church" (1 Corinthians 14:12), having first vividly described the world situation and given illustrations of the witness of numerically small Christian communities within it, he went on to ask how, for example, a University like Cambridge could assist in the task of "building up the Church" in our generation. He then suggested three areas of theological teaching where references to the history of missions could be of vital significance: in biblical interpretation, in church history and in dogmatic theology. Having given striking illustrations of this possibility in the first two areas, he went on to speak of the third:

"Just over one hundred years ago, in Göttingen University, there was a Professor Ehrenfeuchter who decisively influenced the subsequent teaching of theology both on the Continent and in the United States. In both of those countries it has become increasingly commonplace that where theology is taught there should be a Chair of Missions, or at least a lectureship dealing with the scientific study of the subject." After quoting some words of the Professor seeking to justify the study of the work and theory of missions as "a theological necessity" he continued:

"At a time when so much theological energy is being devoted to an understanding of the nature of the Church; when so urgent a need exists that more should seek to 'excel in building up the Church'; when the contemporary manifestations of the Spirit are compelling theologians to wrestle afresh with the doctrine of the Holy Spirit, it is surely of some importance that the theological discipline of any University should include far more serious attention to the contemporary experience of the Church – that is to say, the Church engaged in mission."

This hope, however, was to remain largely unfulfilled. He was invited to give two courses of lectures under the aegis of the divinity faculty at Cambridge and through these he made a notable contribution to the history of the modern missionary movement from Britain and, within it, of the interaction of political, social, economic and religious factors. Almost incidentally he showed, as a reviewer in *The Guardian* commented, "what an immense range of historical studies is being neglected and what a rich vein of research lies practically untouched in the archives of the great societies". But in England, for whatever reason, there has been no such development of the study of missionary history and theology as in Dutch and Scandinavian and German universities or in American academic circles. Max's enthusiasm led to the preservation and ordering of material in the C.M.S. library and archives for future researchers. It remains to be seen whether his vision of a larger place for the study of missions in the theological curriculum in England will ever be realised.

II

Whereas the Psalmist could cry out exultantly: "The heavens declare the glory of God and the firmament showeth His handiwork", Max constantly repeated in one way or another a parallel proclamation: "The movements of human history declare the glorious purpose of God and certain major events reveal his total design." This did not mean that he was impervious to the beauties of nature or to its wonderful order as disclosed by the natural sciences. When he looked back on his travels, he arranged a whole file of passages in which he had tried to express his own appreciation of natural beauty. But he never attempted to keep up with the developments of modern science, much as he admired the efforts of such men as Charles Raven and Teilhard de Chardin who were attempting to do so. In contrast, he himself had been seized at an early age by the fascination of *history*: he had been trained in one of the best faculties of historical discipline, he had read widely in the field of history, and he believed that it was by the aid of records of historical events and movements that he could best perform his own particular theological task.

In his parents' home the Bible had occupied a place of honour as the supreme medium of revelation and instruction. It continued to occupy the same place in his own growth as a committed Christian and in the family life of his own home when that came to be established. It was natural, however, that as his own intellectual life developed, his particular approach to the Bible should have been historical rather than, shall we say, mystical or philosophical or typological. He made himself familiar with the records of the Hebrew patriarchs and of the kings of Israel and Judah, but what seems to have appealed to him most of all was the record of the relationship of Israel (in the broadest sense) to the nations surrounding it in the Fertile Crescent. The story of these relationships could be pieced together from the writings of the Prophets, and it was clear to him that from it there emerged a distinctive *pattern*, a pattern which had significance, not only for Israel itself, but for all men and for all times. Behind and beyond the events which could be recorded as history, the Prophets discerned the guiding hand of One who was in control of history and who was working out his purpose in history. To that interpretation he gave his own glad assent.

The result was that no references to the Old Testament appear in his writings with anything like the same frequency as do those he makes to the daring proclamations of the two Isaiahs, Jeremiah, and Habakkuk concerning the movements of world history in their time. Again and again he returned in imagination to

> Assyria, the rod of my anger,
> the staff of my fury   (Isa. 10:5)

to Nebuchadrezzar, King of Babylon,
    My servant   (Jer. 25:9)

to I am rousing the Chaldeans,
    that bitter and hasty nation   (Hab. 1:6)

to   Cyrus, He is my shepherd
Who shall fulfil all my purpose   (Isa. 44:28).

Affirmations such as these came to form the very foundation of his doctrine of God. God, as he put it, was altogether in control: at the same time God was altogether beyond human control. Moreover, these affirmations not only gave him the justification for the study of politics (which he in any case so greatly enjoyed): much more they laid upon him the obligation to observe the movements of the nations in his own time and to seek to interpret them to his own contemporaries in the way the prophets had done before him. Stalin and Mao, Nehru and Eisenhower could be as significant for our times as Cyrus and Nebuchadrezzar had been for theirs.

Yet this was by no means all the story or even the most important part of the story. For amidst "the march of armies and the struggle of empires" we see, by the help of the biblical record, a small nomadic people being led on through its corporate experience, and through the interpretation of that experience by priest and prophet, towards that growing apprehension of God which gained its crowning expression in the faith that the Word had indeed been made flesh, and that through certain events at a particular time in history the purpose of God for man had been once for all revealed. This "missionary" pattern came to dominate his thinking. God's purpose for Israel was that it should become a "missionary" people: similarly, this was his purpose for the new Israel, the Christian Church. In between, in and through the One who alone fully realised that purpose, the "missionary" pattern had been revealed in all its splendour yet in all its costliness: "As my Father hath sent me [sending = mission] even so send I you."

"If then we take the Bible as our guide to history, that is, the sphere in which we discover God and man – for that discovery is what gives to history its coherence – we can claim that there we discover the humility, the patience and the forgiveness of God, a humility, a patience and a forgiveness which characterises all his relationship with nations and persons, with man in his various collectivities and man in his individuality." (*Interpreting the Cross*, p. 51.)

III

Max's theological writings, which appeared as pamphlets, news-letters, articles or printed lectures rather than as formal expositions, were different in tone and emphasis from the theology which had been dominant in Anglican circles through the 30's and 40's. There the central concerns had been the *form* of the Church, the *structure* of its ministry, the *shape* of its liturgy. He was deeply interested in these investigations. For example, after a most careful study of Gregory Dix's book *The Shape of the Liturgy* which left him "happy but exhausted", but also full of questions, he invited the author to spend an evening with him at the Royal Empire Society. It was a most friendly occasion, though Max had to record: "I could never tie him down to discuss any one point. He just cannot see that there can be any other point of view than his about worship." In point of fact it was this insistence on the possibility and legitimacy of *another* "point of view" which increasingly characterised Max's own theological contribution. He welcomed and appreciated what was being written by Anglicans about the nature of the Church and sacraments but was convinced that it was not the *only* point of view. Theology must be done *dialectically*, in *tension*, *across boundaries*, rather than within the enclosed enclave whether of a single ecclesiastical compound or of an exclusive dogmatic system.

As he became increasingly involved in ecumenical contacts and discussions and in the missionary outreach which transcended national and cultural barriers, he became convinced that truth cannot be expressed through any strictly bounded expression, whether of organisation or of terminology. This did not for a moment result in any belittling of the value of the tradition in which he had been reared and to which he remained loyal. Nor did it lead to any kind of indifferentism about forms of theological expression as if *any* expression of doctrine was as good as any other. But it did mean that he moved constantly and dialectically between, for example, the particularity of the biblical record and the wide panorama of human history, between the heritage of the Judaeo-Christian tradition and the pressures of the immediately contem-porary world situation, between man's life in community and man's own self-identity, between the Christ of the New Testament and the Christ in living experience today. No formulation of doctrine could be final and absolute: theology belonged to mission as well as to worship and therefore must always be patient of new discoveries and new expressions.

This very emphasis on mission meant that he was always suspicious of any attempt to *separate* the Church from the world, whether in theory or in practice. There is obviously a sense in which "the Church", if it is to mean anything at all, must refer to a distinguishable corporate entity and it is natural to try to define this entity by fencing it around, either by articles of belief or by forms of ritual practice or by both. But though natural it is also dangerous, for the inevitable tendency arises to make these articles and forms rigid and immutable. Max wanted therefore to hold together in tension what may at first sight seem incompatible and even contradictory: the institutional and the voluntary, the organic and the covenantal, the controlled and the freely-initiated, the traditional and the innovational. And perhaps because he felt that the second terms within this total dialectic had received less emphasis in theology generally, he did not hesitate to lay the major emphasis upon them in his own theology of mission.

There is a significant entry in his diary for June 1958 which shows the place that dialectic and tension had come to occupy in all his thinking.

If you are to be free to pioneer evangelism you *cannot* be administratively unified. For still as ever "the Spirit bloweth where He listeth". The freedom of the Spirit is antithetical to all mammoth organisations. For mammoth organisation is essentially a power centre designed to be manipulated by fallible men. And power, however disguised, tends to corruption in the hands of sinners. Here is the perennial justification for the protest of the voluntary and free Society. But we must not make our protest as one of negative opposition. We have to see and understand the need for certain kinds of centralisation, and respect those whose vocation is to serve within these "power structures". Our "protest" must be a constructive protest in "love" which seeks always to be serving that against which we protest, the while we ourselves submit to the "protest" of those against whom we in turn protest. Here is a dialectical situation, full of tension and paradox. But we must not be afraid of either tension or paradox for they are the ingredients of real living in the real world God has given us. "Love as brethren, be pitiful, be courteous" seems to me to be the sum of the whole matter in the field of personal relationships, which after all is the place of meeting between those within these mammoth central organisations and those of us whose vocation is to serve outside them.

Even in the context of his passion for historical research and for discerning the working out of the Divine purpose in history, he could still on one occasion say to his hearers in the course of a Quiet Day at St. Julian's: "I have read these words to you (Exodus 19:4) on the eighth day of the Arab-Israel war. Just in passing let me say this: unless you can read your Bible as being both history and symbol, and hold these two in a perpetual but creative tension, then sell your Bible and get what spiritual nourishment you can from Alice in Wonderland!"

IV

In one sense it would be possible to describe his theology as "balanced", in that he tried always to be fair and to recognise the value of doctrinal formulations other than his own. But "balanced" is too static a term. His theology was intimately related to the ongoing movement of history and within that history nothing to him was more important than *personal relations.*

In the course of a lecture given to clergy at Chichester less than two years before he died, he admitted that much of modern life has to be carried out almost anonymously because of the size and complexity of social organisations in our technological world. We so often feel helpless in face of those systems which now dwarf the individual. Yet, he affirmed, "God is not the God in the gap of human incapacity. God is not the God who suddenly enters human history at this point or that to effect some decisive change. God is present in history in and through persons-in-relationship. The greatest of his creations is that supreme mystery, human personality, whose fulness we know in Jesus Christ. And some of his features we have been privileged to see in those we love, in friends, and in strangers."

This model of person-to-person relationship in love and friendship was so central in all his thinking and imagining that it quite naturally became for him the supreme instrument by which he tried to express his apprehension of Divine activity. He repudiated any thought of a *Deus ex machina*: equally, he rejected any concept of a deity concerned only for some chosen elect. Instead, his thinking centred upon the God who enters into personal relationships with men and does so through the modes of patient listening, courteous attention, and imaginative speaking, such as are modelled in any

152

authentic personal encounter in human life. Constantly in his talks and writings he referred to the *patience* of God and near the end of his last book he made this significant statement:

> Several times in this book we have had occasion to speak of the patience of God. Would we be so very wrong were we to say that patience is the greatest of all his attributes? For what is patience but love in action, love waiting, love suffering, love pursuing, love ever respecting our freedom, however much we abuse it? If this is the supreme attribute of God, it must be the supreme attribute of the missionary. He, if he knows himself, knows that he has already tried the patience of God to the limit. He must show to others what God has shown to him. (*I believe in the Great Commission* p. 177.)

A second term to which he often returned in speaking of human relationships was the term *courtesy*. He loved to quote St. Paul's injunction: "Love as brethren, be pitiful, be courteous" and, in his address to the clergy at Chichester, quoted a charming verse of Hilaire Belloc's to direct their thoughts to the courtesy which characterises all God's relations with mankind.

> Of courtesy it is much less
> Than courage of heart or holiness:
> Yet in my walks it seems to me
> That the Grace of God is in Courtesy.

The central model, then, was the personal conversation as enacted between friend and friend: calling for patience, courtesy, attention, listening, outgoing, give and take, recognition of common ground, mutual respect. Such relationships, he believed, were not only invaluable for the growth of the individual: they were ultimately the most influential factors in the whole process of human history. *It was in this way that God had spoken to men* – through his prophets, through his Son, through his missionaries. It was by listening to God and responding in prayer that man could attain his highest destiny.

V

I have referred in passing to the place of the Bible, first in the home where Max grew up and then in his own individual and family life. Nothing has been more characteristic of the Reformed tradition, and within it of evangelical Anglicans, than regard for the Bible as the supreme medium through which the Word of God has been made available to mankind. At a particular time and place the Word "was made flesh", but for all times and places the Word of God as recorded in the Bible has constituted a potential means of revelation. It has naturally followed that the Bible has played a central part in the training and the subsequent ministry of evangelical missionaries.

Ever since the crisis in the early twenties, it had been the aim of the leaders of C.M.S. to hold together within its membership those of more "liberal" and more "conservative" views concerning the inspiration and interpretation of the Bible, and at the same time to insist on its central importance in missionary work. Max's entire wish was to do the same. Yet although he distrusted all qualifications of the term evangelical, there could be no doubt that the direction of his own thought and action was liberal rather than conservative.

Hardly any problem gave him more concern and perplexity of mind than that of his relation to conservative evangelicals. Over a period of fifty years many such had been his valued friends. He knew that these evangelicals who had an unquestioned recourse to the Bible as the guide and inspiration for their own lives were amongst the foremost in seeking to communicate the central message of the Bible to others. To use a familiar phrase, conservative evangelical missionaries had a "cutting edge". They obeyed unreservedly the call to go out into the world and preach the gospel to every creature. Moreover, as he once pointed out, their home supporters usually had "fairly clear-cut ideas" about what they wanted their agents to do.

His heart was with them in affection, in admiration and in sharing their deep concern. But his acute mind, filled with stores of historical knowledge, trained to test evidence with the utmost rigour, rejecting all over-simplifications, ever open to new understanding of the manifold wisdom of God – how could it in honesty subscribe to sweeping statements about the nature and authority of the Bible in any exclusive way? He loved the Bible, lived with the Bible, but did so imaginatively, critically, constantly with a view to relating it to contemporary events. If "conservative" implied honouring a tradition and applying it to present circumstances, he would have gladly found himself in the conservative ranks. But if, as the Oxford Dictionary affirms, it denotes keeping "intact and unchanged", then he was certainly not a conservative. Inflexibility of any kind was to him anathema.

Again and again he returned to this problem in his diaries and letters. To give one illuminating example, we find him one March evening in 1968 going off to Blackheath to celebrate the fifth anniversary of the publication of *Honest to God*, he having been a reader of the original manuscript and having warmly encouraged John Robinson to get it into print. Now, with a few others, he joined in the discussion of "radical theology" and although he confessed that a good deal of the discussion was "right above my head", yet when it came to looking at "world-problems, which pose so fundamentally one's belief about the nature of Man", he felt in tune and judged that it had been a profitable evening.

Ten days later a man who had been a missionary in Northern Nigeria in the service of one of the most conservative of the missionary societies and was now concerned with missionary training, came to Westminster to consult him. He proved to be "a most attractive and open-minded man" and "I think we worked out an exciting syllabus". His later comment was: "I must say I find it very encouraging that these conservative evangelicals are so willing to come and talk about their problems and are so willing to listen to one's ideas about missionary studies. The truth is, of course, that deep down I have their evangelistic commitment and they know that I do. This is our real 'meeting point'. The longer I live the more deeply I feel this affinity as one of the deepest and most priceless of all links. There is a *koinonia* at this point which is really deeper than anything I have with any other Christian group. I don't think that is an exaggeration."

This was the dilemma. Complete affinity with the one group in evangelistic zeal: affinity at so many points with the other group in radical thinking about the world's problems. Alec Vidler has a fine statement in his book *Scenes from Clerical Life* in which he defines liberal as the opposite "not of conservative but of fanatical or bigoted or intransigent. It points to the *esprit large* and away from the *idée fixe*". Max always rejoiced to be in the company of missionary friends who had a deep concern for the world and the salvation of souls: at the same time he rejoiced to be linked with those who were striving to understand the real issues confronting the world and the true nature of the social environment within

which life must be lived today. Narrow prejudice, fear of freedom
to think, the attitude of what he called "mental dinosaurs", all these
were abhorrent to him. Yet he always wanted to see what lay
behind these attitudes, what of good there was to acclaim, even
when there was plenty to criticise and resist. He was evangelical
first, liberal second. Fully committed and also open-minded: this
may seem a paradox but it was Max's unflinching purpose – and
often his pain – to hold both together at whatever cost.

His final attempt to express his thoughts publicly on the problem
was his review of James Barr's book *Fundamentalism*. (This
appeared in *New Fire* after his death.) It displays the same tension
between the passion for intellectual integrity and the profound
respect for religious commitment. He repudiates every form of
"fundamentalism" and makes no attempt "to justify the extravagant and tortuous arguments of those who yesterday tried and today
try, to prove the Bible is inerrant". Yet he defends conservative
evangelicalism in Britain on the ground that its "spiritual basis" is
not at all the same thing as its "biblical basis". Expanding this
distinction he writes: "It cannot be too strongly insisted that the
'hard core' of conservative evangelicalism, what gives it stability, is
an experience of the grace of God which may come through
preaching, personal friendship, or private reading of the Bible but
which is in no essential sense tied either to a view of the inerrancy of
the Bible or its infallibility in the sense attacked in this book." But,
the ordinary reader may well ask: If conservative evangelicalism is
not tied in any essential sense to inerrancy and infallibility, why are
these terms used and defended and what do they imply?

VI

In the history of evangelicalism over the past two centuries two
doctrines have received more attention and greater emphasis than
any others: the doctrines of Atonement and of the Holy Spirit.
Thought and devotion, confessions of faith, and gospel hymns have
all been directed towards Calvary and Pentecost. Assurance of
forgiveness has come to those who have "surveyed the wondrous
Cross"; new life in Christ has become a reality through the power of
the Spirit. Amidst all his many responsibilities and interests Max
never wavered in his loyalty to the evangelical tradition, and it is
not therefore surprising that its two focal doctrines were constantly
uppermost in his own theological thinking.

Yet he never set out his own interpretation of these doctrines in any comprehensive way. Two sets of lectures on the Atonement, given in the last period of his life, I shall consider later. His particular contribution to the doctrine of the Holy Spirit was made, it appears, as a direct result of a difficult situation which arose in the Churches of East Africa.

First in Uganda, then in Kenya, a revival movement brought a wholly new sense of release and fellowship to many within the Christian congregations, while other Christians remained untouched and even critical of what seemed to be excesses amongst the revival folk. There was a real danger of misunderstanding and strife and even of schism. These divisions affected not only the African church members but also the expatriate missionaries. There were appeals for guidance and Max, who never shirked responsibility in difficult situations, set to work to study the incidence of revivals in Christian history in order that he might see the African situation in perspective and help Christians there to understand the manner of the Spirit's working.

Already he had studied with great admiration Ronald Knox's brilliant survey *Enthusiasm – a Chapter in the History of Religion*, and he had also become familiar with the researches of Dr. Edwin Orr on the history of evangelical awakenings during the past two centuries. As always he tried to view the present in the light of the past and in September 1952 he wrote a preliminary paper entitled *The Revival in East Africa – An Essay in Understanding*. This was followed in 1954 by a book *Revival – An Enquiry* and finally, in January 1977, he returned to the subject with an article in *The Churchman*: "Revivals in Religion". In all of these he was concerned to set revivals or movements or awakenings of modern times within the wider perspective of "the whole record of the Christian Church".

His own study of history had convinced him that just as in the life of an individual a mountain-top experience needs to be followed by a period of steady growth towards maturity, so in the life of a corporate body a flood-tide of enthusiasm may need to be followed by an ebb-tide in order that corporate maturity may be attained. "Such an ebb-tide is not lightly to be equated either with an ebb-tide of faith, or spiritual exhaustion, let alone infidelity." (Another example, it may be noted, of Max's dialectical theology.) He delighted to speak of the Holy Spirit as "untidy and unpredictable" by any human reckoning, appealing to John 3:8. Yet he would have been just as ready to appeal to 1 Corinthians 14:33,40 to support a claim that the Spirit is constantly active in promoting order and peace. Commenting in his diary on an occasion when, at a conference in America, he referred to the work of the Spirit in stimulating to some fresh missionary endeavour those who were not "tied in" to the institutional structure of the Church he wrote: "Fundamentally, anyone with a strictly hierarchical view of the Church cannot do justice to the 'untidiness' of the Holy Spirit and generally refuses to come to terms with it. Always untidiness is an affront to order. And, of course, order and the sacramental system belong together." Yet was there anyone more eager than Max to celebrate the sacraments with meticulous attention to decency and proper order?

So he recalled "the search for God by the Desert Fathers, the monastic movements both Celtic and Benedictine, the Cluniac revival, the movement of the Friars, the Old Believers of Russia, with their unexpected development into Baptist communities, the Reformation itself, and the Puritan movement in its many ramifications, and the great movement initiated, under God, by the Wesleys and Whitfield. All experienced a flood-tide of enthusiasm preceded and followed by an ebb-tide." The question of the relation of flood-tide and ebb-tide within the Divine ordering remains intriguing and important.

In dealing with this question, Max never raised doubts about the reality of the "overwhelming experience" inspired by the Holy Spirit amongst communities of believers. At the same time he recognised the perils which attend such experiences and urged that these should be frankly faced: perils of a psychological kind and perils of an intellectual kind. In the latter category he stressed in particular the danger of *over-simplification*, such a concentration upon one form of experience that the manifold work and wisdom of God revealed in other ways came to be forgotten. That revivals had issued in higher levels of moral living and in more devoted service to the world at large could, he judged, be abundantly demonstrated by appealing to historical evidence. It would be foolish to attempt to "quench the Spirit". Yet it would be equally foolish to overlook the dangers inherent in attempts to stimulate enthusiasm by unworthy means, or to live at all times on the crest of a spiritual wave. Max prayed for revival in the Church, rejoiced in evidences of revival wherever seen. But what he wrote in his diary during his first visit to Uganda in 1949 not only expresses his own assessment of the movement in that country, but tells us much about his own attitudes to the wide range of Christian truth and to the lofty demands of the Christian ethic.

I am so puzzled about the revival. It has done some wonderful things in the Africans. I have no doubt about that. But its effect on the Europeans is much less happy. I don't doubt for one moment that it has been used to them and that many have got a deepened vision of God and their own sinfulness. I do not doubt that some even may have experienced a long overdue conversion. I am sure that some have come into a far deeper spiritual life, and that all are in a far healthier relationship with the Africans than they were before. All this is glorious and a positive gain.

What I find so lacking in the movement is any awareness of the range of Christian living and thinking, any apprehension of the complexity of life's problems once you get beyond man to man relationships, any awareness of the place of thought, of theology, of the discipline of order and the place of pattern in life. I am not asking for intellectualism. I'm asking for awareness. All one gets is the exasperating iteration of pious formulae, which one must not allow to exasperate one because they obviously correspond to some genuine experience. But one just longs to say – "Hallelujah, brother – but do try and enlarge your vocabulary." But if you hint at this you are told you are obscuring the simplicity of the truth. Who was the fool who used the phrase "the simple truth" for the first time? Truth is not a proposition. Truth is to be found only in a Person and in personal relationships, if it is to be saving as distinct from purely scientific truth. And the Truth which is personal is as deep and profound and complex as the very Being of God, even though in his mercy he may reveal himself in simpler guise. But the Incarnation is not simple whatever else it may not be.

I am quite sure that the European leaders of the revival are running a serious danger for themselves and the Africans of escaping from the discipline of thinking. Unless the movement grows in stature it will be bogged in emotionalism and infantilism, and from that it will break away into sects. But, of course, to grow is dangerous. Pray God that the revival may not become a "Peter Pan" which will not grow up.

I believe there is a vast potential for God's Kingdom in Africa and elsewhere in the revival. I also believe that what I've written above has some small modicum of sense in it and is relevant to the realisation of that potential, that latent possibility in the movement. But I've not been successful so far in getting anyone seriously to face it. Meanwhile many are being kept on the edge of the movement because of their awareness of these facts and their doubt as to whether they would be welcomed if they came into the movement, but at the same time brought this kind of thinking with them.

What is so frustrating is that any suggestion of such a thing is received by the revival leaders today with a quiet complacent smile, which says "If only you'd join us you'd know that all that is nonsense". But life is not to be won just by "pressing buttons". Life is won in the conflict of loyalties which are never resolved at low levels but always in the agony of tension. Life is always something beyond our grasp, which eludes our possession. Always Life is calling us to that which is beyond our present apprehension. How well I remember Raven, in Holy Trinity, preaching a matchless sermon on "the impracticability of the Christian Ethic", and showing how it was a saving ethic precisely because it was always impracticable, because it had that telescopic quality of always leaving you in the moment of achievement with some new vista to attain, which is the other side of the experience of knowing that at your best you are a miserable sinner.

That is the Christianity I dimly understand. That seems to me what Paul was wrestling with. What worries me about so much Christianity is that it leaves one with the impression that folk aren't wrestling but are resting on the thrill of not having been thrown in the first round.

God forgive me for a miserable sinner. Who am I to judge other men? Yet even a miserable sinner has to make decisions and that means passing judgments. Browning was right: "How hard it is to be a Christian"!

Revivals in the history of the Church brought the doctrine of the Holy Spirit prominently before his attention. Yet he did not attempt to write at length (as he might well have done) on the Holy Spirit in relation to mission. He left this to his successor, John Taylor, who consulted him in 1966 about lectures on the Theology of Mission that he was proposing to give. Max had a series of headings worked out which he readily placed at John's disposal. They show the way his thoughts were moving: the work of the Spirit in evangelism, in the encounter with other faiths, in the world-view of modern science, in the movement towards unity, in the structure of the Church, in the discipline of intercessory prayer, in relation to the Atonement and to the ultimate purpose of God. A full development of these thoughts never saw the light of day. But they may have offered at least some suggestions towards the making of John's fine book on the Holy Spirit – *The Go-Between God*.

In one of the last articles which he wrote Max expressed one of his hopes for the future:

"Is there not need for a far deeper understanding of the prevenience of the Holy Spirit as being continuously at work *within* the religious consciousness in its varied manifestations? Increasingly we are coming to recognise the work of the Creator Spirit in the long-drawn-out and still continuing story of creation. We are much less bold to explore his activities in the collective unconscious of mankind. If we do pursue this exploration we will expect to discover the *presence* of the Holy Spirit in the religious history of mankind *outside* the Covenant of Christ with his Church, as well as within it. It is not for us to define in advance the nature and extent of the discoveries we will make."

VII

Whatever other doctrines may have been neglected by evangelicals, the doctrine of the Atonement has occupied a central place in their thinking. Salvation, forgiveness, reconciliation have been different ways of describing the experience which has come about, they have believed, through the work of Christ on Calvary. *How* the death of Christ effected man's redemption has been the theme of countless books and Max took every opportunity to acquaint himself with them.

The persistent danger in evangelical books on this subject, however, has been precisely that to which Max referred in his reflections quoted in the previous section: the danger of *over-simplification*, of concentrating on one exclusive explanation, of using a single model taken from human experience to define the change in the relationships between God and mankind effected through the death of Christ. Efforts have often been made to derive one consistent interpretative theory from the New Testament and to set that up as the standard of orthodoxy to which all are expected to conform.

Such an over-simplification Max never accepted. In his most extensive writings on the subject, the product of long meditation and mature experience, he approached the Cross from varying angles, and set out his reflections in a synoptic rather than a unitary

161

way. Invited in 1965 to give a series of eight addresses to clergy in South Africa, he chose to speak on "some of the meanings of the Cross of our Lord Jesus Christ" and these addresses were published under the title *Interpreting the Cross*. In a sense it is not a book on doctrine but a very practical series of rallying-cries to men whose ministry was of necessity being carried on "under the Cross". Yet in another sense it is applied theology, for it is the fruit of years of reading and thinking on the theology of Atonement.

Interpreting the Cross is a very beautiful and very searching book. It starts from Paul's striking affirmation concerning the Wisdom of the Cross in 1 Corinthians 1 and 2, and constantly returns to the New Testament to gain some new insight into this many-faceted Wisdom. But Calvary is never a remote event, unrelated to the contemporary world. There is the basic fact, increasingly evident, of human solidarity and this implies solidarity in the world's evil. Yet the central message of the New Testament is that in Jesus Christ we see "the personal activity of God becoming directly involved in our human solidarity . . . Jesus identifies himself with disobedient and sinful mankind, and makes a perfect confession of our sins. He does this, to quote an old divine, by giving 'a perfect Amen in humanity to the judgment of God on the sin of man' . . . Amen has been said, and it has been said by Man – Man completely at one with the will of God, a dual solidarity which is itself atonement."

It was God's complete identification with man in Christ that Max found so compelling. In my human experience I can try imperfectly to identify myself with another, to see things from his point of view, to feel what he feels, to accept the consequences of his decisions. But to do all this in every respect, even to the point of being identified with others as a result of betrayal and suffering and death, this is beyond the capacity of any ordinary man. Yet this, it is claimed, was the nature of God's action in Christ, who identified himself both with mankind in general and with the individual in his particular need. Max was deeply conscious of the difficulty which every missionary must experience in trying to identify himself with the wholeness of a different race and culture and with individuals within it. Yet he was convinced that unless the missionary could, like the prophet Ezekiel, go and "sit where they sat", his work would be in vain. Insofar as he *could* make such an act of identification, he would be sharing in the atoning work of Christ.

Max never tried to work out in detailed fashion a theology of the *finished* work of Christ, though he believed with all his heart that everything for the Christian – victory over sin, death, and all the forces of evil – resulted from the once-for-all offering up at Calvary of the life lived in Galilee. But what he did try to spell out in detail was the way that Atonement must be worked out in the present experience of the Church and of the individual. In particular he saw the missionary's vocation as being in a special way a call to share with Christ in his mission, a cross to be borne, a cup to be drunk, a discipline to be accepted, all in a spirit of glad obedience as a follower of him who came, not to be served but to serve, and to give his life a ransom for many.

So he took up the threefold aspect of the missionary's task to which he often returned – to evangelise, to teach and to heal – and tried to show how in each the pattern of the Cross is bound to be revealed.

(a) *In evangelism.* "It is an inescapable part of the Cross in our ministry of evangelism, the Cross we have to carry, that we cannot persuade men that the Cross has a meaning." "The Hindu, the Buddhist, the Confucianist, the Shinto devotee, and those who have abandoned those systems of belief but have retained their cultural forms, all alike have seen Christianity fundamentally as an expression of cultural aggression, expressed too often with scant respect for their own sensibilities. They have much to forgive. That is something Christians need to remember when they seek to interpret the gospel of forgiveness. It is not enough to know that God has forgiven us. We have to receive the forgiveness of those men of other faiths. This will mean an interpretation of the Cross in our ministry of evangelism which it will be very hard to achieve. We can only seek forgiveness in the light of the universal relevance of the Cross. But how are we to convince the men of these other faiths that we all meet at the Cross and that we want them to forgive us there? That is the essence of the encounter that lies ahead."

(b) *In teaching.* "Jesus Christ lived the Cross before he died upon it. His living was the teaching upon which the Cross itself threw the light of a vast illumination. Unless we can see this and understand that all Christ's living was a dying, we shall not plumb the depths of what is involved for us in our ministry of teaching. For if the Cross stands at the centre of history, as Christians believe, if it is the central key to understanding the nature of God, the dilemma of man, the mystery of life and death: then we have to expound its meaning as the way in which all men are meant to live and die. This carries with it the implication that we too must live it, if we are to teach it."

(c) *In healing.* "Our ministry is to the whole man. To heal means to make every whit whole. We can be satisfied with nothing less than a full atonement in which the man or the woman is made one with God, with neighbour, with environment and with the inner self. Health, wholeness, integrity, holiness belong together." And in a suggestive reference to Galatians 6:1–2 he points out that the verb translated "set him right" ("If a man should do something wrong, my brothers . . . you who are endowed with the Spirit must set him right again very gently") is also the technical term used for the setting of a broken limb. At-one-ment in the body becomes a model for the understanding of the At-one-ment which is the restoration of perfect harmony and wholeness.

Max never forgot that all true missionary work must reflect some aspect of the New Testament interpretation of the Cross of Christ. The watchword of the Willingen Conference in 1952, *Missions under the Cross,* constantly directed his thought and activity. And who can question that he had the right to speak thus, for he had known the fellowship of the Cross in his own missionary experience and never ceased to exercise a ministry of reconciliation wherever his lot was cast.

Yet his emphasis upon life under the Cross was never dark, sombre or strained. He celebrated the Cross as the place of victory, as the source of positive good, as the gateway to resurrection and newness of life. (It is significant that the titles of three of Max's books are *The Gospel of Victory, Strange Victory* and *The Triumph of God.* He once said that Gustav Aulèn's book *Christus Victor* had been seminal for his own thinking.) In addition the Cross was the fountainhead of *hope,* the hope about which he wrote so confidently in *The truth of Vision.* Life, Victory, Hope – all were constituent parts of the Word of the Cross and these enabled him to triumph even in tribulations and to rejoice in hope of the glory of God.

So Max did his utmost to hold together all evangelicals who shared the same love of the Bible, the same assurance of having been justified by faith in Christ Jesus and the same sense of having committed themselves to the spread of his gospel. He was trusted and admired by liberals and conservatives alike. It could not be claimed that he succeeded in formulating a new system of evangelical theology but it is doubtful whether *systems* belong to evangelicalism anyway. He led the way to a fuller understanding of the activity of the living God in the history of mankind, of the Cross and Resurrection of Jesus Christ as the central event securing man's salvation, and of the Holy Spirit as operating within the religious consciousness of men everywhere, leading them to seek after God and persuading them to open their hearts to the message of the gospel. By so doing, it may be claimed, he made a significant contribution to the theological task of his time.

PART III

Towards a Theology of Mission

11

An ambassador sometimes in bonds

I

ON AUGUST 31, 1963 Max ceased to be General Secretary of the C.M.S. The spacious room in Salisbury Square had been his base of operations for more than twenty-one years while for most of that time he had travelled to and from the modest family home in Blackheath. Now he was to carry on his work in the context of the Houses of Parliament rather than that of the newspaper world and his residence was to be one of the most beautiful and desirable houses in Westminster.

His retirement from his post of responsibility did not come about suddenly. Many attempts had been made to induce him to accept some other position in the life of the Church but he held to the conviction that the task of missionary leadership was the one to which God had called him. Yet he also knew that the demands of the post were such that the time would inevitably come when it would be right for him to hand over his responsibilities to a younger man. Early in 1961 he informed the President that he intended to resign in 1963, thus giving plenty of time for consideration to be given to the question of who would be his successor.

In January 1963 he formally tendered his resignation to the Executive Committee but in his characteristic way took immense pains to ensure that his friends and co-workers in the missionary cause would not suddenly become aware of this decision by coming across a notice in some newspaper. He wrote a letter explaining the reasons for his decision and sent copies to all parts of the world. Not surprisingly a flood of replies indicated how deep was the universal regret and at the same time how great was the general admiration for his service to C.M.S. A typical outburst came from an Indian bishop: "Most people wonder what on earth the C.M.S. will do without you." Particularly through his News-Letters he had come to be a wise counsellor and interpreter of world events to such a vast audience that it became almost impossible to think of anyone taking his place. As the Swedish Lutheran Bishop Bengt Sundkler wrote:

> Your decision means a very great loss to the C.M.S. In "this age of querulousness and uncertainty" – quoting your latest News-Letter – your vision and guidance have been of the very greatest importance. Where there is no vision, the mission perisheth – ah, that is our deepest need. Therefore we all who have our little share in this great common cause are always thanking God for what you have given and are giving us of inspiration and insight and hope and determination.

And as an old friend, Douglas Harrison (then Dean of Bristol) wrote:

> Few men can have such satisfaction: to have carried C.M.S. through this critical generation and to leave it stronger than it has ever been in the admiration and esteem of all Anglicans is an immense achievement.

In a more formal way a Minute on Max's resignation was prepared by the President for submission to the Executive Committee and this tells of his remarkable leadership in reconstruction as the Society faced the rapid changes within the post-war world. It pays tribute to his unflagging zeal in travels and at the same time to his mastery of the details of administration at the home base. Finally it sums up the quality of his work in a striking paragraph:

> In his office Dr. Warren has shown himself a many-sided and truly human General Secretary, has united those who differ, acknowledged those who help, and won the respect and affection of all. He has treated people, men and women, as people, open-handedly, with as serious a regard for truth as for personality. He has used his pen in season and out of season, not only for official writing, but to encourage the faint and comfort the mourner. In his conversation he opens up, in a few phrases, a new vista of thought and judgment. Good sense and high enthusiasm are well mingled in his mind. He has been prophetic not only in the old sense of frequently foreseeing the great trends of the times, but in bringing to bear on the transactions of men and nations the healing judgment of the gospel. All have acknowledged his leadership and have been eager to acclaim that in an age when personality is overshadowed by the

machine, here was a man. But Dr. Warren would be the first to plead that all that he has been able to give is of the compassion and tender mercy of God and of the guidance and enablement of the Holy Spirit.

II

It was left to Christopher Driver, writing in 1962 in *Time and Tide* magazine (before the resignation had been made public), to unearth from literature the almost perfect parallel to Max in a different sphere. The figure is that of Professor Moriarty in the Sherlock Holmes saga:

"Aye, there's the genius and the wonder of the thing," Holmes cried. "The man pervades London and no one has heard of him . . . He has a brain of the first order. He sits motionless, like a spider in the centre of its web, but that web has a thousand radiations, and he knows well every quiver of them."

"Warren", Driver commented, "has been general secretary for twenty years and his numerous agents are scattered abroad from Omdurman to Osaka. Yet to the public at large he was virtually unknown until, last year, one or two knowledgeable and influential Anglicans were heard to say that they wished he might be Archbishop of Canterbury."

In fact it was far more than "one or two" who had this idea. But whatever the selectors may have thought at the time, it is clear from hindsight that physically Max could not have borne the burden of the office and that, in any case, he would never have regarded himself as fitted for such a post. The big question was what niche he could now fill which would give him relative freedom from institutional responsibilities and at the same time ample scope for communicating the results of his world-wide experience. Lord Fisher, on hearing the news of his resignation, wrote: "Down in a little country village I hear no gossip and I pull no strings but if I saw you going to Canterbury as Dean, or nearer us to Salisbury as Bishop, I should rejoice."

However, neither a bishopric nor a deanery was to claim him for the last stage of his active ministry. A canonry at Westminster had fallen vacant and when this was offered to him by the Prime

Minister he decided to accept. It is difficult to think of any other position in the Church of England which could have given him such a base and such opportunities of personal service. Not that it was without its problems as we shall see. But it kept him in London at the very cross-roads of the world's traffic, and during large sections of time he was freed from official duties. No longer able as before to go into all the world, friends from all parts of the world came to him.

So on July 15, 1963 Max was installed, amidst such ceremonial as he was hardly accustomed to, as one of the canons in the ancient Abbey of Westminster, with all its royal associations. He who had never sought the limelight would figure, with other members of the Chapter, at the centre of the picture on great occasions. He who had shrunk from using mass-media of communication would constantly be required to preach to crowds of transient visitors. He who had been entirely at home in small meetings for prayer or in services with a missionary outreach would now find himself called upon, when in residence, to participate regularly in the liturgical offerings, with elaborate musical accompaniment, which belonged to the tradition of the Abbey. It was certainly a change from being "in the centre of the web" of the great missionary enterprise at 6 Salisbury Square.

Happily, however, there was not only the Abbey with its rights and responsibilities: there was also the beautiful Canon's house in Little Cloister. This could be a veritable spider's parlour, not in any menacing sense but as a home of unbounded hospitality, gracious and romantic in its setting, an oasis of refreshment for body and soul amidst the hurly burly of the cars and buses swirling around the environs of Westminster. In Blackheath Max had a tiny study just inside the front entrance, with books on all sides and just enough room for two to sit and talk cosily by the fire. At the Westminster home a visitor went up a splendid staircase, often to be greeted by Max emerging from his study at the top; he was then ushered into a glorious room with windows giving views of the Houses of Parliament, with ample room for files and book cases, and with everything arranged in that perfect order which Max loved to create. A few weeks before the end of his time at the Abbey he wrote in his diary: "No memory of the Abbey and its precincts will mean more to me than the memory of *this superb study* in which I'm writing this diary. The dimensions of the room, the bookcases and books, everything has made it the most perfect study I have ever had. Gratitude is a feeble word to express what I feel."

The dining-room and kitchen were on the ground floor while next to Max's study there was a spacious drawing-room which could be used by the various groups which met at the Warren home from time to time. From the beginning of the new life at Westminster the two dominant notes at 3 Little Cloister were hospitality and friendship. How Mary coped with the endless stream of guests for lunch, tea, supper and overnight accommodation is a mystery. She and Max were determined that the emphasis on the personal and on people which had governed their life at C.M.S. should remain uppermost in the more formal and institutional surroundings of their new abode. And pilgrims from all over the world came to Westminster, not as in certain former times to visit the shrine of a saint, but rather to enjoy the living welcome and to seek the living counsel of the seemingly tireless pair who made their home a little London sanctuary.

One of Max's heroes was Gaius, referred to by Paul in Romans 16:23 as "my host and host of the whole congregation". It was in this tradition that Max and Mary saw their opportunity and their task in relation to the Lambeth Conference of 1968. Bishops and their wives would be coming from all parts of the Anglican world and then would be scattered in residences in different parts of London. To entertain them and, especially in the case of bishops from Africa and Asia, to make them feel at home was a continuation of their missionary calling. Max duly recorded the names of all those who visited 3 Little Cloister that summer and gave as the final count:

> During Lambeth Mary served 294 meals to bishops and others attending the Conference, not counting many others. In all 102 bishops, 47 bishops' wives, 8 consultants and 3 other observers came to receive hospitality, some many times.

For months the Warrens had prepared for "the Lambeth flood" and when it came Max wanted to re-name their house Lyons' Corner House. Not only during this Lambeth period but throughout their time at Westminster they practised the New Testament virtue of hospitality to friends and strangers alike, to a degree that few others can ever have emulated. Max did not enjoy "going out", especially to formal parties, but to have someone in for a meal and a talk was perhaps his supreme delight. Except during the time of his serious illness in 1967 all paths led to 3 Little Cloister and there, unless Mary decided that he was not well enough, a visitor was met by the unforgettable smile, the twinkle of the eye with some gentle witticism apt for the occasion and then a period of conversation in the study, always invigorating and mediating that realism mixed with hope which lay at the centre of Max's own life. *Hospitality Unbounded* could well have been inscribed over the doorway of the house with its peaceful small garden in Little Cloister.

III

Though Max disliked "going out" in person, the number of personal letters that went out from the new home could hardly have been less than those which went out from Salisbury Square. There, however, he sometimes kept two secretaries fully occupied, having mastered the art of fluent dictation. At Westminster secretarial help was spasmodic, secured mainly for manuscripts to be printed or for documents to be circulated. This meant that hundreds of letters went out in his own hand-writing and these were by no means brief replies to casual enquiries. Always deeply interested in his friends' concerns – their work, perhaps as missionaries, books they had written, personal problems on which they sought his advice – he gave himself unceasingly to the activity which from student days to the end of his life continued unremittingly, the activity of personal correspondence. In Cambridge as many as thirty a day: in Westminster the tally was often comparable in number.

On the one hand Max declared that he enjoyed letter-writing most of all his activities: on the other hand he lamented the "impossible" amount of correspondence with which he had to deal, leaving him far too little time to read and write. A day which he described as "more typical than exceptional" was July 18, 1968. This is his account of it.

This has been one of those days when one wonders if one will ever be anything but a writer of letters! I worked solidly at letters from 9.15 a.m. – 1.0 p.m. I got off No. 170 to Pat, most of it written earlier in the week. Then I had to send a Covenant form for the College of Preachers. The Registrar of Makerere University wanted a letter testimonial for X. Norman Sharp had to be sent his ticket for the Lambeth Service on July 28. Norman Campbell in Uganda wanted me to tape-record two Bible Readings at Skegness. Peter Baelz wants me to preach at Jesus College. Professor Arberry, in a moment of insanity, recommended me to the Director of the Islamic Cultural

174

Centre as a likely person to write articles for his Journal! I replied to the Director offering either "The Encounter of Islam and Christianity in the 20th century" or "The Challenge of Communism to Christianity and Islam" but said I could not let him have them until Jan. 1, 1969. Then a letter to Robbins Strong in Geneva enclosing a copy of Roger's comments on my earlier letter. Then a letter to Captain Lousley, R.N. accepting an invitation to speak at the Royal Naval College on "Christianity in an Age of Technology". Then letters to Bishop of Guildford, John Taylor and Douglas Webster . . . What a morning!"

The record of such a morning vividly reveals the width of his concerns and contacts. The references to Pat, Max's daughter, and Roger are specially interesting. They had met while each was in training for missionary service. After their marriage in October 1964 they went out to India where they were to spend some thirteen years under C.M.S. Nothing could have given Max greater pleasure. He entered with enthusiasm into their plans and hopes and made an arrangement by which he would write in turn to each week by week. These letters of course gave family news and dealt also with matters of interest in English life. In addition, however, they became the medium of a vital partnership within the task on which the young people were engaged. Max was ever on the look-out for significant books, articles, clippings to send; he rejoiced, as in times past, to receive return reports from the field. More than six hundred letters were sent out, and these rarely contained less than four quarto sheets. In these, as in his diaries, he "let himself go", commenting shrewdly on current movements, ecclesiastical and political, praising generously yet also criticising severely, though never spitefully, above all wrestling with the problems which missionaries were facing as they sought to bear their Christian witness in the new independent India.

Writing in 1968 about the unpredictability of world events and the uncertainties of tenure surrounding missionaries in any country where for the time being they were located, he urged Pat and Roger not to be too disturbed by estimates of what the future might bring:

The great thing is to make all the friends you can for this is the way Christ will be best recognised. And become as fully proficient in the language as possible. Who can possibly tell for what God is preparing you both in the years ahead? But he is preparing you for something. He's given you both a love for

175

people, a sensitiveness to the local scene (India at the moment) and a gift for language. How joyful a thing it is to be so enabled that every day and in every way you are all of you being prepared for whatever God may want of you in the unknown future.

If I were you I would shout and sing. Indeed I often do, even not being you, for I've been on the job long enough to know that God never wastes any experience which he allows his servants to have.

Clutch avidly at everything India offers you and having offered it to God you can be gloriously detached while deeply involved! How I envy you both! And remember, "your days in India are *not* numbered" only "every hair of your head"!

So he delighted in every bit of news from India, especially when Roger and Pat were allowed by C.M.S. to take up residence in the sacred city of Varanasi with Roger enrolling in the Sanskrit University for studies in Hindu literature and philosophy. To and fro the letters went, with Max joining in the dialogical pattern of ministry which Roger was developing. At the same time, in spite of his concern that missionaries should identify themselves as far as possible with the culture of the country to which they were sent, he was eager that they should never lose touch with ideas and movements in their homeland and to this end he constantly reported and commented on what seemed to him significant features of the life of the Church in England.

In the same letter in which he had expressed some of his own deepest convictions about the nature of the "foreign" missionary's task, he turned back to the home scene, raising the question how far it was possible to carry on an effective ministry within the traditional parochial system. After referring to a certain young man as providing "a supreme illustration of what a man can do when he combines a real love for people, real tact and a head which can think and who insists on making the most of the material for liturgical and preaching reformation now available" he continued:

I think there are vast possibilities in the traditional ministry. But it needs to be seen from a lot of new angles and without any legalistic controls. *Slavery to rubrics* is the real curse! If once we can see that rubrics are guide-lines and no more, I believe we may be able to get Anglicanism moving. But clergy love rubrics because they make us feel safe. Abandon rubrics

176

and anything may happen. But to treat them as useful guide-lines and then to feel free, is to make possible within our Anglican worship the "freedom of the Spirit". This is the great merit of Series II which leaves so much freedom of choice.

I have given these two brief extracts as examples of the keen and lively interchange of ideas, suggestions, plans, information, which continued over a period of thirteen years. Max's enthusiasm never flagged. However poor his physical condition might be, once he had a pen in his hand ("I can only think with a pen in my hand") the ideas began to flow ("I am bubbling over with ideas") and the pages began to fill up. Only rarely was a letter a thing of one or two paragraphs. A friend wrote him about a sentence in the Open Letter to the Archbishops on Intercommunion which Max had signed: the reply did not defend the sentence, which he agreed was unfortunately drafted – but it proceeded to give a careful and measured statement, running to several pages, of his own theology of the Incarnation. A letter was the next best thing to a personal conversation and to each Max gave of his best: listening to the other, generous in his appreciation of the other's point of view, setting out his own clearly and persuasively.

Some paragraphs from one of his letters to India seem to me to provide a vivid example of the width of Max's reading and the wisdom of his judgments. He had referred to the writings of John Buchan in one of his letters and this had raised the question of how different generations respond to well-known writers.

"John Buchan's generation, the generation that was for the most part killed off at Loos, Paschendaele and the Somme, the half-generation older than mine, was still romantic at heart. But for my generation it is impossible to forget an older brother killed at Loos when he was 20 and Mum's brother killed at Ypres when he was 20. That generation went to War in a way no subsequent generation has been able to go. For that generation still believed a lot of things that few believe today. The world of their schooldays was stable (to all seeming), politics looked as if they would deal with social injustice given time, the Empire was still primarily the White Dominions + India. And the vision that inspired the *best* of our people was a great vision. The weakness was that it had not come to terms with the *beast* in man. And when the beast was discovered in the human heart in that post World War I situation I think that Lloyd George and Clemenceau killed the vision.

"Now Mums and I were at Cambridge when hope had not yet died. The Cambridge we enjoyed as undergraduates was indistinguishable from the one to which my brother has gone up in 1913. To us the world was still our oyster.

"Now Buchan was the novelist *par excellence* who described the Britain of 1920–1926, who loved it, but who in all his later novels showed that he knew its weaknesses but hated what he saw taking over the human spirit. And he was right to hate it. The insecurity of your generation, the sense that science is depersonalising man, the mass media with their trivialities, and the whole negative mood of debunking every thing is the background against which you have had to hammer out your ideas. That is the real difference between the generations. But we can meet, thank God, because the background of your growing up has been the foreground of our living.

"For both of us there is a vast insecurity. For both of us there is the faith of Abraham and what is much more important the God of Abraham.

"That said I can still enjoy reading Buchan for he describes something into which I was born. But I don't expect you to enjoy him! But in a curious way James Bond still hangs on to a lot that Buchan valued, tho' superficially he belongs to another world. Buchan and Bond both believed in Dragons and in dealing with them at the risk of one's own life!"

IV
‽

From the earliest days of his Christian experience Max had been a "servant of the Word". He loved the rhythms and cadences of well-ordered sentences: "What a marvellous relaxation it is to read superb English!" (from his diary). Possibly this was in part the result of the childhood days in India when (like Sartre who described his own experience in the book *Words*) he lived more with books than with other boys. When the wonderful words of the Bible became familiar to him he embraced them whole-heartedly, not only because they became a lamp to his feet and a light to his path but also because they satisfied his sense of what was beautiful in literature so completely.

Words, then, were his chief medium of communication, primarily through personal conversation, also through personal correspondence and lastly through written articles and public addresses. At Westminster the flow of articles and essays, often on missionary topics, continued and the series of lectures on missionary history, delivered at Cambridge, appeared in book form. But the new challenge, which the new position at the Abbey presented, was that of preaching regularly to large audiences of people whose origins and interests and concerns were almost entirely indeterminate and unknowable. Hitherto he had preached in churches where residence in a particular area and regular attendance at Sunday worship established common religious outlooks and expectancies. But now the task was to find any common ground linking preacher with hearers, while any continuity of teaching the Christian faith seemed quite impracticable.

Max found this situation very perplexing. He had strong convictions about the importance of preaching. He believed it was the preacher's privilege to communicate the Word of God to all who would listen. But how could this be done when those listening had little or no knowledge either of the text of the Bible or of the world out of which it came? Where could any point of contact be found? And if this was the case with preaching, which allowed room for explanation and interpretation, how much more was it so with the lections, especially when they came from the Old Testament? What sense could a quite heterogeneous collection of people make of a chapter from the Pentateuch or the books of the prophets when they had no idea of its context or of its relatedness to the world of today?

Only rarely did he criticise the sermons to which he listened in the Abbey. Normally he was generous in his appreciation of those who brought new light and encouragement to his own soul. If there was no obvious exposition of biblical truth he was disappointed: he felt that the Bible had a message for every significant human situation. But it was the task of finding a vital connection with the generality of contemporary desires and needs that he found so puzzling. He was meticulous in his preparation of sermons and tireless in his searching of the Scriptures. But how could the Bible and the twentieth-century mind really be brought together?

On September 28, 1969 he preached at Evensong in the Abbey on Revelation 5:1–7. "Folk listened. But I'm sure I'm no preacher for any but those who are already committed Christians. I think I can in one way or another strengthen faith and help some to understand what their faith is meant to be about. But I don't think I register with the fringe folk and, of course, the real unbelievers don't come to Westminster Abbey. I'm not on the wave-length of most people today. I wish I were able to strike it. But I'm sure I do not do so.

"Sometimes I can help folk a bit in face-to-face conversation but not from the pulpit."

Trying to analyse his problem in more detail he wrote:
"I find it difficult to avoid mere exhortation.

"I wish I were better at illustration. I can get people's attention but I can't give them anything they can remember. I can quote from contemporary sources but for the most part my quotations are abstractions which I find congenial and people do not. In this I miss C.M.S. very much for there I was always getting magnificent illustrations."

"Fringe folk" and "Illustrations". Max pinpoints two of the crucial problems in Christian witness today. "Fringe folk" are curious, wistful, searching, but often without knowledge of the Bible and of the Christian tradition. To plunge them straight into the midst of a full liturgical service can have little effect upon them except to awaken a certain feeling of admiration for sound and colour and movement. Ritual may perhaps serve as a *preparatio evangelica* but there is still the problem of communicating the gospel in such a way as to convey some sense of its relation to the ordinary life of today. Increasingly it has come to be realised that no medium is more effective to this end than the *story*, a story of the gospel in action, a story of someone being brought out of darkness into light, out of futility into a life of meaning.

While he was at C.M.S., corresponding with missionaries and reading their reports, Max constantly received fresh stories about the liberating power of the gospel message and used these to good effect, for example in his News-Letters. But although his heart was still in the missionary enterprise and although he retained contact with many missionaries, reports from the field were not coming to him in the same way and he felt himself deprived of those stories of contemporary experience which would have brought the Bible stories more within the range of imagination of the "fringe folk" who flocked to the Abbey services.

He was so dedicated to the ministry of the Word that he willingly gave time and energy to committees and consultations in connection with the establishment of a College of Preachers in England. For a long while such a College in Washington D.C. had served the Episcopal Church through courses designed to improve the quality of preaching amongst its ministers, and the aim in England was to do something of the same kind. But those attending the courses had chiefly to minister to regular church-goers, and improvements in preaching techniques could serve to provide more efficient instruction in the faith already accepted. The problem of the "fringe folk" remained unsolved.

It is more than possible that Max underestimated the effect of his

Abbey sermons. He came to be regarded as a true representative of the prophetic tradition, preaching from the Old Testament more often than his colleagues, looking out upon events in the world and seeking to see in and through them evidences of the activity of the living God, courageously dealing with current issues such as the entry of the Ugandan Asians, race relations, Rhodesia, and Britain's entry into the E.E.C. The deadly peril which he saw to be threatening his fellow countrymen was that of *introversion*, a retreat from the wider world in the hope of preserving fancied privileges. He lived with his Bible and at the same time kept his windows open to the world and its needs. Often he felt discouraged: there seemed to be so little response. But he never lowered his standards. Thorough in preparation, persistent in prayer, unemotional but deeply in earnest in delivery, he fulfilled his appointed preaching assignments to the best of his ability and offered his efforts to God to be sanctified and used by his Holy Spirit.

V

The fact that Max had been relieved of his vast responsibilities at C.M.S. and was now relatively free from prescribed duties except for the months when he was in residence, meant that requests came to him from all sides to preach, to lecture, to serve on commissions or committees, to assist worthy causes in varying ways. Five years after going to Westminster he was begging the C.M.S. Secretary in South Wales to save him from having to refuse yet another request. "I'm completely snowed under with requests. Two others came by the same post as yours. This goes on day after day, everyone assuming I've got nothing to do! So I'm just going on strike. Oddly enough, apart from the Abbey I've got a very heavy programme of writing and lecturing and I just know I've got to draw the line at this kind of request. I hate saying 'no'. The trouble is I've acquired a reputation for being soft-headed and always saying 'yes'. The worm is turning at last."

Such was the situation less than two years after he had suffered a severe thrombosis which put him out of action for several months. It was on February 16, 1967 that he collapsed. Through the ministrations of a devoted doctor that night, the watchful professional nursing by Mary's sister through the succeeding weeks, and the regular attentions later by members of the staff at St. Thomas's

Hospital, he was granted ten more years of astonishing activity with "Brother Ass", as he often referred to his body, often causing him frustration, frequently creating a sense of weakness and exhaustion but, nevertheless, supporting that active mind and buoyant spirit which nothing seemed able, except for very brief periods, to quench. His courage was amazing. Some time in 1968 he found himself coughing up blood one morning. Yet he was due to go to Chislehurst to lecture and off he went to perform his duties before going to the Hospital in the afternoon to ascertain the cause.

Yet the thrombosis had caused him to wonder seriously about the future. "What does God want me still to do?" he asked in his diary. "Be just a vegetable? I pray that when I recover my energy I may be a co-operative vegetable! I do not think the location of Westminster Abbey will allow me to get too isolated from the affairs of mankind." Any prospect of isolation, however, was soon dispelled, seeing that before the end of the year he and Mary were in India delighting in its sights and sounds and above all participating at first hand in the mission of Pat and Roger. And in 1970 there were two more journeys overseas, one to Uganda to address Church leaders, the second to Israel to take part in a significant colloquium on the subject of Religion, Peoplehood, Nation and Land. In spite of his modest disclaimer in his autobiography, Max's paper was an imaginative and discriminating tracing of the theme of *the land* and its significance in the religious traditions of the West. It was a remarkable feat on his part to take up an unfamiliar subject in the presence of a group of distinguished scholars and to make so positive a contribution from the Christian point of view. Since 1970 the question of the land and its symbolism has received increasing attention, and Max's paper can still be regarded as a valuable pioneering effort within this context.

Journeys overseas both before and after the thrombosis kept him in touch with the missionary enterprise which ever remained nearest to his own heart. In addition he devoted special attention to two areas with which he had been closely associated for many years and each of which, during his time at Westminster, was passing through a time of travail. In the Sudan the conflict between North and South entailed severe problems for the indigenous Church while, in Nigeria, the Biafran crisis brought suffering and hardship to multitudes of innocent people. In the former area Bishop Oliver Allison bore the chief responsibility of Christian leadership, and Max kept closely in touch with him, supplying him with information appearing in newspapers and keeping a close watch on attitudes and policies adopted in Whitehall. In Nigeria Archbishop Patterson, facing enormous difficulties, turned to Max for counsel and for practical assistance when his clergy had lost much of their belongings. Though he was no longer at the centre of missionary activity at C.M.S. headquarters, Max was nearer the centre of political manoeuvring at Westminster and, like his hero, the prophet Habbakuk, he tried to be a watchman, relaying to his two episcopal friends the signs of likely developments and giving them every possible support from England as they struggled to encourage and hold together the Christians in their respective areas when antagonisms were tearing their countries apart.

All in all, Max's contribution to the missionary cause during his ten years at Westminster was outstanding. Less the pioneer, he was now the statesman, with years of experience behind him and an unrivalled knowledge of the Christian world. Those concerned with the growing problem of relationships with immigrants in Britain, those involved in the Minority Rights Group, leaders in the missionary societies, bishops intending to speak on world issues in the House of Lords, all sought his advice. Old colleagues from America visiting Britain made their way to 3 Little Cloister and shared with him their continuing concerns. The fictional Professor Moriarty seemed to have taken actual shape at Westminster and quivers of radiation emanating from the Cloister study were felt in a thousand parts of the world.

VI

From what has been said so far it might well be inferred that the canonry at Westminster proved to be the ideal position for Max to occupy after resigning from the General Secretaryship at C.M.S. In many ways it was. In fact it would be hard to think of any other office in the Church of England which would have kept him in such a central position and given him so great freedom to continue his missionary interests. Yet his diaries and family letters reveal what he would never have talked about in public – that in certain respects life at the Abbey brought disappointment and a recurring sense of frustration. These it is clear were due partly to the character of the regular liturgical worship within the Abbey itself, partly to the lack of a closely integrated corporate fellowship amongst those responsible for the Abbey's affairs. It was the former which led him at times to register feelings of complete exasperation.

It was never the case that Max despised or disregarded *order* in worship. At Holy Trinity, Cambridge, he had given the utmost attention to every detail of every service which it was his duty to plan. He had no wish to deviate from the general structure of services authorised by the Book of Common Prayer but he was convinced that there ought to be a coherence and unity in any service if it were to minister effectively to the needs of those present. Hence he selected psalms and hymns and appropriate lessons such as would, he believed, unite with the sermon to form a total offering-and-receiving which would have meaning and relevance for people's lives. He believed, in short, that true *order* could be achieved by wise selection within a given framework rather than by strict adherence to rubrics and calendars. And he believed, furthermore, that every effort must be made to encourage the congregation to enter intelligently into the whole movement of the service.

In contrast, he felt bound to record sadly about so many services in the Abbey that they bore the marks of complete inflexibility and unrelatedness. He saw the multitudes flocking around, with large numbers of them staying for one or other of the daily Services. Then he would find that the Psalms appointed for the day were of inordinate length and often unintelligible without some knowledge of their context. He never forgot that his own installation had been on the fifteenth evening of the month and that this had entailed the singing of Psalm 78 in its entirety. Further, in spite of his love for the Old Testament and of his *penchant* for preaching from it, he was often uneasy in his stall while listening to some lengthy passage being read which he knew conveyed little to the majority of those present.

What he found most trying of all was the fact that an Abbey service was so often indistinguishable from what he called a "sacred concert". He was quite ready to admit that he lacked musical knowledge and musical sensitivity but so, he suspected, did a large proportion of those present at the liturgical services. Did a 10–15 minute anthem, in which the words were in Latin or inaudible, really redound to the glory of God and the edification of the people? Again and again he wrestled with these problems in his daily diaries, often with a light and witty touch but sometimes after the iron had really entered into his soul. For example, after the *Missa Brevis* by Leighton he wrote (with a sigh?): "The sheer cacophony of sound without a single word being distinguishable was the ghastly ordeal I, and many others, had to endure when attending the Sung Eucharist this morning. The enormous sense of relief at the said

184

portions of the service could almost be felt. After the uproar the still small voice. What quaint musical conceit induces organists to produce this ghastly cacophony?"

He tried to sympathise with those who delighted in fine music. "I'm sure the musical folk revelled in it. To me it was anything but an introduction to heaven." And again: "I assume that very musical people derive some sort of inspiration by listening to certain noises made by the human voice. It must be so, otherwise why do choirs exist? However, as long as they do, their efforts provide persons like myself with the opportunity to ponder other things and do so in a setting which has its own peculiar restfulness and inspiration." Long processions, in which members of the Chapter wore excessively heavy copes, were also not entirely to his liking. He never complained publicly and never tried to evade his duties. But he often chafed within the Abbey discipline, most of all because he felt that opportunities were being missed for a relevant presentation of the gospel to the throngs of visitors who were vaguely feeling towards a religious dimension for their lives.

"I stood in for Edward at Evensong and was once again utterly depressed with its irrelevance to the real needs of the congregation. There were about 60 'cubs' present who were, of course, bored to tears. How I wish we could see what the Abbey ought to be doing. It is obvious what it is not doing, but it is much more difficult to see the real role. I for one cannot see clearly what its role is in the field of worship. At the moment it is simply hanging on to a Benedictine tradition by the most tenuous of links but the link is not obviously meeting the needs of today which the Benedictines met in the Middle Ages."

The second major source of disappointment was the absence in the Precincts of that intimate fellowship created by involvement in a common enterprise. This it was which characterised the life of the great company at Salisbury Square. When he had occasion to go over to C.M.S. House, even though it had by now moved to Waterloo Road, he immediately and instinctively felt "at home". For so long he had been united with others in a common task and, though differences arose from time to time on points of detail, there was never any doubt about the common purpose. But at Westminster the Chapter consisted of a group of men, each of whom had gained distinction in some particular area of the Church's life and so was constantly being called upon by agencies outside the Abbey to share the results of his experience with them in some way. The Canons came together in Chapter Meetings, but these were often concerned with unexciting matters relating to the maintenance of the services and fabric of the Abbey. It seemed almost impossible to define some common objective towards the attainment of which all could bend their energies. "I only wish," he wrote in a letter to the Dean in 1967, "that *qua Collegium* we all knew each other better at a deeper level than Chapter meetings and casual encounters and liturgical 'presence'." But how this could be achieved when each member of the Chapter had his own particular interests to pursue (just as Max himself was still deeply involved in the whole missionary enterprise) was hard to envisage.

Life then at the Abbey provided a mixture of intense activity in personal relations, continuing concern about the burning issues such as race and world poverty confronting the C.M.S. as it moved into the 70's, a sense of deep responsibility for the proclamation of the Word to the great Sunday congregations – all this combined with disappointment at the lack of some deep unifying corporate purpose, and periods of depression when he felt that the Abbey services of worship were almost wholly unrelated to the needs of people in the twentieth century. The nearly ten years spent in one of the most fascinating environments of the world brought unnumbered joys and blessings, privileges and opportunities. Yet in 1973 he prepared to lay down his office without regret and with a large measure of relief.

On January 14 these were the opening sentences in his diary. "In these Abbey diaries I have had many occasions in the past to comment with less than enthusiastic approbation on some of the things done and sung here. The more right, then, to record those things about which I have been unaffectedly glad. So I start today with my marks of G R A T I T U D E. They will not follow any order but that in which on the day concerned I have been particularly grateful." With complete regularity over a period of a hundred and forty days, he proceeded to record day by day some aspect of the Abbey itself or of its activities and its personnel for which he was grateful.

These expressions of Gratitude form a remarkable series. They are not forced or artificial but genuine reflections of a sensitive and observant subject. A window seen from his stall in the Sanctuary, the friendliness of the Vergers, the many magnificent sermons he has heard, the flood-lit lace-like tracery of the Henry VII Chapel, the beauty and quietness of the front garden, the pervading sense of history, the dignity of the Abbey ceremonial, the memory of family wedding and christening, the chestnut tree in Dean's Yard, and so on. Many colleagues are named and many happy occasions remembered. It was Max's *Benedicite,* celebrating the works of the

Lord in creation and redemption, in human skills and human friendships. It all had been a wonderful experience but now it was time to go. Happily, a house was awaiting them down in Sussex which they had acquired in 1969 and which they had already come to love. The furniture removers arrived at 3 Little Cloister on June 4 and by June 6 Max and Mary were beginning to straighten themselves out in their new home.

12

The Uniqueness of Christ

I

BEFORE GIVING SOME account of Max's life in "retirement" I shall attempt to summarise his writings about what came to be the central question in his theological thinking: How can we best bear witness to the uniqueness of Christ in a world which has become conscious of its many religious and its many cultural forms?

Max felt the same constraint as the Apostle Paul to proclaim the good news and to relate it directly to the social conditions which were inevitably affecting people's needs and attitudes. His over-mastering concern was to communicate the gospel into what he knew was a rapidly changing world: to continue the apostolic mission in a new age: to evangelise in an increasingly secular environment. It would not, I think, be unfair to say that, whereas in the first half of the period 1942–77 he regarded it as his special task to make people aware of the new world and the new age into which the gospel had now to be proclaimed, in the second half he became more and more concerned about the nature of the gospel itself and its relation to the other faiths of mankind. In the first period the gospel could be virtually taken for granted: the question was what was the world situation to which it could be meaningfully related. In the second period the world situation could be largely taken for granted: the question was what was utterly distinctive about the Christian gospel, and how could this distinctiveness be maintained in the context of a dialogue with those belonging to other faiths or to no religion at all.

In a letter sent early in 1975 to Father F. E. Furey, S.M.A., who had written an academic thesis on *The Theology of Mission in the writings of Max Warren*, Max declared:

> From 1942 to 1963 while I was in office as General Secretary of C.M.S. my major preoccupation was with the political issue of

188

nationalism and the quite certain emergence of independent nations, previously part of the old Colonial world. I was convinced that this development would be far more rapid than was thought possible even by Government authorities. Also I knew well that the Churches in Asia and Africa had benefited enormously by the "umbrella" provided by Colonial Governments which did cherish a liberal ideal more particularly with regard to minorities. The Churches in Asia and Africa, whereever they did grow, owed much to the fact that life and property were safeguarded for minority communities. Now this tradition had lulled the thinking of missionaries *and* of local Church leaders and the rank and file Church membership into a negative attitude to politics. Only rarely did missionaries show active sympathy with the desire for political independence.

My primary task, as I saw it, was to warn them of what was going to happen and to try to prepare them *and* the Churches they served for the very different political climate which would follow independence.

This was an all-absorbing task. It is, I think you will agree, clearly expressed in my News-Letters and in most of my books written during those years. And it explains why, until the end of my period in office, I only gave passing attention to the question of the Christian faith in relation to other faiths.

Later in the letter he went on to say:

A large part of my thinking and writing today deals with the Christian in his relationship with men of other faiths. On that subject I have to take seriously the spiritual experience of those ·whose faith differs from my own . . . So far as my published writing is concerned I have limited myself to trying to get missionaries and others to have a right attitude to other faiths and to those who live by them. On a minute basis I have attempted to give a few of the biblical pointers to this right attitude. In a tentative way, for instance, I have tried to consider the question of idolatry from a biblical sociological standpoint . . . Whether my exegesis can be justified is for scholars to say.

Finally he referred to his continuous correspondence over the previous ten years with his son-in-law, a missionary in India. He had, he said, a distrust of all writing which is done from "Ivory

Towers". To write about other religions it was necessary, as far as possible, to live or to have lived with them. His own interpretation of them was therefore necessarily limited. But this did not prevent him from trying to set forth as clearly as possible his own position in regard to *The Uniqueness of Christ*, while never forgetting to be on the watch for all evidences of God's prevenient grace amongst other peoples of the world.

II

In 1967 he was due to take a leading part in a conference on *Ecumenical Principles and the Christian Encounter with other Faiths* in Israel. Although ill-health prevented him from attending, his four Lectures were read and discussed and made available in duplicated form. In the first of the Lectures he made a statement which is fundamental to an understanding of his particular task as he conceived it during the post-war years.

"It is impossible to deny that, in the past, cultural imperialism pervaded much of the presentation of the Christian gospel." This had led to an "easy-going optimism" which assumed that "the walls of other Jerichos would collapse before the concerted sound of gospel trumpets and the march of missionaries." (One remembers Max's own use of martial metaphors at an earlier stage of his career.) Such an attitude, he affirmed, had survived in many quarters even after World War II. Even those who were unhappy about many features of the colonial past had been shaped by it. Its influence was still to be seen in the structures of the missionary enterprise.

Yet the rise of national consciousness, followed by the growing awareness of economic under-development, had changed the whole situation. This was affecting Christians in former colonial territories. "Whereas in the past, being a Christian, linked by religious affiliation to those in authority, was a source of prestige, this condition has already largely disappeared. [This was written in 1968.] Where being the member of an international society [the Christian Church] and the recipient of substantial foreign aid, strengthened the position of the Christian minority, tomorrow it is more and more likely to make Christians the objects of suspicion. This is already happening."

Even more marked was the effect of the changed conditions upon those in the Third World who had not thus far embraced the

190

Christian faith. The whole psychological atmosphere had changed. Resentment towards former colonial rulers was easily extended to missionaries who were assumed to have been under their protecting care. Nationalism was to become increasingly linked with religion and, in consequence, to change one's religion became tantamount to rejecting one's own national allegiance. As Max wrote after Suez when missionaries had to leave Egypt and Jordan:

> The basic reason why the missionaries had to withdraw was not that they and their work as Christians were obnoxious to the people or the governments of the countries concerned, but that so many of *every* country are completely unable to draw any kind of distinction between religion and nationality.

He then proceeded to comment in a more comprehensive way:

> The proclamation and working out of the gospel has to be in the vernaculars of time and place if its real saving power is to be discovered. The very proof of the universality of the gospel lies in its power to take *local* form everywhere. But to become genuinely local is to become involved in race and nationality and tribe. At the very centre of our task we are confronted with this paradox. It enormously complicates the task of the Christian mission in a world such as our own in which revolutionary political changes are occurring at such a feverish pace and in which, for many, Christianity is still wrapped in the swaddling clothes of the West.

I do not think that any Christian leader in the 50's saw this more clearly than Max did. His phrase "the vernaculars of time and place" is a striking one. He knew that even to become expert in the vernacular language was not enough. There must be, as far as was humanly possible, a sympathetic understanding of the *local* situation and of the *historical* circumstances within which any particular society was living. In consequence he was tireless in gathering information by reading, by travelling, by questioning, by corresponding, by conversing – all with the aim of making those who were in any way concerned with the missionary enterprise aware of the real situation in those parts of the world to which the gospel message was being sent. It was not going into a vacuum nor into a static and uniform social context. Max was determined to do everything in his power to reflect through his writing the "vernaculars" of particular localities as they existed at the time of writing. He was convinced that only on the basis of understanding and humility could any missionary gain entrance to the true vernacular of any people.

In another striking passage, written later in 1968, he spoke of this approach through the medium of a different image:

> Whether the pattern of events in China is going to prevail elsewhere or not, it can be safely assumed that we are going forward into an era in which none of the material or social securities of the past can be assured. As a friend wrote to me recently on this whole subject, both the Church and the individual Christian have got to be prepared for what, he called, a new "nakedness". In the colonial era both Church and individual Christian were "clothed", often inappropriately no doubt, but nevertheless clothed. Perhaps now they have to be "unclothed", both for their own salvation and future resurrection and also for their equipment for mission.

The image is obviously too extreme: no missionary can go into a new situation completely stripped of his history, his language, his culture. But Max's point, again and again, was that he must be stripped of all attitudes of superiority and privilege. He often referred to the terrible resentment of the coloured races towards the evidences of *contempt* which they discerned even in the white man's eyes.

> The peoples of Asia and Africa are distinguished from those of the West not only by the pigmentation of their skins but also by their relative poverty. Both distinctions help to explain the emotional drive of resentment, of mounting racialism, which is at bottom a revolt against that attitude of contempt which has been the traditional attitude of the "White" world to the world of "Colour".

Psalm 123:3 and 4, perfectly expresses this mood:

> Have mercy upon us, O Lord, have
>   mercy upon us,
>   for we have had more than
>   enough of contempt.
> Too long our soul has been sated
>   with the scorn of those who are
>   at ease,
>   the contempt of the proud.
>   (RSV)

192

This sense of being sated with scorn and contempt . . . has had as one of its results a resurgence of the other religions of mankind, a resurgence often explicitly directed against Christianity. For Christianity has been commonly identified with the West, with Western imperialism, with Western domination. In Asia and Africa, for many, their ancient religions have been found to provide a cement for their traditional culture, their race-consciousness and even their nationhood.

So, in News-Letter after News-Letter, in booklets and letters and interviews, he steadfastly pursued his aim of bringing the missionary movement face to face with the realities of the second half of the twentieth century. He did not in the least denigrate the achievements of those who had laboured so magnificently in the first hundred and fifty years of the Society's history. But he knew that a major crisis, a turning point, had come. He knew that it was desperately hard to change patterns of thought and behaviour which characterised so many of the loyal and worthy members of the Society. Yet, like his hero Habakkuk, he must be faithful to his calling and mount to the top of his watch-tower and give an honest report concerning what he saw. The Mission, the sending of the missionary with the message, must continue. But the missionary must know the kind of social environment into which he or she would inevitably be plunged, and the supporters at home could pray the more earnestly if they had some idea of the difficulties from which there would be no escape.

III

During his term of office as General Secretary, then, Max did everything in his power to make members of the Christian Church, and in particular those who felt a deep concern for the Church's Mission, aware of the revolutionary movements which were taking place in the post World War II world. He believed that only in the light of such an awareness could missionary policies be framed and the central task of evangelism performed. But another more serious problem was looming up. With the casting off of the old colonial dependencies and the rise of independent nations and the development of national self-consciousness, were there not signs of a determined repudiation of the Christian gospel as part of the Western culture from which the new nations wanted to be emancipated? Did not the peoples of Asia and Africa possess their own ancestral religions which were part and parcel of their cultural heritages? On what grounds could it be claimed that the Christian gospel had a universal relevance? Why could not Islam, for example, become the national religion of the newly independent Pakistan? Or why, indeed, need there be a religion at all? Were not the words of Chairman Mao sufficient for the moral and social needs of China?

From the early 1950's onwards Max's News-Letters reveal an increasing awareness of the renaissance of the non-Christian religions, and this led him in turn to concentrate his attention more and more upon the relationship between Christianity and other world religions. What claim had the Christian gospel to be a *universal* gospel? Was it still possible to proclaim the *uniqueness* of Christ? If so, how could this proclamation be made to those who were apparently entirely satisfied with their own religious affiliations? And what was to be said about the place of non-Christian religions within the eternal purpose of God? Could it be denied that his activity was universal, and that in some way therefore his Spirit had been and still was prompting all religious aspirations? Such questions as these were never far from Max's mind in the last twenty years of his life. It could perhaps be said that the awareness of the renaissance grew through the 1950's, and that from about 1960 he poured everything that he had into studying the theological justification for the Christian mission; to re-assuring those engaged in the mission about the validity and urgency of their work; and to exploring the implications of *dialogue* which now, as never before, seemed to be the way of approach to those belonging to other faiths.

As long ago as April 1953 Max's News-Letter was entitled *The World of Islam*. In it he spoke of "the spectacular advance of Islam" in Africa: of the new Muslim state in Pakistan: of the reaction of the world of Islam to the threat from the West, politically, economically and culturally. "Are we then," he asked, "to view the ferment of the world of Islam as a great revival of religion?" During the next six years he devoted five more of his News-Letters to further enquiries about the Islamic revival and its significance for the Christian mission. In addition he wrote Letters on *Missionary Hinduism*, on *Buddhism on the March*, and on the advance of paganism in Africa under the striking title, *Great Pan is not Dead*. In the letter on Hinduism he quoted words of Professor Radhakrishnan: "The Hindu religious revival is partly the result of Western research, partly reaction against Western domination and partly the revolt against Christian missionary propaganda." In that on Buddhism he stressed the importance of the sixth Buddhist Council in 1956 as an attempt "to revitalise Buddhism and to prepare for its growth and expansion throughout the whole world". In speaking of paganism, he dwelt upon the immense power of the emotions in African life and the consequent appeal to witchcraft and to the imagined powers of the spirit world. Finally, in a comprehensive Letter in November 1959, he tried first to give a series of possible explanations of the indisputable fact that a renaissance of non-Christian religions was taking place, and secondly to draw out some of the most important implications for the missionary outreach of the Christian Church.

Explanations in terms of national "cement" and the assertion of cultural value he developed more fully than before, and to these he added a suggestive new factor – the search for psychic security. "Our generation has seen the sweeping away of countless landmarks by which men have tracked their way across the wilderness of human life. Slowly we are accustoming ourselves to the startling fact that our physical universe possesses no known margins . . . A vast insecurity envelops us . . . In such circumstances the souls of men draw upon the deep wells of the past for their psychic security, or go mad. Here is one vital reason behind the present renaissance of the non-Christian religions. They represent for the ordinary man the reservoir of his people's past history, past security. In the crisis of our times he turns back to the old gods, either with an uncalculating devotion, or with not unreasonable faith, or even with the sceptical cynicism of a man who tries to cover his bets. There are plenty of examples of all three of these reactions in our contemporary world in the renaissance of the non-Christian religions *and*, if we are honest, in the renaissance of Christianity as well. Whatever the motives of the return to religion, and commonly these are mixed, there is no doubt but that in the return something does happen, and there is a recovered sense of assurance – at least for a time. We are living through the time of this re-awakened assurance. How long it will last we do not know. There are enemies at the gate. There are forces at work in our world which aim to change human nature radically and claim that they can do so, changing it for servitude not for freedom. We do well to be aware of our enemies. Yet we also do well to remember that we are living through the time of renaissance and it has certain things to say to us in the actual NOW of our responsibility."

Max was vividly aware of the powerful revivals of zealous devotion amongst the adherents of the ancient religions and he shared with Dr. Hendrik Kraemer the conviction that for the first time since the victory of Constantine in A.D. 312, the Christian Church was heading towards a real and spiritual encounter with these religions. Words written by Dr. Kraemer are set in the forefront of his own deeply-felt message.

"Not only because the so-called younger Churches, the fruits of the work of modern missions, live in the midst of them, but also because the fast growing interdependence of the whole world forces the existence and vitality of these religions upon us, and makes them a challenge to the Church to manifest in new terms its spiritual and intellectual integrity and value" – for these reasons encounter was now inevitable.

IV

In his writings Max often pointed out that no *religion* could encounter another: encounter is between *persons* and this meant that his dominant concern was to know how best the Christian missionary can today approach the devotee of another faith, and in what form the Christian gospel can then best be presented. He never wavered in his determination to follow the apostle Paul in setting forth "Jesus Christ and Him crucified". But to the very end he continued to wrestle with the problem of how this could be done when meeting a man of another religion and culture and history and language and general attitude to life. In thought and in prayer he pursued his missionary vocation, hoping that by the mercy of God some might thereby be brought into the fulness of Christ.

As he continued to think and write and preach after his retirement from the General Secretaryship, he formed certain major convictions which he expressed in varying ways according to the demands of any particular occasion. First and foremost, his mind and imagination dwelt upon the wonder of the *prevenience* of God. In a notable lecture at Westminster Abbey in March 1966, for example, when his topic was *The Relationship between Christianity and other World Religions* he declared:

"Paul the missionary was never in the slightest doubt that however much God had called him to be a missionary, God had always arrived in every situation before Paul got there. Paul's task,

196

the essential missionary task of the Church in all ages, is to unveil the God who is already there."

Nearly three years earlier he was given the high responsibility of delivering the opening address at the Anglican Congress in Toronto. His theme was *The Church's Mission to the World – On the Religious Frontier*. By common consent his was one of the great utterances of the Congress and its effect is still remembered amongst those who were present. I doubt if he ever expressed his conviction about the prevenience of God more dramatically. Beginning with man's religious quest through the long ages of the past, he went on to insist that this quest was not man's initiative but rather his response to the divine initiative.

"At this start of our deliberations let us put ourselves humbly under that affirmation – 'in the beginning God'. In the beginning of every religious experience, in every one of mankind's religions – God! In the beginning of every political change and of every political revolution – God! In the beginning of all culture, and of every mutation of culture – God! In all our action, in all our organisation for action – in its beginning, God! And, with due humility we believe that God was in the beginning of the Anglican Communion, whatever the date at which we place that beginning. Only let us in these coming days beware of the subtle temptation which so easily pervades all Anglican gatherings, the temptation to believe that in the beginning was the Anglican Communion, with the tacit assumption that in the *eschaton* all will be in the Anglican Communion.

"No, in the beginning, God. In the end, God. And, surely we have to learn to say – 'in the middle, God. In the centre, at the heart of things, God'.

"But if to speak of man's quest is not to deny God's initiative, still less is it to call in question the reality of that continuing divine initiative which we call revelation. God has revealed Himself in divers manners. We should be bold to insist that God was speaking in that cave in the hills outside Mecca, that God brought illumination to the man who once sat under the Bo tree; that the insight into the reality of the moral struggle and of man's freedom to choose the right, which was given to Zoroaster, came from God; that it was God who spoke to a simple Japanese peasant woman, a hundred years ago, of sin, of righteousness, and of judgment, and that God is at work among the four million Japanese who follow her teaching; that, indeed, the God of a hundred names is still God. Thus boldly to insist is in no way whatever to hesitate in affirming, what we believe, that in a quite unique way He revealed Himself in

197

Jesus Christ our Lord. I wish I knew how best to insist on that uniqueness. Perhaps I must content myself with the *Incarnatus* of our Creed and say simply that once upon a time the Word was made flesh at Bethlehem."

Towards the end of this statement the word *uniqueness* occurs and this was the term to which over the next period of years he constantly returned in lectures and articles when speaking of the revelation in Christ (though at the last he inclined to substitute "distinctive" for unique). He set to work to edit a series of books entitled the *Christian Presence* series. The *presence* of Christ, even in lands where Islam or Buddhism or Hinduism were the outwardly acknowledged faiths – this was his second emphasis. In one of the most influential books of this series, *The Primal Vision*, John Taylor described the missionary encounter as "a meeting of three, in which Christ has drawn together the witness who proclaims him and the other who does not know his name, so that in their slow discovery of one another each may discover more of Him" (pp. 26f).

The third emphasis, which proved to be a distinctive note of Max's writings in his later years, was upon "that common humanity which we share with all mankind". He was convinced that, in spite of national and racial conflicts, there had come into existence in this century such a sense of man as a universal creature that it could be called one of the great emotional discoveries of our time. Modern communications had done much to bring this about: the movements of peoples as a result of two world wars: the impact of modern psychology (he was particularly impressed by Jung's theory of the "collective unconscious"): the explorations of social anthropologists and the researches of historians of religions (he was an eager student of the writings of Mircea Eliade) – all these had helped to make us aware of our common heritage and of our common humanity. "Today we, of every race and culture, meet each other on the level as, with sadly rare exceptions, men and women have never done before."

What then are the implications of this recognition? If there is a common humanity and if God has not left himself without witness in any section of this humanity, no man dare approach his neighbour with any attitude of superiority or self-sufficiency; he goes to *listen* to his neighbour and, if possible, to *learn* from him how God has already been active in his life. Moreover, if God's central activity towards mankind is that of reconciliation and if that reconciling activity was supremely disclosed through Christ, then it follows that there are marks or vestiges of Christ's work of reconciliation even amongst peoples who have never heard the Christian Gospel.

In making such an affirmation Max recognised that he was treading on dangerous ground and was likely to cause unease amongst many devoted followers of Christ. Did not this way of thinking open the door to certain forms of idolatry, to an approval of syncretism, to a vague theology of universalism? Some of his most interesting writings of this later period are devoted to a careful examination of these possible dangers in the light of the Biblical evidence. He recognised how fiercely his heroes, the Old Testament prophets, denounced idolatry. Yet in the main these denunciations were addressed to the *covenant* people, those who had been chosen by God. They had come to know something of the judgment and grace of God and then had defected, transferring their allegiance to gods of wood and stone. But what of the peoples outside the Covenant? Had their worship in ignorance, and often out of a deep yearning, been totally unacceptable to God? Max wrestled with Paul's words, recorded as having been spoken on his missionary travels in Lystra and Athens (Acts 14:16–17 and 17–30). What was the meaning of the phrases, "God overlooked" and "God allowed"? At least they must mean that God did not crush and repudiate those stretchings out towards reality, those dim recognitions of mystery, those attempts to worship through focussing attention upon visible objects, which have characterised other religions of the world.

If, however, "God allowed" the nations to walk in their own ways, what were the implications of this for the whole concept of the Covenant, so central in Old Testament theology? To answer this question he wrestled with the early chapters of the Epistle to the Romans. Though Jesus himself made a new covenant with his disciples and thereby fulfilled the old covenant, he himself transcends the covenant and in his total reconciling work relates himself to those outside the Covenant. Truly he is the *cosmic* Christ. (And this was his fourth emphasis) he is the judge of the human heart everywhere seeing that he is the "proper Man". He is the saviour of mankind everywhere seeing that "Through him God chose to reconcile the whole universe to himself, making peace through the shedding of his blood upon the Cross."

Max never gave a full systematic exposition of the thinking which became the vital inspiration of his missionary outreach in this late period of his life. He rejected any form of *syncretism*, which he defined (following the Oxford Dictionary) as an 'attempt to combine different or opposing tenets or systems'. In other words he made no attempt to combine Hebrew monotheism with Hindu monism, or the concept of *nirvana* with that of eternal life: but he wanted instead to *synthesise*, "to put together or combine into a complex whole" by concentrating upon "universals of spiritual experience" rather than upon formulated doctrines. These universals are "synthesised" as we attribute them to "the same source – God, the God we have seen revealed to us in Jesus Christ".

The fifth emphasis was upon the nature of the missionary's approach to those of other faiths, an approach which Max described increasingly in terms of *dialogue* rather than of preaching. There can be no doubt that Kenneth Cragg's book *The Call of the Minaret*, published in 1956, made an indelible impression upon Max's whole philosophy of mission. In 1966 he described it as "that great Christian classic". When it first appeared he devoted a whole issue of a News-Letter (March 1957) to expounding its main themes. Again and again he acknowledged that Kenneth Cragg had been his teacher and had led him to explore in a new way the relationship of the Christian missionary to those of other faiths.

In point of fact he had himself written the striking News-Letter in 1955 on the Christian approach to Islam, in which he pleaded for *real* meeting, an overcoming of ignorance and suspicion, legacies of the past, and the establishment of a new atmosphere of trust. He defined the way as one of sympathy, of humility, of service, of understanding, and of personal friendship. The call in Kenneth Cragg's book was not very different. It was for understanding, for interpretation, for patience, and for service. Somehow, however, Max felt that *The Call of the Minaret* had set out in a more comprehensive fashion, and out of a deeper knowledge of Islam and its language, that which had already been stirring in his own imagination. To explore more fully the way of personal respect and friendship, of listening and sharing, of interpreting and understanding, became his dominant concern. It was based on his theological conviction that it is the Spirit of God who is ever preparing the way and making real dialogue possible and that, within the context of a common humanity, each partner in the dialogue can assist the other to a fuller apprehension of the reconciling work of the cosmic Christ. Indeed the ways of dialogue and encounter could be viewed as the external expression of that spirit of reconciliation which was the living heart-beat of the Christian gospel.

In his important Letter on the renaissance of the non-Christian religions, written in 1959, he summarised the implications for the Christian Church as demanding understanding, service, retrieval (in the sense of redeeming the tragedy of past mistakes), interpretation, and finally, patience. Christ must be proclaimed but "proclamation takes many forms and often a very long time. For as Cragg reminds us and perhaps we need the reminder – 'The purpose of the Christian Mission is not cultural displacement. It is the presentation of Christ as Saviour within every culture . . . conversion is not *migration*, it is the personal discovery of the meaning of the universal Christ within the old framework of race, language and religion'. The Christian mission in a word is an organic process intimately related to the whole organic life of man and the whole organic purpose of God with whom one day is as a thousand years and a thousand years as one day."

V

Max entered with enthusiasm into the task of drawing out the implications, theoretical and practical, of the new concept of Dialogue. The sense of commission to *go* was as strong as ever: to cross frontiers and sit with those of another race or culture or religion, sharing experiences and ideas and worth-while activities and thereby establishing mutual trust and confidence. But there was a deepening sense now of the need to respect others and to learn from them: to seek to present Christ as the fulfilment of their common humanity and the reconciler of their natural alienations. And what Max was speaking about and writing about he was actually engaged in doing, vicariously, by sharing in every way possible the mission of his daughter and son-in-law as they carried on their dialogical mission in the city and university of Varanasi in North India.

All this gave immense zest to his continuing obedience to mission after his official leadership of C.M.S. came to an end. But there was one haunting question which was obviously troubling many missionaries as they tried to adjust to the new world situation and to enter with sympathy into the traditions and outlooks of devotees of other religions. It was: How far can we any longer speak of the *uniqueness* of Christ? Are all religions to be regarded as paths up the mountainside leading to the same God at the summit? Or is there just one path by which all must travel if they hope to reach the top? These alternative images seem definite and easy to grasp. But what happens to the traditional Christian confession of Jesus as the unique revelation of God's saving activity if the belief be held that, through other religious systems, revelations of God's saving activity have also been disclosed? Max wrestled with these questions not only for the clarification of his own mind, but also out of a sense of

201

deep responsibility towards those who might find his attitude to non-Christian religions puzzling and even offensive.

In 1968 he was invited to address a conference of missionaries on leave, and chose to speak on the question which had become urgent in their minds. Characteristically, he selected passages of Scripture as the basis of meditation, and then considered the uniqueness of Christ under four headings:

1. As a revelation of the nature of God.
2. As a revelation of man as he is meant to be.
3. As a revelation of what man is.
4. As a revelation of God's trust in man.

He spoke eloquently of Jesus' revelation of God as holy love, of man as meant to be free from anxiety and fear, of sin in man causing Jesus' suffering and death, of the gracious trust by which God transforms weak men into agents of his Kingdom. The addresses conveyed the speaker's deep devotion to Christ and his sense of utter indebtedness to him. But they made no mention of other religious teachers or of the spiritual experiences of adherents of other faiths. The theological question still remained open.

Five years later, however, he was asked to prepare a memorandum for a Working Party of the British Council of Churches on the crucial question of uniqueness and this was subsequently published in *The Modern Churchman*, during 1975. In my judgment this is one of the finest articles he ever wrote. After an introduction in which he portrayed an Anatolian Turk, a devout Muslim, coming to work in a factory in Munich and trying to maintain his religious practices there, "a man of faith, another Faith than my own", he went on to show how, from the age of Constantine onwards, an attitude of "triumphalism" had existed in the Christian Church, and how that attitude had been all too often present in missionary work during the past three hundred years. But the death and resurrection of Jesus did not immediately settle all human issues nor could the significance of that death and resurrection be embalmed in a static formula. The mystery of death as the gateway to new life has been frequently perceived, however dimly, by those belonging to other religions. The uniqueness of Christ consists in the fact that what has been felt after, and even implicitly believed in other systems, has been explicitly demonstrated in his Cross and resurrection.

Further, Jesus' own intimacy of communion as son with Father is distinctive. If to be saved is to know God with a confidence such as a son experiences with his father, then there is no other Saviour than

202

Jesus Christ. From within humanity the "proper man" appeared, who both fulfilled the promise of past ages, and opened up the future for all whose faith came to be centred on him. Forgiveness for the past and hope for the future are alike available to those who ground their faith upon the life and death and resurrection of Jesus the Christ.

At this point Max joined issue with John Hick, the author of *God and the Universe of Faiths*, who in that book had called for a Copernican revolution to establish God, rather than Christianity, at the centre of this universe. Max expressed his readiness to accept the need for a revolution, but only of such a character as to place at the centre not a theological term "God" but *an historical person Jesus in whom God is to be recognised as uniquely revealed* (my italics). He registered doubts about Hick's use of non-personal language in relation to God and about his seemingly too static view of the universe. He concluded his article with some striking sentences which are worthy of quotation:

"The mission of the Christian is not to take Christ to some place from which he is absent but to go into all the world and discover Christ there, and, in a Christly way, there to uncover the unknown Christ. The uncovering will be as much of a surprise to the Christian as to the Hindu or the Muslim or the Buddhist. There is no question of presumption in 'going into all the world' on this quest. If you have knelt at Bethlehem, received the Bread and Wine in the Upper Room, faced the Cross, as far as possible, in its squalor and its glory and have walked the Emmaus road – you must go. In the unique experience of this going you prove in your own experience the uniqueness of Christ."

Professor Hick was invited to comment on the article and in doing so expressed his appreciation of its "constructive and sensitive" character. But not surprisingly he concentrated his criticism on what he felt to be its most vulnerable point – the attempt to frame a universe revolving around a centre simply defined as "an historical person, Jesus". In a letter thanking Hick for his criticism, Max tried to make his meaning clearer. (This letter seems to me so important that it is printed in full as Appendix II, p. 239.) I believe that Max made a most important point in the debate in stressing the need to include the model of *historical movement* when attempting to describe the universe, whether in the case of the universe of our ordinary experience or in the case of the universe of faiths. At the same time, his very enthusiasm for history exposed him to the danger of trying to deduce more from historical studies than they could legitimately provide.

He continued to wrestle with the problem during his remaining years. Significantly the last paper that he was able to give in public was to a group of clergy in Norwich in October 1976 when he addressed them on *The Uniqueness of Christ*. In this I do not think he added anything substantial to his previous writings on the subject though he did not simply repeat himself but drew upon his most recent reading of books – in particular Professor C. F. D. Moule's *The Origin of Christology* and Professor J. A. Cuttat's *The Encounter of Religions*. The invigorating *tension* which had played so large a part in his life and thought, was never allowed to slacken. The distinctiveness, and yet at the same time the inclusiveness of Christ: the Christ to be proclaimed, and yet the Christ already present: the missionary with a message, and yet also the humble listener to what the other man had to contribute: the theologian of the world's faiths, and at the same time the ardent evangelist who never forgot his calling to be a "fisher of men" through friendship and personal encounter: he lived within the tension and yet few men have appeared less tense in his daily life, for that life was "hid with Christ in God".

13

The Sage of "Waymarks"

THE TITLE OF this chapter I owe to Edward Carpenter, Max's colleague on the Chapter, who was later to become Dean of Westminster. Sending greetings for the year 1974 Edward wrote: "What precisely the world will be like in January 1975 is anybody's guess, but I think history teaches us, however minimally, that human nature is pretty tough and resilient, and seems to have remarkable powers of surviving its own stupidity. Here is a theme which I am sure the sage of Waymarks can alone handle! You may have heard that he was quoted by E.S.A. [E. S. Abbott, the Dean] to great effect in the latter's Christmas sermon."

Waymarks was the name chosen by Max and Mary for the house near Eastbourne which was to become, like 3 Little Cloister, a centre of attraction for people from all parts of the world. Visitors were not quite so numerous (161 in 1976) but Mary organised what was virtually a taxi-service, ferrying folks to and from Eastbourne Station and providing her usual hospitality in the much smaller home. "Waymarks" was derived from the Revised Standard Version of Jeremiah 31:21: "Set up waymarks for yourself, make yourself guideposts, consider well the highway, the road by which you went."

Westminster, as Max often affirmed, was a most wonderful place in which to be. Yet "what a boon this cottage is going to be to us all – a place to call a home where we shall be as little disturbed as we want to be" [written in 1969]. So, for rather more than four years he and Mary enjoyed one another's company, entertained Rosemary and Greg with their children on their regular visits from London (Max and Mary were deeply interested in the parents' commitment to mission on behalf of handicapped children), rejoiced in the near presence of Pat, Roger and their children when they were on furlough in 1974, and worshipped in the small churches of the Sussex Downs instead of in the great Abbey.

Max chose for his study an upstairs room, reasonably capacious, with windows looking out northwards and southwards. Many of his books had been disposed of but quite enough were left to fill the cases which lined the walls and gave him the miniature reference-library which he still needed. From now on this was to be his base of operations. He liked to take short walks and to go in the car to Eastbourne or to neighbouring villages from time to time. But he did not any longer attempt to go far afield and only rarely went up to London. His physical capacities were already limited and tended to diminish and he adjusted the pattern of his life accordingly. Yet nothing could damp the ardour of his enquiring mind or halt the pen which continued to register the wise thoughts of one who could deservedly be called *The Sage*.

However exhausted he might feel, he somehow managed to write his daily diary up to the last day before he was finally taken to hospital. He had an extraordinary facility for writing just the right amount to fill the substantial page allotted to each day. (Between 300 and 400 words.) It was an exercise which he enjoyed and which, as a trained historian, he felt to be of real importance. When it came to the writing of his own autobiography he discovered how much his task was lightened by being able to refer constantly to his travel diaries. So in a letter to his son-in-law he exhorted him to "Keep the diary going. You will never regret it. And it is the only way in which impressions can be held and preserved." He admitted that in his diaries he expressed his feelings "at the moment" and not "in perspective". "I'm Irish in my reactions which are always immediate and generally have to be repented. I could be no sort of use as a missionary in a Hindu setting and I think the good Lord saw that I'd have been a disaster in the world of Islam. So he removed me!" It is however just the immediate and vivid reactions contained in the diaries which make them such fascinating reading. And rarely a day passed without some shaft of wit (a clever turn of speech, a lively metaphor) reflecting on the written page the twinkle that was seldom absent from his eye.

There is a revealing page written less than two months after he and Mary had settled in at Waymarks. It begins with a note of "shame" because for once he had failed to write up the diary at the end of the previous day. "With me to pass from one day to another is to relegate the previous day to oblivion." Yet he remembered that he had read passages from his travel diaries and had tried to fit them in to the pattern of his autobiography, on the writing of which he was then engaged. Then comes this revealing passage:

"Each day I'm having a short 'quiet time' between 6.0 and 7.0

p.m. which I spend in the bedroom looking out through the window which gives a view of the sea. It is a rather lovely picture window. Sitting back a bit, one sees a rooftop of our neighbour but then only a few homes in the distance, a brief glimpse of East Dean Church, and the trees. Then in the distance fields with cows. The Downs run down to meet each other, one tree-covered, one bare. But there is a fine stretch of sea and even if there is a mist one knows the sea is there. I'm coming to love this little bit of quiet, which helps to give the day a pattern.

"In the evening, after supper, I finished the book on Coleridge. It was pretty heavy going but I'm glad I read it. It has given me one key quotation for the Ecumenical Chapter in the book. What a strange natural genius the man was. But he seems to have been a really seminal thinker. I did not think the author of the Study had really given us the man in the round. His impact on theology was far greater than emerges from the book. His essay on 'Church and State' was especially important and is still very relevant."

II

The reference to the book on Coleridge leads me naturally to comment on one aspect of Max's life which I find completely astonishing. It was his ability to *devour* books. Correspondence far larger than any ordinary person would contemplate; the writing of books, essays, memoranda, diaries; the reading of *The Times*, *The Economist*, theological and other journals; and still time to read innumerable books and that with only one eye! Back at Linford, the surgeon had told Mary that Nature had so ordained it, that the power of the removed eye is transferred to the remaining unaffected one. Whether or not this is generally the case, in fact Max had much better sight than Mary both for distance and for reading. He not only raced through book after book, but also wrote down lengthy quotations from them for future use and retained in his mind the major themes of any particular volume. Often he wrote a précis in his diary. To any author who had sent him a copy of his latest writing he would reply in appreciation or occasional questioning but always with obvious attention to its contents. How he found time for all this remains a mystery.

At Waymarks he could read with less disturbance than had ever been the case since the three years of enforced seclusion after his breakdown in Nigeria in 1928. He tried to keep abreast of developments in biblical and theological studies: he sustained his enthusiasm for history: he loved biographies and memoirs: he relaxed with novels and travel-books. On one day for example we discover him struggling with a book of essays on the Message of the Resurrection, one of which entirely baffled him. "It seems to be one vast playing with words and quite detached from commonsense and probability." From this he turns to the *Memoirs* of George Kennan, "probably the ablest American diplomat of this century, perhaps the ablest of any country. It is superbly written". On another day he begins with Reports on "Colour and Citizenship" and on "Community Relations", continues with David Anderson's *The Tragic Protest*, a book on religion and literature, and ends the day with John Baillie's *And the Life Everlasting*. Max comments: "How particularly valuable to read a number of books at the same time, each illuminating the other – the real way to read."

Such an illumination he found on another day when, having finished Gordon Haight's biography of *George Eliot* in the morning, he turned to George A. Panichas's *Promise of Greatness: The 1914– 18 War* in the evening. The latter, he wrote, was "a bit of history which really has made us today. George Eliot belongs across the great divide". Yet the contribution of her novels to the understanding of nineteenth-century evangelicalism and the sudden retreat from faith amongst intellectuals fascinated him. It could throw light on his study of Henry Venn. He determined to pursue the matter further.

Reading was a duty, a pleasure, in some senses a hobby. At one point in his diary he regrets that he has no hobby except reading. Stamps? His fine collection gave him real relaxation. But, as he reflected, the trouble with a large stamp album is that you cannot carry it around from place to place. So, for recreation, reading remained his first priority. When only six weeks before he died he was asked by an old friend living in Eastbourne to come one evening to help a group discussing certain books, he had to decline, partly because of his commitments to writing and reviewing, partly because of his not having read any of the books under consideration. "My reading has taken me along a very different line of country. I just haven't got the time or physical energy to launch into what I do not doubt is a most rewarding field. The snag is that so many fields are rewarding!! I am asking the Lord to arrange for the Bodleian and the Cambridge University Library to be transferred to heaven about the time of my departure so that I can start some serious reading before being asked to do anything else!" Max had no great interest in heavenly choirs. But to read without the restrictions of time and place – that indeed would be bliss.

III

Much of his reading over the years had been concerned with politics, in the history of his own people and in the constitutional developments of the new independent nations. At Waymarks, by the help of newspapers, journals and the media, he continued his lively interest in the political scene and made many wise – and caustic – comments in his diary on leaders and their policies. There is no doubt about where his real sympathies lay: it was with the Liberal Party. But he felt that in the Eastbourne area, he was in "the *Daily Telegraph* belt" and that it would be difficult, considering his physical resources, to make any worth-while contribution to political activity. He deplored the apathy, blindness and resort to expediency on the part of both of the major political parties and at one point, while at Westminster, exploded with the comment: "Surely this is the most pathetic government that has ruled England in this century!"

In March 1973 we find him indignant at the Tories on the one side, for their failure to grapple with land values and with racketeering over development areas, and at the Trade Unions on the other side, for their refusal of the secret ballot and their perpetual insistence on differentials without real care for the underprivileged. He then makes the shrewd point that "the real tragedy of this country is the almost total failure of the State Education to instil an element of economic common sense into the heads of those at school. Everything today seems to be designed to make things easy and to suggest that the world owes us a living."

In July of the same year there came the exciting news of the victory of the Liberals at two bye-elections. "Oh if only this Liberal revival", he exclaims, "could sweep the Conservative party and the Labour party into the dust-bin. Then, purged, they can come back with their souls cleaned of political clap-trap and ideological nonsense." He admits that this may be asking for the moon but "what a lift to the spirit this kind of political news gives me even though it has little bearing on the grim economic situation. I wish I understood the economic language in which everyone talks and which I sometimes suspect few of the talkers themselves understand. What, however, is really serious is that as long as the Watergate affair goes on there can be no responsible leadership of any kind from the U.S.A. As they appear to be the cause of half the economic trouble, there is no prospect of an easing of the situation till Nixon gets out of his scrape he is in or is ceremoniously sacked. We live in exciting times."

Max was a fervent patriot but also a stern critic of many of his country's policies, just as he was a convinced Anglican but critical of many aspects of the life of the Church of England. What he could not abide, in State or in Church, were any attitudes of *hubris*, of complacency, of introversion, of blind conservatism. He did not minimise the high ideals and fine achievements in Britain's imperial past but he saw how radically the world had changed in the twentieth century and that any attempt to cling to the past was futile. He gloried, too, in the riches of the Anglican tradition, but saw no hope for the Anglican Communion if it tried to remain a self-contained island within the on-going ecumenical and liturgical and theological movements of our time. He regarded cries for disestablishment, and for change in the manner of appointing bishops, as irrelevant to the main challenges facing Christians in the world today. His ideal was that of Church and Nation striving together in every way possible to promote the welfare of mankind. *People matter* was a guiding principle, and it was doubtful whether the election of bishops by some kind of popular vote would bring much benefit to the wider world.

At times he was deeply despondent about the future. A book in the great Liberal tradition to which he responded instinctively was Charles Morgan's *Liberties of the Mind*. It was the enclosure of *the mind*, the ghetto mentality, that he feared most of all. "Once again so it seems to me," he wrote in 1973, "it is 5 minutes to 12 but with a take-over of the human mind, rather than World War III as the real probability. And things are far farther advanced in Britain than we yet fully recognise." In face of this situation he felt "utterly paralysed". "I know that God for his own purpose withdraws from sight, allows us to think of Him as *Deus Absconditus*, but this faith does not make endurance as 'seeing him who is invisible' any easier. These days one just has to hold to one's deep conviction of the ultimate rationality of things which derives from the Reason that is *Sancta Sophia*. This and the fact of Jesus and the lives of holy men and women keeps one going on." The threat of irrationalism, of mind-control by other humans, of denial of freedom to read and think and make personal judgments, this, to Max, was the direst threat of all.

On international affairs he was probably one of the best informed men in Britain. He had his "ambassadors" in Asia, Africa and North America with whom he was in constant touch. They were men and women living amongst ordinary people and sensitive to their moods and aspirations. He had also travelled far and wide and taken particular care to record first-hand observations. Occasionally those in authority in London paid some attention to his views but it is hard not to feel that far more use could have been made of his sympathetic understanding of the new nation-states and of their likely developments in the future.

IV

Only a little less pleasant than reading was writing. The postman at East Dean must soon have learned that since the Warrens' arrival his labours had increased substantially. What Max called the unceasing flow of correspondence continued without a break, one morning bringing "a huge mail" and another morning spent almost entirely replying. The letters came from all over the world and each one was given proper attention and a considered answer. One who had spent only two and a half years as a missionary of the C.M.S. yet received from him letters relating first to her vocation and then to her marriage, clear evidence as she put it of "Max's care and love for the little person". Similarly a young incumbent, whose Parish Magazine Max had seen, received a note from him commenting on his "magnificent" letter entitled *People Matter*. "You deal faithfully with what is perhaps the most difficult of all the problems facing a parish priest, outside himself. We remain our own chief headaches to the end! But I've been where you are over this business of time for individuals." And finally: "Please accept this letter as what it is, a grateful sharing in your ministry even if at long range and very indirectly." This was written in March 1977 at a time when, as he wrote to another friend in the following month:

"Having only about three-fifths of my lungs working and with the old ticker being a bit temperamental, I am happily reconciled to writing – something I've always preferred to most other activities. My energies are slowly drying up!".

But his "drying" energies did not hinder him from writing two important books during his four years at Waymarks, together with numerous articles and reviews. He developed a very happy association with Christopher Bryant S.S.J.E., who was prepared to accept any article that Max felt able to write for the magazine *New Fire*. This gave him an outlet for a number of his concerns, especially on missionary matters, and the articles reveal how deeply he was still committed to the missionary enterprise. He seemed to capture once again the excitement which he experienced when writing his monthly News-Letter. "The Threat of Religious Pluralism", the implications of the forthcoming World of Islam Festival in London, the nature of the missionary movement in the nineteenth century, the suggestion often heard that Western missionaries should now withdraw from Asia and Africa – all these were themes which gave him the opportunity to share the fruits of his reading and to put forward positive proposals.

The most substantial of his contributions was that on Religious Pluralism which appeared in two numbers in 1975. In this he outlined a concept which was much in his mind during the last years of his life – what he called a theology of *difference*. Difference, he claimed, is something to be welcomed, not feared. A ghetto mentality, seeking safety in any kind of closed circle, should be impossible for the Christian to contemplate. What is needed is a theology which both holds fast to belief in one God, and at the same time rejoices in the fact of religious pluralism. Such a theology will recognise more fully the working of the Holy Spirit in the history of mankind *outside* the covenant of Christ and his Church as well as within it. It will also recognise the possibility of new ways of expressing the Manhood of Christ against the background of the religious and cultural inheritance of non-Western peoples. Basic, in Max's view, was the conviction not only that God in Christ was reconciling the world to himself but also that in and through the religious consciousness of mankind, in its varied manifestations, the Holy Spirit was working towards its full redemption. Thus, differences of experience, differences of understanding, even differences of interpretation can be for enrichment rather than for confusion. Yet he still needed to spell out his claim that this new vision would enable us to "find freshly minted the divine imperative to offer Christ to other men with greater humility than in the past no doubt, but also with even greater enthusiasm".

This he attempted to do in the last book he wrote. Invited by Michael Green, the Editor, to contribute a volume on mission to a new series bearing the general title *I believe*, Max undertook to do what he had never done before, viz. to survey the progress of the Christian mission from the time of Jesus himself, who *is* the Great Commission, down to the latter half of the twentieth century.

It was an ambitious project. It involved first a study of the New Testament evidence, secondly a sketch of the history of the Church down through the ages, and finally an application of lessons from the past to the life of the Church in the contemporary world. Some doubts have been expressed about his success in the first section for he hardly took into account much of the work done by New Testament scholars over the past twenty-five years. The second section, considering the small amount of space available, brilliantly revealed the skill of an experienced historian. The final section concentrated on the issue of Religious Pluralism and concluded, in typical "Maxian" fashion, by listing seven positive qualifications needed by anyone prepared to commit himself or herself to the missionary enterprise today.

Writing to his friend Norman Goodall about the book in November 1976 he said: "I have poured into it all I have of real concern for mission, though I hope with reasonable moderation. I am most deeply concerned at the sheer loss of nerve in the Churches of this country and the main-line Churches of North America as regards the missionary task. There are huge new problems, yes, but a theology of commitment is still vital. And history has lessons to teach us."

This book was Max's last will and testament, reiterating ideas and convictions which had been in the forefront of his own consciousness over more than fifty years and yet still expressed in a fresh and challenging way. He never grew stale. He never simply repeated himself. He was too keenly aware of the day to day changes in the surrounding world and the need of the Christian to relate himself to them. At the same time he was ever alert to receive new light and truth from God's Holy Word and to focus that light upon the world's dark places. Perhaps he experienced some disappointment that his book did not appear to make a greater impact, especially in those quarters for which it was particularly intended (though it soon had a second printing and was translated into German and Spanish). But it stands as a noble last attempt to summon Christians everywhere to consider him who in his *sent-ness was* the Great Commission. Commitment to him must imply commitment to that same sent-ness which has no boundaries but is directed to all the world.

Had the other demands of his life allowed, Max might well have written a big book on the theology of mission, a theme in which he was passionately interested and for the writing of which he was perhaps uniquely qualified. There has been little serious attention to missiology in Britain. On the continent the situation in universities has been different and Max's writings have gained careful

213

attention there. But at an early stage in his career he declined an offer which could have led on to a life of historical and theological scholarship. He wanted to be in the forefront of the Christian mission, never neglecting the theological background but too much involved in the demands of the moment to set aside long periods for research and for the writing of books. He might have written a definitive biography of Henry Venn or a major theology of mission. But he was content to deal faithfully with pressing situations as they arose, *To Apply the Gospel* (the title of one of his books) rather than to attempt a comprehensive theology of mission.

One other book written early in his retirement to Waymarks gave him immense pleasure and excitement. He accepted an invitation to write an autobiography for publication by Hodder and Stoughton. This provided the stimulus to go back over his travel diaries, to consult some of his intimate friends from C.M.S. days, to share memories with Mary and to plan chapter after chapter of what he deemed to have been the most significant aspects of his life. The actual writing went with a swing and was completed in three months, months which Max in his characteristic way, described as a period of "uncommunicative broodiness while I was conjuring up the past". *Crowded Canvas* was a striking and appropriate title and each chapter was prefaced with a favourite quotation. (In another book, he remarked, he had tried to "curb his passion for good quotations".) It was published in September 1974, just after his seventieth birthday and a launching party was held in Mowbray's London Bookshop on September 25 at the invitation of both the publishers and Mowbrays. Happily Pat and Roger were home on leave. In consequence they were able to join Mary, Rosemary and Greg, and a host of friends in celebrating the occasion. It was all a big strain, but Max survived and soon became aware of the great pleasure that the book was giving to his friends. The first edition quickly sold out and a reprinting was arranged.

Max's forebodings, recorded almost exactly a year before the date of publication, were in large measure dispelled. "The more I reflect on it the less I feel that I ought ever to have been asked to write it. I cannot for the life of me see how more than a handful of people will want to read it. It simply does not tell of anything interesting but of a single life built round a happy family life and a particular enthusiasm. Also it is dated. Its connection with the world of letter-bombs and hijacked air-lines, inflation and Juggernaut lorries, is tenuous in the extreme. What an incredibly stable world it was, though one was all the time living with the growing instability. But in those days morbid nationalism had not become a disease.

The struggle for political independence had dignity. The portentous figure of Gandhi-ji brooded over it, and men like Kaunda and Nyerere and Nkrumah and Banda and Jomo Kenyatta and Nasser had 'something' however much one deplored some of the things some of them did. But the 'squalid' had not yet come to dominate the scene, a 'squalid' typified by South Vietnam – the senseless idiocy of the U.S.A., repeating 'Suez' on an even more fantastic scale of outdated imperialism. For all the strains and stresses they were days of hope. Today the world is sickening with despair. Also there was still some vision in Britain, not a yelp for more money and less work from every section of the community. Is the Liberal Revival an enduring thing? If so then there may be some hope for they are at last stressing moral values which both the other parties have long since abandoned except in 'word'.

"Well, I'm glad I have lived when I have and known the folk I have known."

Perhaps the chief reservation on the part of readers of *Crowded Canvas* was that it told them so much more about "folk I have known" than about the author himself! It is generous to a degree in its references to the vast assembly of relations and friends and colleagues and correspondents who influenced and enriched his life. Except for the great chapter on "Nigeria and Illness" it tells us less about the struggles and triumphs of his own experience. The fact was that he never found it easy to "let himself go" in any *public* way and indeed he pointed out that the book was never intended to be an autobiography in the strict sense but rather an account of "the experiences of a life-time". His lasting memories were of people and events, not of his own feelings and reactions (though impressions were recorded in his diaries). And in any case there was an inherent modesty and even diffidence which never allowed him to say much about himself. Nevertheless *Crowded Canvas* is a beautiful book, handsomely produced, skilfully planned, vibrant with stories of movement and encounter, written in a style which is always a delight to read. He feared it would become a period piece, but it is in fact a valuable piece of missionary literature which tells much of the adjustments to change which have had to be made in the twentieth century, particularly in those fields in which the Anglican Communion has held major responsibility.

V

This record of the years at Waymarks may seem to have stressed unduly the more serious side of Max's life. As a long term friend of his remarked to me, he was never in fact *not serious*. And yet there was plenty of laughter when his friends came to see him and always the ability to turn a phrase or puncture a situation in a humorous way. He was serious because he was always realistic about the world situation: he could smile and laugh because of his complete faith that God was in control and able to bring good out of evil.

And there were the special events and periods of relaxation: the return to Westminster Abbey to receive gifts from his colleagues after his retirement, luncheon at Buckingham Palace to meet General Gowon of Nigeria, visits to St. Julian's and occasionally to the homes of close friends. There were walks, often somewhat laboured, around East Dean and his delight in the views of sea and Downs. There were also the periods watching television, a relaxation which he enjoyed increasingly in the last years of his life. Cricket and tennis gave him special pleasure while in the winter rugby football was a good substitute.

One event during his retirement deserves special mention, for there is no doubt that it gave him particular pleasure and afforded a singular opportunity for the expression of the esteem of some of his close friends. It seemed altogether desirable that his seventieth birthday should be celebrated in some way and the first idea was that a collection of essays might be published in his honour. But publishers are hesitant to embark on such collections except in academic circles and it was decided instead to organise a small private dinner party for September 12 which, through the good offices of Douglas Webster, took place in the congenial setting of St. Paul's Cathedral Chapter House. Twenty-two were invited to be present and only two were unable to accept because of engagements which could not be broken.

All were friends with whom, to use his own words, he had shared "significant adventures". Both Archbishops were present, together with the retiring Bishop of Winchester, who had been chief steward at Max's wedding, and the Bishop-elect who had become General Secretary of the C.M.S. after Max's resignation. In addition there were men who had been intimately associated with him on the C.M.S. Executive, in the Evangelical Fellowship for Theological Literature, on the Council of Ridley Hall, in the Conference of British Missionary Societies, in evangelistic and literary activities.

The Archbishop of Canterbury who presided made a happy and affectionate speech in proposing Max's health. He remarked that he had only known two other Max's – Max Beerbohm and Max Beaverbrook: he hoped that something would be written on theology summing up the contributions of these three! He then referred to Max's missionary vocation which had ended in Nigeria *sadly* but, as he immediately added, part of the gospel is the redemption of adverbs. He did not forget to speak of Mary's share in Max's ministry and included her in the toast of the evening. Max must have known that the twenty friends who had the privilege of being with him that evening were simply favoured representatives of a vast company of those who had been his companions on those "spiritual adventures" in which, again and again, he had led the way.

VI

From Waymarks Max accepted few outside engagements. He was prevailed upon to speak to groups of clergy in the Chichester and Norwich dioceses, though the effort involved for the latter in the autumn of 1976 caused him serious strain and he never attempted anything of the kind again. More and more his activities were confined to the home and to his ministry to those who sought him out for advice and counsel.

In a letter to an American friend in 1975 he wrote: "I'm in touch with 15 people doing research and am official supervisor of one man working for a Cambridge Ph.D. All this, with the reading involved, masses of correspondence and *no* secretary just means I can't do all I ought to do or want to do."

As those who sought his advice on missionary history and theology have good cause to remember, he was prodigal in expenditure of time and interest on their behalf. Father Furey who had chosen to write a thesis on *The Missionary Theology of Max Warren* received every kind of help while his work was in progress, together with an extensive appreciation and rejoinder when the dissertation had been completed. I was myself in touch with a Roman Catholic layman in Oxford engaged in research on Christian-Muslim relations in Nigeria. I suggested to him that he should seek an interview with Max. The immediate consequence was an invitation from Max and Mary to spend a night at Waymarks and

217

this was only the beginning of a fruitful association in historical investigation. Moreover, in addition to this eagerness to help anyone working on the history of missions (he gave an immense amount of time in assisting Gordon Hewitt who, at his suggestion, undertook the first part of the mammoth task of writing the history of the C.M.S. in the twentieth century), he retained an unceasing interest in the nineteenth-century evangelicals and readily put his own knowledge at the disposal of those writing on any aspect of their history.

But ultimately he began to feel the strain of even personal interviews. Early in 1977 he spent a good part of a day discussing a thesis with a doctoral student and then woke up the next day "completely drained". "Very reluctantly I am coming to the point of realising that I can no longer carry on a long discussion advising someone about their thesis. I get mentally too excited and this plays on 'Brother Ass' in a most exasperating way."

Gradually he was compelled to lessen his direct counselling of individuals. Yet this did not mean any reduction in the time and attention given to the other side of his personal ministry – to regular and ordered intercession on their behalf. One of his closest friends, Bishop Oliver Allison, once used the fine phrase in speaking of Max: "his heart embraced the world". This was abundantly true of his prayer-life. In part, his diary was his medium of devotion, for he noted on succeeding days the names of those who over a period of many years had entered into his life and remained friends, even if he saw them but seldom. Most important of all, however, was the daily outreach to those known to him who were labouring in the mission field. He often had first-hand knowledge of the places where they were working and so could imagine their special needs. He often lamented his own inadequacy in this ministry of intercession but there are enough hints scattered around in his writings to make us aware that this man of commanding intellect and imagination was also a man of meticulously ordered and wide-embracing prayer.

The one place to which Max could still go for refreshment, and where he could still speak without strain in the quiet of the Chapel, was St. Julian's. His last Easter was spent there and at the evening service on Easter Day he gave the address. His theme was: Christ suffers with his Church and must win his final victory, in the Church and through the Church, in the world.

"This seems to me," he wrote afterwards in his diary, "to be a vital part of the witness of the New Testament. There is an element of unreality about so much Easter rejoicing because it sends him away to Glory with a cheerful wave of the hand while all the time he is standing, showing his hands and his feet, and saying 'So send I you'. And this is more than we can bear and we allow Easter and the Ascension to be very beautiful escapes from a world needing redemption and the message of the crucified King."

The summer passed happily with many visitors coming to Waymarks. On August 13 he celebrated his 73rd birthday and in his customary way looked back on the goodness of God throughout his life.

The diary for August 20 records "a day devoted to letter-writing. First came a letter to Sister Marjorie of S.L.G. [quite lately Max had established a happy relationship with the Sisters of the Love of God at Fairacres, Oxford and had written a long review of Hans Kung's book *On Being a Christian* for their magazine] who has had to go into a terminal home for cancer. She has several times told me of her illness. This may be my last touch with her till she is over Jordan and we meet on the other side." Then followed letters to Uganda, to the U.S.A., to Australia, to Northern Nigeria, nine in all. "It was a good day's work." Visitors came to lunch and after tea he saw "some superb batting" in the traditional battle of the Roses between Yorkshire and Lancashire. "Then I completed a 12 times round the perimeter of the garden which is 50 yards or so over the mile. In the evening we started reading Vernon Sproxton's *Good News in Revelation*, which is quite magnificent, full of vision and meat and superbly written. Quite a day!"

Next day, Sunday, began with a chapter from William Temple's *Nature, Man and God*. "Temple can be heavy going at times and just now is all caught up in mathematics, logic and philosophy, three subjects which are not my strongest." Then to church for Matins, two letters to Tanzania and Israel respectively, six rounds of the perimeter, and more reading of *Good News in Revelation*, "one of the most exciting things we have come across in the book line for a long time". But after the writing up of the diary there came a greatly disturbed night and this was followed by an equally disturbed day. His doctor, however, having found a rise in blood pressure, thought that rest would put him right. But later he suffered severe pain and Mary called for an ambulance. Next day she saw him in an intensive care unit. Then the news came that he had quietly departed and, as she loved to say, all the trumpets sounded for him on the other side.

14

The *Archegos*

IN STUDYING MAX'S career, I have often been reminded of one of my favourite titles in the New Testament. It occurs four times in its Greek form *Archegos*, and in the Authorised Version is translated alternatively as Prince, Captain, Author. The New English Bible twice uses the title *Leader* and on a third occasion uses the phrase "who leads the way to life".

In 1936, Max began the very first of his many publications by quoting the famous passage from Albert Schweitzer's *The Quest of the Historical Jesus* which reads: "He comes to us as of old by the lakeside he came to those men who knew him not. He speaks to us the same words: Follow thou me – and sets us to the tasks which he has for our time. He commands. And to those who obey him he will reveal himself in the toils, the conflicts, the sufferings, which they shall pass through in his fellowship and, as an ineffable mystery, they shall learn in their own experience who he is." In 1962, near the end of his tenure as General Secretary, he concluded a sermon at Great St. Mary's, Cambridge by quoting the same passage, this time underlining the words "to those who obey him". When the time came to celebrate his seventieth birthday he wanted the company to consist of *fellow adventurers* with whom he had been associated in his journey through life.

If there is one main theme in the Epistle to the Hebrews, it is the adventure of faith in which Jesus is set forth as the *archegos* (pioneer, leader) and the *teleiotes* (finisher, perfecter). It would obviously be inappropriate to apply the second title to Max but if anyone ever deserved to be associated with his Master in bearing the first title it was he. For a great band of his contemporaries he became the *Archegos*, the Knight of faith, the Leader in thought and action. I know of no title which more adequately describes his role in the Christian mission of the twentieth century.

In what areas of life, then, was his leadership most signally manifested?

II

In the field of *evangelism*

In his teens he committed himself, by an act of personal surrender, to Jesus Christ as his Saviour and Lord. He had grown up in a family entirely dedicated to the service of Christ but it was through the Crusaders' Union and the Childrens' Special Service Mission that he was led to discover his own identity and calling as a Christian disciple.

He never ceased to be grateful for what these two evangelistic movements had done for him. One Sunday morning, while on holiday in Yorkshire, he and Mary turned on the radio during breakfast and heard a Welsh choir singing hymns and choruses he had learned nearly fifty years previously.

"I can never thank God enough for the fact that these simple evangelical hymns were the ones with which I first entered into a conscious and deliberate discipleship, through the C.S.S.M. and Crusaders. They do not represent the whole gospel: they do not look beyond a deep personal experience: they lack the horizontal dimension. But continuing discipleship brings in the horizontal. I believe with all my heart that we must start with the vertical . . . God comes first in the Bible and it is of far reaching importance that God – the Other – comes first in experience."

In these circles it was an unquestioned consequence of discipleship that some part should be taken in sharing "the things concerning Jesus" with others. This, in simplest terms, was evangelism and Max never ceased to be an evangelist. A few months before listening to the familiar hymns he had been preparing Bible-readings on the uniqueness of Jesus for a Missionaries' Conference. This time he wrote: "I think I really have managed to say something which, by God's grace, may help some of the folk gathered there. Anyhow I always rejoice at the opportunity of talking about Jesus and making people see some aspect or another of 'the King in his beauty'. What an amazing privilege it is to be able to speak for him. I haven't got much emotional content in my religion. It is, I know, a terribly over-intellectualised affair. But if I ever get a 'thrill' in religion it is from talking about Jesus, whether to an individual or to a congregation in Westminster Abbey. Can there be any more wonderful experience than to be allowed to testify to him even if one's own spiritual experience is a very thin affair indeed?"

To follow Jesus in humble discipleship and to talk about him – these were his responsibilities as an evangelist. But he recognised fully that *methods* of evangelism must be open to change and the *language* of evangelism must be adaptable to new circumstances. After reading the life of Canon Christopher, a famous Rector of St. Aldate's, Oxford in the late nineteenth century, he commented: "For my part I find it far easier to enter sympathetically into a man's doubts and to try to help him to discover a way through than to challenge him in the way a Simeon or a Venn or a Christopher would have done. Again old Christopher was for ever giving away tracts. To me this is wholly uncongenial – in part through coward-ice, in part through lack of conviction that they have any value. I simply cannot commend 'oversimplifications' which is the essence of tracts. But the challenge of an earlier day remains – 'Am I concerned for souls?' I can honestly say 'Yes' but I cannot go after them in the way an earlier generation did."

It was his insistence on the legitimacy of differences and novelties in the methods and language of evangelism that helped to make him a leader in this field. He spoke of variations between "siege operations" and "commando operations". He commended en-thusiastically the book of *Twenty-four Bible Stories* composed by the lay-evangelist George Ingram and his wife, "to turn the eyes of simple people to Jesus". At the same time he enthused over such massive books as Hans Küng's *On Being a Christian* or John Baker's *The Foolishness of God* because he regarded them as containing the finest kind of apologetic for the true understanding of the Christian faith. He had no place for shibboleths. All who bore a living witness to the living Christ were his friends.

Occasionally he accepted an invitation to lead an evangelistic mission but it is doubtful if this was really his forte. It was in the establishment of person-to-person relationships that he excelled, never forcing an issue, never imposing his own interpretation, but seeking at all times to dispel false conceptions and to unveil the Christ of the gospel. Yet he fully supported those engaged in evangelistic missions on a larger scale provided that they did not seek for numbers rather than for true personal commitments. No man in the Anglican Communion over the past fifty years has been more fully engaged in city-wide and parochial missions than Bryan Green whom Max first knew as his own leader in a Junior Crusader Class. Bryan has written:

We have discussed evangelism together, formulated policies and tried to promote action. I suppose that, in theological and evangelistic theory, I owe more to Max Warren than to anyone else.

III

In the field of *mission*

Even before he went up to Cambridge as an undergraduate, Max had a compelling sense of his own vocation to be a missionary. Then, in his first term, this vocation came to be specifically directed towards Northern Nigeria with Christian literature as the chief means of approach to the Muslim mind. His parents were both missionaries, his brother was a missionary, he had been brought up on a missionary compound, the missionary challenge was often heard in the evangelical organisations with which as a boy he was associated. But his own call to mission was in no sense second-hand or a mere conforming to a tradition. It was, he believed, a direct call from God which it was his bounden duty to obey. Though the attempt to carry it out was to involve suffering in body and mind, he never lost the conviction that for him the Divine imperative was to mission in one form or another.

Never to my knowledge did he question the validity of the vocations of those who felt no sense of call to the *foreign* mission field. He respected every one's right to make his or her own decision and recognised that health or family circumstances must be taken fully into account. Nevertheless he was profoundly convinced that *sending* and *being sent* constituted a part of the Divine mystery and that the simple verb "to go" should hold a place of supreme importance in every Christian's vocabulary. It was not necessarily a question of going to another country but rather of going out to the frontier – geographical, cultural, social, ecclesiastical. To remain complacent within some well-guarded fastness was for him the denial of the crucial revelation of God in the sent-ness of his Son.

He knew well that missionaries to other lands had often been guilty of insensitivity and attitudes of superiority, that they had often failed to commend the gospel either by word or by action. There were ugly caricatures of missionaries in fiction and caustic comments in history-books, but this did not lessen his admiration for the heroic self-sacrifice and untrumpeted devotion of thousands who had gone out to proclaim the gospel and heal the sick. He gave the most careful attention to Geoffrey Moorhouse's book *The Missionaries*, and admitted that its criticisms were often fair and justified. Still, the summons to go out to the world's frontiers was at the heart of Christianity, it was the Great Commission, and those who obeyed, whatever their faults, were seeking to be faithful to their Lord's command.

His strong conviction about mission has reminded me of Browning, one of his favourite poets. Verse 6 in *Rabbi Ben Ezra* seems singularly appropriate:

> Then welcome each rebuff
> That turns earth's smoothness rough
> Each sting that bids not sit nor stand but go!
> Be our joys three parts pain
> Strive and hold cheap the strain
> Learn nor account the pang; dare, never grudge the throe.

Perhaps even more in line with Max's conviction of Mission as belonging to the very life of God himself is R. S. Thomas's poem, *The Coming*.

> And God held in his hand
> A small globe. Look, he said.
> The son looked. Far off
> As through water, he saw
> A scorched land of fierce
> Colour. A light burned
> There, crested buildings
> Cast their shadows: a bright
> Serpent, a river
> Uncoiled itself, radiant
> With silver.
> On a bare
> Hill a bare tree saddened
> The sky. Many people
> Held out their thin arms
> To it, as though waiting
> For a vanished April
> To return to its crossed
> Boughs. The son watched
> Them. Let me go there, he said.

To go, to bear witness, to heal, to teach – such was the Divine imperative. Max's genius and his outstanding leadership were revealed as he set himself to re-think and re-frame this commission within the post-war world. The War had brought vast uncertainties and discouragements to missionaries already in the field. Many saw the old colonial frameworks dissolving and new national self-consciousnesses emerging. Max knew that the movement of peoples in Asia and Africa was bound to create a totally new political and social climate.

What was perhaps even more important, he was convinced that the work of mission could never be pursued in isolation. Man is not simply an individual. He is a social being, deeply affected by his social environment. The gospel must be related to men and women in their actual situations through the languages and symbolic forms with which they are familiar. His mission, as he saw it, was to help missionaries and missionary supporters to *understand* what was really happening in the world, and to try to relate themselves to people living in the twentieth and not in the nineteenth century.

Two vital ingredients of this new strategy were first the training and pastoral care of missionaries, secondly the devising of new means by which the realities of the new order of things could be communicated. He could not possibly do all this himself but he became the *leader*, on the one hand of the band responsible for missionary-training, on the other hand – particularly through his News-Letters – of the team responsible for disseminating missionary information. He did not just hand over these responsibilities, though he was ever ready to delegate authority. He knew that his chief contribution must be made in the realm of *ideas*. His role was to be that of an inspired journalist, keeping in vital touch with what was happening in the world, spotting items and events which were of major significance and then relaying them in a form which could readily be understood. He never relaxed during his period of leadership. Twice he was tempted to abandon the News-Letter: it became ever more difficult to recruit and equip missionaries. But, amazingly, he went on, travelling to all parts of the world, strengthening the hands of missionaries by personal visits, encouraging his Headquarters Staff by taking them constantly into his confidence. He gloried in the title *missionary* and in the whole ethos of the Church Missionary Society which it was his privilege to lead. The crisis brought about by World War II was surmounted and few would deny that C.M.S. became better equipped for its task than ever before.

IV

In the field of *missionary history and policy*

The field of history is now so vast and contains so many labourers that it would have been impossible for Max to make a distinctive contribution to historical studies except within a quite specialised area. He had a horror of over-specialisation. In course of time, however, the history of missions in the nineteenth century became his particular field of study and although he never produced a big book on either of his heroes, Charles Simeon and Henry Venn (as he might well have done), he managed to write articles and books of considerable value on important features of the missionary movement in the nineteenth century.

Within a few years of his assuming office as General Secretary, the C.M.S. was due to celebrate its one hundred and fiftieth anniversary. This led him to study its history the more carefully and to remind members of the Society of their forefathers' aims and achievements. Yet there was no time to write at length about the history as a whole. He encouraged others to undertake particular studies and gladly shared with them the results of his own research, but it was not until retirement from C.M.S. gave him opportunity to undertake more detailed investigations that he felt able to publish serious historical studies.

Three substantial books appeared during his years at Westminster. *The Missionary Movement from Britain in Modern History, Social History and Christian Mission*, and *To Apply the Gospel*. Each bears the marks of his early training in historical research: a full and accurate bibliography, careful annotation, no facile generalisations. His strength was in *analysis*, discerning significant forces and trends in history, examining the principles by which men directed their lives, asking how far the past is involved in the present and how far present policies should seek to conform to those which were framed in an earlier age. He was fascinated by the fluctuations in the relations between Church and State in England during the nineteenth and early twentieth centuries and he tried constantly to see how Government policies in the Empire affected, or in some cases were affected by, the overseas expansion of the Christian Church.

It is clear that the legacy of Henry Venn greatly influenced his missionary thinking. He pored over the Venn correspondence and ultimately edited a fine edition of the letters in the book *To Apply the Gospel*. In his introduction he shows how deeply he had entered into Venn's mind regarding the establishment of the Church of England, the role of bishops, the maintenance of voluntary associations, the validity of evangelical missionary policy alongside whatever other policies might be pursued within the Church, and relations with other Christian communions: on all these matters Max was convinced that Venn had planned wisely and that the principles he had advocated could be applied, with proper adjustments, within the changed situation of the mid-twentieth century.

There is a significant paragraph in his Introduction. Referring to Venn's anxiety about the attack being made upon the constitutional position of the Church of England he comments: "Not only his heredity but his whole reading of history made him a strong upholder of the Church of England as by law established. For him the Church Establishment was a safeguard of spiritual liberty, and by spiritual liberty he had in mind liberty for different opinions to be held within the Church and in particular for evangelical opinions. And his concern for evangelical opinions was no narrow party preoccupation. He was essentially concerned for the freedom of the gospel. No doubt he did too narrowly identify the gospel with an exclusively evangelical interpretation both of its meaning and the way in which to apply it. But it was a passionate conviction about the gospel that dominated his thought and determined his action. This was the source of his anxiety."

At first reading this may seem to contain a paradox, even a contradiction. The Establishment as a safeguard of spiritual liberty? At various times Max's references to *national* Churches or to the state as a "Beloved Enemy" caused puzzlement or disagreement. But what, following Venn, he resisted was every attempt to establish a monolithic Church under the rule of an unchecked prelacy. He did not deny that the planting of the Church overseas under episcopal jurisdiction was *one* way of missionary expansion. But he was convinced that it was not the *only* way. There was also the way of preaching the gospel and gathering converts into Christian congregations and ultimately uniting them, where appropriate, within an episcopal organisation. He wanted to act at all times as a loyal son of the Church of England. But he continued to struggle for a theology and polity of *difference*, allowing varieties of interpretation and method within the one embracing whole.

For him the Epistle to the Galatians was a kind of Magna Carta of Christian liberty. He sensed the dangers inherent in every closed system, whether of papacy or of episcopacy or of fundamentalist sectarianism. In the changing circumstances of the twentieth century, the power of bishops in the Church of England was declining but the power of the Church Assembly (and later of the General Synod) was increasing. In consequence he became deeply apprehensive about the possibility that all aspects of the Church's activity would be governed from the Church House in Westminster, with bureaucrats throttling the dynamic of all voluntary associations. He was a liberal through and through, in matters both political and ecclesiastical. Flexibility was, for him, a key-word. He was ready to live and work loyally within an ordered framework but the urge to experiment, to initiate, to adventure, to *go* must never be quenched.

V

In the field of the relationship of *Christianity to the non-Christian religions*

In Chapter 12 I have to tried to outline the way in which Max tackled this problem. To him it was the most serious issue in the theology of mission.

During the earlier part of his career the leading emphasis in missionary circles had been on the Christian's duty to proclaim the gospel wherever he could gain a hearing: to do it with sympathy and understanding but still with the strong conviction that only by receiving the message and by responding to its challenge could those living in bondage be delivered into the liberty of the children of God. But towards the end of his period of office as General Secretary the term "dialogue" began to appear, both in missionary and ecumenical contexts, with the implication that the missionary's calling was less that of imparting truth to the ignorant and misguided than that of entering into dialogue with adherents of other faiths with a view to joining in a common search for ultimate Truth. Max gives a clear definition of "dialogue" as he came to conceive it:

"Dialogue, properly conducted, is not a way of soft-pedalling truth, an easy pursuit of superficial agreement, a compromise on fundamentals. Essentially 'dialogue' is an expression of that utter humility which acknowledges that Truth is always more than one has yet discovered and which is prepared to learn more about Truth from the discovery of what another has found. And this humility is based on the deep conviction that because Jesus Christ is the Truth no real truth, wherever discovered or by whomsoever communicated, can ever be inconsistent with 'the truth as it is in Jesus'."
(*The Missionary Movement from Britain in Modern History*, p. 178.)

This did not mean that henceforward he would refrain from proclaiming the gospel through preaching or through writing. But it did mean that a sharper tension developed between the method of proclamation and that of dialogue. Most, I think, would allow that Max's own preference and greater strength came to be towards the latter and some of his most distinctive labours in his later years were directed to this end. In a revealing letter to a friend in 1975 he wrote: "I can never get an evangelical answer to what God has been doing throughout the vast range of human history during which the huge majority of mankind have been *outside* the covenant with Israel and have never heard whether there has been such a Person as Jesus Christ, let alone the Holy Spirit.

"What has God been doing? And I want to personalise the issue down to the individual men and women of all nations and races who have never heard any gospel at all and all the individual men and women who lived before the Incarnation. Every individual is an object of the creating and redeeming love of God. That is an axiom which I hold as fundamental, and I know you do too. Well, then, what has God been doing all down the ages with individual men and women?"

He endeavoured to answer this question in two ways. First by his concept of *Christian Presence*, the conviction that even outside the covenant with Israel or the Church, Christ is present, incognito, in mystery, and yet in ways that are consonant with the revelation of the mystery which the New Testament unveils. Secondly by his stress upon the activity of the Holy Spirit in the religious consciousness and conscience of mankind. "It seems to me", he wrote "that conscience is something imparted by God and what he plants he nourishes. Who is the Nourisher if not the Holy Spirit? He is the agent in sanctification as we Christians believe. Can we doubt that he inspires to holiness wherever holiness is to be found?"

This concept of "dialogue" in thought and practice has its difficulties as appeared in Chapter 12. Yet Max's own activity, in the last ten years of his life, was so much concerned with individuals, meeting and talking with countless men and women in person, writing to still more with whom he was in personal correspondence, that the way of "dialogue" could hardly have failed to be uppermost in his mind. This was reinforced by his regular correspondence with his missionary deputies – for such they were – in India. The tension was there, theologically and in practice. Yet once again it was within the tension that he was glad to live.

VI

I have tried to outline some of the more formal qualities of Max's leadership. But his friends will look back upon other aspects of that heroic character. There was his determination to travel in order to see situations at first-hand and to establish friendly relations with missionaries or with local ministers and their supporters, in their actual day-to-day circumstances. The extent of his missionary journeyings is astonishing and perhaps unparalleled. Then there was his determination to share his experiences with his fellow Secretaries, with the wider constituency of C.M.S. and, as it turned out, with those interested in missions all over the world. He set an example in missionary journalism which is also, so far as I know, without parallel. He had a genius for writing, especially for correspondence. His pamphlets, printed lectures, articles, books, all reached a high standard but when writing a *letter*, either to an individual or to a particular group of readers, he reached the heights. His mastery of the English language stood out clearly and scarcely a letter was written, at least to a friend, which did not contain some example of his superb Irish wit. These witticisms were never artificial or forced. They just seemed to flow naturally as the appropriate and yet altogether memorable thing to say.

In his diaries, where he felt entirely free to converse with himself, he frequently *sparkled*. When speaking in public he knew that he was a representative man and he was cautious. But in his diaries he could let himself go, in reflection, in praise, in criticism (often self-criticism), in prophecy. Comments in letters or in the diaries show how often he was ahead of his contemporaries in interpreting the moods and aspirations of the peoples of Asia and Africa and how frequently he was accurate in forecasting the way in which political, as well as ecclesiastical, affairs were likely to develop. He wrote always in a lively and easily readable style. In fact I know of no one in the Church of England to have equalled him in this respect since the days of Hensley Henson and Dean Inge.

He was not an artist so far as any of the musical or visual arts are concerned. But in the use of words he was an artist of high distinction. John Sheffield's couplet, written in 1682, could appropriately be applied to Max:

> Of all those arts in which the wise excel
> Nature's chief masterpiece is writing well.

Other qualities can be enumerated which set a high and challenging example to those who were in any way associated with him. He never gossiped about church affairs. He never sought public recognition or promotion to higher office. He never made the ordinary person feel inferior, but instead enlarged him. He loved debates and may at times have seemed to press a cause too hard but he never tried to bring any pressure to bear upon an individual in situations where a personal decision had to be made. When he gave the address at the memorial service for Lord Fisher, the quality in the Archbishop to which he drew special attention was his *trustworthiness*. He might have been speaking about himself. If ever there was a man whom you felt you could trust completely, it was Max.

These qualities never deteriorated. He was spared the time which comes to some when mental powers grow weaker and memory begins to fade. In the very last letter sent to India we find him still as concerned as ever about the Christian mission and the "spiritual strategy" of those responsible for carrying it on.

"Meanwhile really able recruits are just not coming forward, part of the national malaise; this makes Secretaries even more nervous. No one is going out and putting his hand on this man or woman's shoulder and just saying quietly – Here is a situation – have you really asked God whether, perhaps he may not want you to do that, to go there. This isn't putting pressure on people: it is just presenting an actual situation and asking a question. But no one is doing this. No effort is being made to nurse the universities. The basic assumption is that the day of a foreign missionary is over. This is nonsense. Take the Arabian Peninsula. In the Persian Gulf States there are more expatriates, Pakistanis, Indians, Europeans and Americans than there are local Arabs. Saudi Arabia has over one million expatriates and the authorities there say they need another 500,000 if they are to complete their five year plan!! There is a missionary opportunity here in some ways unique in history. We could put twenty men and women of real calibre into this area alone and we need far more than that.

"I'm sure we have to see many of these 'missionaries' doing quite new jobs and some will operate in very queer disguise. But they would be missionaries of the gospel – a gospel more desperately needed than ever".

The fire was still burning. The *Archegos*, the Captain, was very near the end of his earthly pilgrimage of faith. Yet he was still calling for a new strategy and for new recruits to share in the great adventure. *Archegos*, Missionary, Apostle: it is possible to describe

231

him as such just because, from start to finish, his aim was to be a loyal follower of him who was God's *Archegos*, Missionary, Apostle, to the world.

Words written by Doctor Louis Birtagna about André Malraux seem singularly appropriate:

He lived right up to the moment of death.

With these I couple words written by Elspeth Huxley about her friend Denys Fitch Hutton:

A man never forgotten or explained by his friends, who left nothing behind him but affection, a memory of gaiety and grace.

15

"Into all the world"

I

The news of Max's death came as a shock, though not a surprise, to his world-wide circle of friends. Many knew how uncertain, even tenuous, his life-expectancy had been since 1967 and how the maintenance of reasonable health had been made possible by the watchfulness of Mary, the devotion of physicians and nurses and a regimen of what one old friend called an "inordinate" number of pills. His courage and uncomplainingness in the face of physical weakness were phenomenal. Writing to another friend, less than two years before he died, he said:

> I've not had a very pleasant autumn, Brother Ass having been somewhat contrariwise. It is sickening being in this somewhat crotchety state, the more so as there is nothing seriously wrong. So please don't go looking in the obituary columns of whatever paper you prefer. I hope not to be mentioned there for some time yet.

He would, I am sure, have been vastly surprised to open *The Times* on August 25, 1977 and see, not only a photograph of himself but the greater part of two columns recording the life and work of the man headlined as *Influential Anglican leader*. It was a magnificent synopsis of the qualities and achievements of the man referred to by a Canadian Dean in 1963 as the "greatest Anglican in the Anglican world today". The Church papers dwelt particularly on his combination of convinced evangelical churchmanship and passionate commitment to the missionary cause with an open and liberal mind and a humble and charitable spirit. Further tributes appeared in journals and magazines, none of which was more sensitive and perceptive than that of John Taylor, his successor as General Secretary of C.M.S.

Writing in the magazine *New Fire*, he began by recalling an

233

incident which had happened in 1946. A new missionary, a few weeks after her arrival in a strange land, received by post a particularly attractive catalogue of dress designs and fashion lengths produced in America by the best colour printing. It came from the General Secretary with a note hoping that it would bring cheer by reason of its gaiety.

"That incident", the Bishop commented "epitomises many of the characteristics which added up to greatness. Here was that originality of mind which never ceased to see value or significance in something that lay right outside the accepted categories of spiritual concern. Here was the humorous, but perfectly sincere, self-depreciation, and the imaginative interest in individuals with never a thought of their comparative 'importance'. Here was the defiance of normal bureaucratic consideration: four only of the glossy catalogues had come his way and there were four hundred missionary wives, but he understood that the economy of God – a favourite phrase of his – was personal, arbitrary and uninhibited by tidy principle. So he was free to exercise his most characteristic gift of all, the light but intimate gesture of recognition, the hand laid momentarily upon a particular shoulder, which endeared him to countless people because it was the unaffected offer of a totally trustworthy friendship."

Later in the article came this significant testimony, significant because John had originally consulted Max about his own missionary vocation, had ultimately worked alongside him as Africa Secretary in C.M.S. and had, as he said, come to regard him as a central reference point in his years at Westminster and Waymarks.

> He was the most single-minded man I have known and all that "purity of heart" was devoted supremely in obedience to the Great Commission of the Master who had claimed his love. Even his major hobby was concerned with world communication. In all the multiplicity of his practical concerns, he could never forget the Kingdom.

II

Letters poured in to Mary from every quarter. I cannot attempt, and perhaps it would be superfluous, to summarise the expressions of deep affection and sense of bereavement which they revealed. The most notable outward and visible sign of these inward feelings was the presence of so great a throng at the 'Service of Thanks-giving for the Life and Ministry of Max Warren' held at West-minster Abbey on October 11, 1977. Rarely can the Abbey have been filled with such a company at such a service. Scores were there who had served, often for long periods, in far parts of the world. Clergy and laity representing all kinds of Christian ministry in Britain were present together with nationals from overseas. It was a "great cloud of witnesses" thanking God for a leader and a friend.

After an opening hymn of praise, the former Dean, Dr. E. S. Abbott, who had been a friend of Max's since undergraduate days, read the opening bidding in a way which set the tone for the whole service.

> We come together as Max's friends and admirers to thank God for a life dedicated without reserve to Christ and his kingdom. We recall the largeness and fertility of his mind, sharpened by extensive travel and omnivorous reading; his perceptive aware-ness of a world in the process of change, with the consequent need to shape Christian mission to a new cultural, political and religious environment. We remember the sensitive and out-standing leadership given to the Church Missionary Society, through which he exercised a prophetic influence on the Church of England, on the Anglican Communion and the congregation of Christian people dispersed throughout the world. We recall his openness to other faiths; the pastoral help and wise counsel which he gave to the many who came to him for guidance and support; and the wide influence of his books. Nor can we forget so rare a modesty, a courtesy shot through with Christian grace and understanding; a strength of character seen in his willingness to champion unpopular causes, though without self-assertiveness or pride.
>
> Here at the Abbey we remember him with affection, and give thanks for ten happy years when he helped to direct our corporate life towards a greater world concern and a more comprehensive vision.
>
> In remembering Max, we remember Mary; their mutual love and delight in one another, to the enrichment of their friends.
>
> May God be praised that he called Max to the service of his kingdom "at such a time as this".

The Choir, whose renderings Max had not always appreciated, sang Psalm 139 most beautifully. Dame Diana Reader Harris, President of the C.M.S. and Dr. John Huxtable, representing the Free

Churches, read the Lessons. Dr. Coggan, Archbishop of Canterbury and, again, a long-time friend, preached the sermon in which he commented particularly on Max's alertness of mind, sense of responsibility, prophetic discernment and faithfulness in prayer. After the singing of the movingly appropriate hymn, "Blest are the pure in heart", the Dean committed the ashes to their resting-place in the Abbey. The Anthem "This sanctuary of my soul" was equally appropriate for it was one of Max's favourites and the words had been composed by a fellow Old-Marlburian who had died in the First World War. The great congregation rejoiced in the mercies of God and the memories of his servant as it sang "Tell out my soul, the greatness of the Lord" and the Dean gave the final blessing. So Max's grave is in the great church, at the heart of one of the world's greatest cities, not far from that of David Livingstone over which he used constantly to walk as he went in and out of Services in the Abbey. "What a humbling and disturbing privilege," he wrote on May 1, 1973. "At least one cannot easily forget one's missionary vocation which continues right up to the end."

On June 29, 1979, the Abbey celebrated its annual Festival with a joyful Eucharist. At the conclusion of the Service a small procession formed and made its way to the place in the South Cloister where a tablet had been inserted in the floor. The Dean, Dr. Edward Carpenter, read the fifteenth psalm and recited appropriate prayers. Then, at his request, Mary, proudly and courageously, unveiled the memorial to the man whom she had supported for better for worse, in sickness and in health, till at length death had parted them for a while. The tablet reads:

MAX WARREN

1904–1977

———

Vicar of Holy Trinity, Cambridge
1936–42

General Secretary of
The Church Missionary Society
1942–63

Canon and Sub-Dean of Westminster
1963–73

"INTO ALL THE WORLD"

———

Appendix I

Directions concerning the Diaries

These diaries are in the possession of the family, pending other arrangements which may be made for their accommodation.

Essentially personal documents, containing reflections on many subjects, and reporting many conversations with friends and strangers, these diaries contain, in particular, a great deal of material which could be of value to those engaged in research into the history of the Missionary and Ecumenical Movements, and of the Anglican Communion during these years.

Almost all these volumes have each its own very detailed index. But this index has in mind more particularly the interests of those researching into the history of

1. The Church Missionary Society.
2. The Ecumenical Movement in general and the work of the International Missionary Council up until its integration with the World Council of Churches in 1961.
3. The Anglican Communion, and in particular
   - (i) The Churches in which the C.M.S. missionaries were working
   - (ii) The Anglican Church in U.S.A., Canada, Australia, New Zealand and South Africa.

TRAVEL DIARIES 1943–1970

1943–1944	2 volumes	U.S.A., Canada
1947		U.S.A., Canada, China, Hong Kong
1948 (see *Crowded Canvas* pp. 191–193)		Germany
1949–1950	4 volumes	Australia, Egypt, East Africa (Kenya, Tanganyika, Uganda), Sudan
1952		Germany

1954		Germany
1954	3 volumes	U.S.A.
1955		U.S.A., Canada
1955		Switzerland, Hawaii, U.S.A.
1955		East Africa (Tanganyika, Kenya)
1956		Germany
1957–1958	4 volumes	West Africa (Nigeria, Liberia, Sierra Leone, Ghana)
1958		U.S.A.
1958		U.S.A., Canada
1959		Japan
1960–1961	4 volumes	U.S.A., New Zealand, Australia, Malaya, N. India, Pakistan, Iran, Lebanon, Jordan, Israel
1962		South America
1962		Iran, Greece
1963		Denmark, Norway, Sweden, Finland
1963		Canada
1964		U.S.A.
1965		Canada
1965		South Africa, Kenya, Uganda
1967		Israel
1967		India
1969		Holland
1970		Uganda
1970		Israel

As can be seen from his list, the only regions not visited were those where either Roman Catholic or Eastern Orthodox were the major Christian bodies in occupation.

Appendix II

After thanking Professor Hick for his Book *God and the Universe of Faiths* and for his comments on the article in *The Modern Churchman* Max wrote as follows:

By way of a return comment there are several clarifications I would like to make in this letter. Indeed, if I ever come to write further on the subject, I will try to develop these more adequately. But I must not weary you with these now.

1. Increasingly I have come to feel that the word "uniqueness" in relation to our Lord is not the right word, failing a great deal of definition. It is legitimate to use it within the circle of disciples but when one moves out into the world of other men's experiences it begs too many questions.

2. I accept without reserve the point you make that in my article there is a lack of clarity – indeed, I accept "profound un-clarity" – where I contrast the term God as you use it, with "an historical person Jesus in whom God is to be recognised as uniquely revealed". A besetting sin of mine is telescoping an argument. In this case I compounded the sin by a far too loose expression "an historical person Jesus". I am grateful to you for challenging me.

3. I would, at once, want to accept your second suggestion that what I wish to assert is that "God has acted savingly towards mankind in the life of Jesus, a claim which leaves open the possibility [I would say "certainty"] that he has acted savingly towards mankind in other ways as well." This, beyond question, is my own conviction and, I think, it emerges fairly clearly in the course of my argument. Indeed, towards the end of the article I say, "To be saved through Christ is an ex-

perience which cannot be given an *exclusive* meaning. It must be given an *inclusive* meaning." The "unknown Christ", as I understand him, transcends all Ptolemaic categories. But I agree that such a statement needs a lot of spelling out.

4. Am I right in thinking that one premise from which you start in your thinking on this whole subject is your total repudiation of the dogma *extra ecclesiam nulla salus*? And, you have a suspicion that I, and others who think as I do, have not made this same repudiation. I do want to assert that I repudiate that dogma *in toto*, and am on record as doing so. Salvation is a word far too great, and an experience far too glorious, to be defined and limited by a dogma. Strictly speaking only God knows what it encompasses.

5. Now, in repudiating the dogma without reservation, I do not think that I re-enter the world of Ptolemaic thinking if, in jettisoning the word "uniqueness" as inapt, I go on to say that in the Jesus of history together with the Christ of faith (without at this point trying to distinguish them) I claim that there is a saving distinctiveness which is valid for all men. And it is this which justifies Christians witnessing to this conviction before all men: which is what the missionary movement, in spite of its many aberrations, is all about. *Pari passu* this applies no less to the missionary implications of Islam, and to any other faith held to have universal relevance. But this in no way invalidates the authenticity of what others have come to know of God. On precisely the same principle I must accept truth about God from whatever source it comes.

6. I would want to add that for me God cannot be less than what can be discovered of him in Jesus – taking Jesus as the Middle Term between the insights of the Old Testament and the experience of Christians down through history. Here as I see it the whole question of history comes into the debate. A biblical understanding of history is essentially teleological. It discerns in history the purpose of God. Is this to take a Ptolemaic view? Surely it is equally compatible with a Copernican view. Without developing this point I suspect that somewhere here is an important challenge to *all* religions as to how they understand the meaning of existence, the nature of man, and with all that the experience of salvation in this life and not only a matter of man's ultimate destiny.

7. I do not think it is a jump out of a reasonable argument to continue by saying that, if my interpretation of Jesus as the Middle Term in the biblical revelation is sound, then, to quote Michael Ramsey, "God is Christlike and in him is nothing unChristlike at all." This makes no denial of anyone's religious experience. But it does seem to me to entitle me to say to other men in deep humility (lest they cannot hear what I say because of what I am), "Look at this Christlike God. Reject him if you will. He conscripts no followers. But do look at him. Meanwhile help me to see what God means to you."

Do I then, after all, mean that "all men must sooner or later come to worship Jesus, and that faith in him is the only way to the new life which is the Life of God?" I make no such claim. I refuse to tell God how to save men. That is not my business. My business is to *offer* Christ.

8. Where I have found your argument most difficult to follow is where, in your book, you suggest that a theology of religion can be based on "The Divine as non-personal". Having just read Maurice Wiles' book *The Re-making of Christian Doctrine* I see that he is feeling his way towards a profounder use of the word "Personal" in relation to God than has hitherto been generally recognised by Christian theologians. But I think he is asking for the word "Personal" to be given a new dimension rather than to be treated as mythological language legitimate for Christians only. Nevertheless I do see that far more thought must be given to how one uses the term "Personal" in relation to God. I am grateful to you for forcing me to think much more about this in relation to other faiths. For the moment, however, I find myself compelled to treat as necessary for faith in God, and indeed for all faiths such as deny God as do Jainism and Hinayana Buddhism, a MODEL which, in a myriad of forms, seems to be a universal constituent of Man's religious awareness – a MODEL that is to which to look, as for instance a Muslim looks to Muhammad, or a Jain to Mahavir. I find in Jesus the most comprehensive MODEL. I do not throw that conviction in anyone's teeth, but if I am to be true to myself I must offer it as my conviction.

9. Ultimately in all this enormously important debate we are moving in the realm of faith – not just faiths. In a disconcertingly fundamental way it is only possible to speak from faith to faith. All communication partakes of the miraculous!

For me then it is the way in which I respond to Jesus which is far more important than anything I say about him. This Jesus to whom I respond is the Jesus of the New Testament (understood in terms which take seriously New Testament scholarship) *plus* that Jesus who has been further illuminated in the experience of others who have also responded to him by faith-obedience all down history. I refuse to confine him within the terms of any theological definition, which must in the nature of things be more or less inadequate. It is from this experience that I go out expectantly to discover him in other men, and from other men to have my understanding of him corrected and enlarged so that I come a little nearer to the Vision of God.

Appendix III

Bibliography

Max Warren compiled a very careful record of his writings and recorded addresses and this may be seen at the C.M.S. Library, 157 Waterloo Road, S.E.1. It includes:—
Books; Articles; University Sermons; Sermons at Consecration of Bishops; Sermons on Special Occasions; Broadcasts; Pamphlets; Reviews; and Books of Essays, either edited by himself or to which he contributed.

In addition to books mentioned in the text, the following are especially important for understanding his theory and practice of Mission:—
The Christian Mission 1951
The Christian Imperative 1955
Partnership 1956
All published by S.C.M. Press.

Index

Index